Unparalleled Reforms

Unparalleled Reforms

*China's Rise, Russia's Fall, and the
Interdependence of Transition*

Christopher Marsh

LEXINGTON BOOKS

A division of
ROWMAN & LITTLEFIELD PUBLISHERS, INC.
Lanham • Boulder • New York • Toronto • Oxford

LEXINGTON BOOKS

A division of Rowman & Littlefield Publishers, Inc.
A wholly owned subsidary of The Rowman & Littlefield Publishing Group, Inc.
4501 Forbes Boulevard, Suite 200
Lanham, MD 20706

PO Box 317
Oxford
OX2 9RU, UK

British Library Cataloguing in Publication Information Available

Library of Congress Cataloging-in-Publication Data

Marsh, Christopher, 1969–
  Unparalleled reforms : China's rise, Russia's fall, and the interdependence of transition
/ Christopher Marsh.
    p. cm.
  Includes bibliographical references and index.
  ISBN 0-7391-1287-2 (cloth : alk. paper) — ISBN 0-7391-1288-0 (pbk. : alk. paper)
  1. Russia (Federation)—Relations—China. 2. China—Relations—Russia (Federation)
  3. Soviet Union—Relations—China. 4. China—Relations—Soviet Union. I. Title.
  DK68.7.C5M315 2005
  303.48'4094709049—dc22   2005027903

Printed in the United States of America

♾™ The paper used in this publication meets the minimum requirements of American
National Standard for Information Sciences—Permanence of Paper for Printed Library
Materials, ANSI/NISO Z39.48–1992.

For Ashlyn Elizabeth, with all the love a father can have for his daughter.

Contents

Tables and Figures

Preface

In *Orientalism*, Edward Said outlines how over a period of centuries the West constructed the Orient as an act of hegemonic discourse. Said's main point is that scholarship of the East was a project passed on from one generation of scholars to another, and that the field was based upon texts that had hitherto been gathered. This process eventually reached the point where there were two Orients — the first a real place comprised of diverse people and customs, and the second an "Orient" comprised of what Foucault would call an "archive," that is, a discourse on the people of the East. The essence of Said's critique is that to understand any culture and society one must not rely solely (if at all), upon the existing discourse on a particular culture in the observer's society. Rather, one must look within the culture itself and let its own members speak for themselves. Otherwise, the observer will be overly constrained by a potentially flawed existing conception of the world and what Said calls "comparativism."

Alongside "Orientalism" we can place the Western construct of totalitarianism, which itself is perhaps nothing more than a later offshoot of Orientalism's concept of Oriental despotism. Study of the Soviet Union, the successor states, and China are as much victim to the Western discursive project as was the Orient. Taking Said's work seriously, I have sought to let the Communist and post-Communist world speak for itself as much as possible. My ability to do this, to the extent that I have been successful, is probably more due to my own particular life circumstances than to any particular skill that allowed me to break away from the constraints posed by Orientalism. Having close relatives who are second-generation immigrants from the Russian Empire, who had been able to flee during the turbulent days of the 1890s and the 1905 Revolution, my introduction to the East was delivered to me by those who had experienced it firsthand, from those who had suffered under the tsarist regime to those who had been persecuted for their religious beliefs, including survivors of the Holocaust.

Once in college, I had the great fortune of becoming the protégé of a former Yugoslav diplomat, Gavro Altman, who himself had fought against the Nazi terror in his homeland. A long-time member of the Yugoslav Communist Party, and an outspoken critic of Soviet totalitarianism, the education he did his best to provide me was not based on Western views of the Communist world. With the

Soviet collapse, I then immediately found myself in Russia, where I was able to study firsthand life in the emerging post-Communist world.

My upbringing and academic training up to the doctoral level, therefore, was not one of indoctrination into Western views of the East. All that changed with my doctoral studies, however, where I was fully indoctrinated into the concepts of democracy, market economics, modernization, and social scientific discourse. It was at that point that I, now armed with my conceptual tools, turned my eyes further East, toward China. My initial expectation was to map out the ways in which China was going to follow the inevitable model of reform and democratization, along the lines that Western social science models predicted.

My studies of the post-Communist world, however, had already formed me to the extent that, although trained primarily in the Western literature on China, I was never convinced of the veracity of its main tenets, and remained unsatisfied with its explanations. Once my Chinese language skills progressed to the necessary level, I was then able to see for myself how the Chinese viewed their situation, and just how wide the gap was between Chinese society and the Western construct of China, in the fullest flower of Orientalism.

This is how I arrived at the present study, which in many ways has allowed me finally to answer in some sufficient fashion (at least in my own mind) some of the questions I first began to ask myself as an undergraduate student, and particularly when writing my senior thesis under Gavro Altman. While I was initially more interested in the differences between the Soviet and Yugoslav cases of transition from Communism, which became the topic of my master's thesis, I eventually turned my focus to the Communist giants. In the pages that follow, I try my best to articulate my views on the broad question of transitions from Communism and the dynamics at work and the evidence I have relied upon in forming this view. While I suspect my findings will be controversial, prior to the criticism I am likely to receive I take solace in the belief that the late Professor Said would probably consider my interpretation at least as valid as the contemporary discourse on China and Russia that abounds today.

In completing such a project, an author accumulates a tremendous number of debts, both intellectual and personal. To my wife, Melissa, I owe all of my thanks and appreciation for her support and encouragement, all the way from my days as a poor undergraduate student to my current life as a busy academic, father of two, and husband. Without her understanding and help, I could never have been able to juggle my various responsibilities. Any success I have I share with her. To my children, Ashlyn and Evan, I apologize for the evenings I had to hide away in my office to finish this manuscript, and I hope to make it up to you before I embark on my next book project. My sincere gratitude also goes to my in-laws, Steve and Mary Ann, whose support and encouragement have been so invaluable. Among the rest of my family, I am in particular debt to my grandmother for raising me with raising me with faith and strong convictions, and my father who taught me to think for myself and respect knowledge and education.

In Russia, my many friends and colleagues have assisted me in innumerable ways, but particular thanks are due to Gregory Klutcharev, who has spent many a night on a train with me and who has helped me clarify my ideas on a variety of issues. Thanks also go to Alexander Lustov, Pavel Petrov, Valeri Patsiork-ovskii, and my many friends at the Institute of the Far East, especially Andrei Ostrovskii and his wonderful wife Elena. Thanks go as well to my many friends in China, who have opened my eyes in so many ways, including Shen Yunzhen, Hu Nannan, Sun Jue, Wulan Tuoya, Yang Guangbin, Li Qingsi, and He Xiaoy-ing. Last, but certainly not least, thanks to Fredo Arias-King, the man whose country is the world, for his very close read of the manuscript in draft form.

Finally, thanks to my many students and colleagues at Baylor University who have listened to me rant on for hours on many of the points I argue here. My ideas are much clearer thanks to their feedback, suggestions, and insight. I would particularly like to thank Jerold Waltman, Xiaheng Xie, Xin Wang, Justin Page, Cole Bucy, Zach Daniel, Kevin Sheives, Mike Long, and the many stu-dents in my courses on Russian and Chinese politics. I am also in debt to Amanda Napoli for all of her assistance in editing the manuscript and compiling the index, and in general for helping keep my affairs in order. Finally, I would like to thank Peter Berger, a mentor and friend who continually goes out of his way to help me in any way he can, and who has influenced me in more ways than he knows.

Christopher Marsh
Waco, Texas
June 6, 2005

Chapter 1

Russia's Past and China's Future

It seems that socialism has been weakened, but people . . . can learn from these lessons. This can help us improve socialism and lead it on the path to healthier development. . . . Do not think that Marxism has disappeared, has fallen out of use, or has failed.

–Deng Xiaoping[1]

The disintegration of the Soviet Union and the collapse of the CPSU is not the defeat of Marxism or Socialism; however, it is the final result of separation from, deviation from, and even betrayal of Marxism, Socialism, and the basic interests of a majority of the people.

–Hu Jintao[2]

THE collapse of Communism in Eastern Europe and the former Soviet Union was spurred on to a significant degree by nationalist aspirations, and the post-Communist period remains characterized to a considerable extent by ethnic conflict and regional separatism. More than a decade after the fall of Communism, headlines from the region remain strewn with accounts of ethnic cleansing, restless minorities, and civil war. From Bosnia, Kosovo, and Chechnya to Abkhazia and Nagorno-Karabakh, the collapse of Communism in Eastern Europe and the denouement of the Soviet state have been characterized perhaps as much by suffering, displacement, and death as by freedom, democracy, and prosperity. And despite the turbulence and turmoil that has come to characterize post-Communist transitions to democracy, it most certainly could have been even worse.

With the world's most populous country standing ready to enter its transition phase, moreover, we may only be experiencing the quiet before the storm. While the idea of Chinese transition is welcomed by the West, the example of Communism's collapse in Eastern Europe and the Soviet Union must be borne in mind. As this experience suggests, along with similar experiences in Africa and Latin America, warlords, disintegration, ethnic strife, and religious conflict all become more likely as states democratize.[3] Given its particular characteris-

1

tics, including almost 100 million members of minority ethnic groups scattered all along the country's borders, a recent history of political repression, and the country's sheer size in terms of territory and population, by all accounts a Chinese regime collapse would be an earth-shattering event. No matter whether it is due to the state's implosion or a peaceful democratic revolution, political change in the People's Republic of China (PRC) will most certainly entail increased secessionist calls from Tibet and Muslim separatists in Xinjiang. The potential also exists in Inner Mongolia and perhaps among the numerous ethnic groups of southern China as well, some of which, such as the Dai, may seek to join their ethnic brethren across the borders of the Middle Kingdom. And with one-fifth of the world's population, a nuclear arsenal, and neighbors that harbor territorial ambitions, the fallout from a Chinese transition could make Bosnia, Kosovo, and Chechnya look like mere skirmishes by comparison.

While this potential is all too real, the likelihood of such a scenario actually unfolding depends upon several theoretical considerations. Those that consider the chances good for a Chinese collapse typically hold two assumptions. The first assumption is that there exist numerous points of similarity between the Soviet and Chinese transitions from Communism. While those who hold this opinion acknowledge considerable distinctions and differences between the two cases, they argue that they are similar enough that the outcomes will be the same, i.e., regime collapse. As Gilbert Rozman has stated, "Despite the many twists and turns along the way, the eventual outcome appears to be the end of the old system of communism."[4] The only way to accurately assess the implications of the Soviet past for China's future is to empirically test these assumptions by systematically comparing the reform experiences of the two countries and their characteristics and to seek to identify factors in China that played key roles in the disintegration of the USSR. Only then can one understand the true causes of the Soviet collapse and the likelihood that China will follow a similar path.

The second assumption, which follows logically from the first, is what I call the teleological fallacy. Scholars who fall into this trap believe that, even if the reform processes were dissimilar and the underlying characteristics of both countries are vastly different, they will nevertheless share the same *telos*, or end point, of regime collapse. As Dickson has so clearly and frequently phrased it, "the historical record suggests that communist governments do not evolve, but collapse."[5] From such a viewpoint, the failure of Communist rule is not related to the reform process, but rather inherent in the system itself.

The evidence examined in this book suggests that both sets of propositions are lacking in theoretical rigor and explanatory power. For one, I find that the Russian and Chinese transitions have been "unparalleled," that is, they have evolved along two quite different trajectories. Not only did China begin its reforms only after expending considerable efforts reconceptualizing Communism, it pursued its reforms in a quite different manner in terms of sequencing, speed, and substance. While this means that Chinese political reforms remain incomplete even to this day, the result has also been that its economic reforms have been overwhelmingly successful in comparison to the countries of the former Soviet Union. Additionally, and perhaps just as importantly, as Chinese leaders abandoned Communist ideology they sought to replace it with Chinese national-ism in an attempt to prevent the void from being filled spontaneously by various ethnic and religious loyalties.

As for the teleological assumption, it too is found wanting due to new his-torical evidence and recent reinterpretations of the fall of the USSR which lead to the conclusion that, rather than being inevitable, the implosion of the Soviet state was in fact the very improbable result of a series of accidents of history and misguided policies that were attempted without any clear understanding of the actual political, economic, and social circumstances of the country, not to men-tion the psychological makeup of its population. If the collapse of the Soviet Union was not inevitable, a Chinese collapse is therefore also avoidable. Such facts seriously warn against drawing too rigid an analogy between the collapse of Communism in the Soviet Union and the future of Chinese Communist Party (CCP) rule in the Middle Kingdom.

A thorough examination of the Russian and Chinese reform processes not only disproves these two propositions, it also highlights the great extent to which reforms across the Communist world were interdependent, insofar as events in one country significantly affected those in other countries, with both leaders and publics acting and reacting to the tide of events as they unfolded. Communist reform in the Soviet Union and China, therefore, was not separate processes initiated independently of each other, but rather a single, multifaceted global phenomenon that played itself out in both the domestic and international spheres.

Mikhail Gorbachev's visit to China in mid-May 1989 stands as a good ex-ample of the interdependent nature of Communist reform. Gorbachev's visit to Beijing to negotiate improved Sino-Soviet relations actually spurred on student demonstrators, with the number of protestors swelling to over 300,000 in the days prior to his arrival. As Kristof observed at the time, "there is a sense of hope in the air. . . . Mr. Gorbachev's visit is contributing to the expectations, even though few people expect him to do anything specific to encourage democ-racy in China."[6] Student demonstrators in Tiananmen Square even carried ban-ners—some in Russian—calling Gorbachev "the great reformer," "the libera-tor," and "the democratic envoy."[7] A scholar at Peking University even went so far as to predict that "the flowers of political reform blossom in the Soviet Un-ion, but the tree will bear fruit in China."[8] While the fruit of democracy was plucked from the tree before it had a chance to ripen, it is clear that Gorbachev symbolized political reform and liberalization to the demonstrating students, and that his presence in Beijing impacted to a significant degree the way events un-folded.

Likewise, the crackdown on the peaceful student demonstrations in Tianan-men Square on June 4, 1989, affected the course of further reform in the Soviet Union. As Tucker has compellingly argued, the Tiananmen demonstrations may actually have been a factor in the collapse of the Soviet Union, insofar as "the

Chinese democracy movement helped to create an environment in which citizens of other Communist countries dared to aspire to a new political order." The fact that "the Chinese themselves succumbed to a brutally repressive regime," therefore, "did not stem the tide elsewhere."[9] This experience also affected Gorbachev himself, who saw what can happen when the speed of reform does not keep pace with the expectations of the people. Perhaps most significantly, however, it affected deputies in the newly elected Soviet legislature and ordinary Soviet citizens who were avidly watching live television coverage of the first session of the Congress of People's Deputies, where reformist legislators and opposition leaders spoke out vehemently against the events and demanded that the Soviet government take decisive action against Beijing.[10]

One reason that the Tiananmen events were taken so seriously in the Soviet Union is that the "massacre was directly linked in the mind of the public to the brutal clamp-down in Tbilisi which happened only weeks before . . . and was seen as an indicator of the possibility that perestroika in the USSR could be discontinued."[11] The sad irony of the situation is that, according to CCP insiders, Deng Xiaoping had apparently "held up as an example of good public discipline" the Soviet troops in Tbilisi who had brutally killed 20 demonstrators and wounded several hundred more with "tear gas, shovels and clubs."[12]

Even a brief examination of the synergistic and interdependent nature of the events that unfolded in Communist regimes between 1989-1991 shows that events in one country affected those in others, as significant interaction occurred and as leaders and groups drew lessons from both successful and unsuccessful events elsewhere. In the end, this is one of the primary reasons why the collapse of Communism "in Poland took ten years, in Hungary ten months, in East Germany ten weeks,"[13] in Czechoslovakia ten days, and Romania only ten hours, since the collapse of the first Communist regime in Eastern Europe led to a snowball effect[14] whereby opposition forces became emboldened and leaders saw the writing on the wall.

These facts suggest that lesson-drawing may have fundamentally altered the dynamic of reform, a point that has remained almost entirely overlooked in the literature on transitions. One of the most significant questions this raises then is what kind of lessons did Chinese reform leaders, who viewed the collapse of Communism as a failure, attempt to draw from the collapse of Communism in the Soviet Union and Eastern Europe? Certainly, the collapse of the Soviet Union in December 1991—one of the most significant events of the twentieth century—was of particular significance to Communist leaders in China, as it signaled impending doom. This event, therefore, most certainly affected Chinese thinking about Communism and its viability and thus impacted their reform strategy. Moreover, how did the resurgence of Communist support in Eastern Europe and the former Soviet Union during the mid- and late-1990s affect the CCP? An examination of public statements made by Chinese leaders, scholarly research by Chinese scholars, unofficial documents, and interviews with party insiders yields compelling evidence that the Chinese have been profoundly affected by the collapse of the Soviet regime, and that they are attempting to draw lessons from the collapse that can serve to buttress their political power.

What about the impact of Chinese reform on the USSR and the lessons that Russia has been able to learn? Gorbachev flouted the initial successes of Chinese economic reforms when he formulated his *perestroika* agenda, seeking to launch simultaneous economic and political reform. Likewise, he perhaps felt his plan was vindicated by the relative stability in the Soviet Union in May and June 1989, during the height of the Tiananmen demonstrations. Simply experiencing this turmoil, however, must have then affected his own thoughts on reform as he witnessed these events firsthand and considered the implications for the USSR. Returning to Moscow, Gorbachev perhaps then began to realize that many of those living under Communist rule in the Soviet Union and Eastern Europe were as discontent as the Chinese who had gathered in Tiananmen Square. Finally, the eventual collapse of the Soviet Union and the continued economic success of China must today force some living in the new Russia to question how perestroika was superior to the Chinese model of reform. The answers to these questions are crucial for understanding the current struggles in both Russia and China to develop effective and responsive governance and will shed light on the future of these influential international actors.

Russia and China: Comparison, Interaction, and Lesson-Drawing

By now it should be clear that analyses that look at single cases in isolation or simply compare reform processes between two or more cases may in fact neglect potentially significant variables. When conditions of interaction exist between the cases being studied, the interdependent nature of political events must be considered. In previous studies comparing Communist reform in Russia and China, however, this fact has remained almost entirely neglected. Nevertheless, several such studies are valuable contributions to the field and inform the research presented here, as they provide detailed information on the structural changes that accompanied the reforms in each country and identify significant differences and similarities between the Russian and Chinese experiences with reform.

The path-breaking research on Sino-Soviet mutual assessments, conducted by Gilbert Rozman beginning in the mid-1980s, first highlighted the fact that Chinese and Soviet scholars were keenly interested in the theoretical significance of events and debates in each other's country. The most comprehensive accounts of this phenomenon, however, his *A Mirror for Socialism: Soviet Criticisms of China* and *The Chinese Debate about Soviet Socialism, 1978-1985*, were completed prior to the most significant period of reform, i.e., before Gorbachev's rise to power and the political turmoil of 1989-1991.[15] Rozman's later work did examine events during this period, but it failed to address the issue of lesson-drawing and interaction effects in the transition process.[16]

The first comparative analysis of Communist reform in the Soviet Union and China, which also included discussion of the world's other Communist states, was Zbigniew Brzezinski's *The Grand Failure: The Birth and Death of Communism in the Twentieth Century*, the publication of which actually preceded the major events of 1989-1991. Despite this fact, the conclusions of this study were validated by subsequent events and those that have not yet come to pass remain valid assessments of the future. By analyzing such factors as the nature of the reforms initiated, underlying structural conditions, and cultural influences, Brzezinski was able to conclude in 1988 that "The reform of Chinese communism is probably fated to be successful . . . unlike its organic rejection by Eastern Europe, communism in China faces the prospects of organic absorption by the country's enduring traditions and values."[17] Brzezinski's cogent analysis also highlights the way in which China and other Communist states emulated the Soviet model. Despite its comprehensive account, this study also fails to consider the implications of interaction and lesson-drawing in a theoretically rigorous manner.

The first study to compare the processes that resulted in the collapse of Communist rule in the Soviet Union with similar processes underway in the PRC was Minxin Pei's *From Reform to Revolution: The Demise of Communism in China and the Soviet Union*.[18] In this study, Pei finds that the success of transition depended upon preexisting social structures and economic institutions as well as upon the mobilization of social actors. While this analysis provides an excellent comparison of the Soviet and Chinese paths to reform, and resulted in a unique theoretical model of transitions from authoritarian rule, it too paid insufficient attention to the interdependent nature of Communist reform in both countries.

One final noteworthy study is Peter Nolan's *China's Rise, Russia's Fall*, which seeks to explain the success of Chinese reform and the failure of Soviet restructuring. Nolan's finding that the Soviet collapse was due in large measure to the reform recommendations offered to the Soviet bloc by the West is problematic, especially given the fact that Gorbachev was not compelled to follow Western reform advice nor were his most crucial policy initiatives related to Western advice, e.g., perestroika and demokratizatsiya. The most significant contribution of this study is perhaps its focus on the role of policymakers and their decisions. With this study, Nolan moves significantly beyond the work conducted by others in that he attempts to explain the differing outcomes of Soviet and Chinese reform by pointing to specific policies chosen by the respective leaderships.

Nolan also goes farther than anyone else in initially identifying the interdependent nature of reform in both countries, finding that "Events within each of the communist giants reacted back upon the choice of policies in the other." The fact that the "radical Russian plans of 1990" were formulated based upon a perception that Chinese reforms were failing is not overlooked by Nolan, nor is the fact that the "Chinese leadership's fear of the consequences of large scale political change was hugely intensified by the acceleration of political disintegration in the USSR in the late 1980s, and by the collapse of communism in Eastern Europe in 1989." In the end, however, Nolan fails to recognize the theoretical significance of this finding and its continuing impact, concluding only that "the collapse of the USSR provided a source of confidence to the Chinese leadership that their incremental reform path was broadly correct and that they had been correct to avoid the alternative of rapid system change."[19] As I will argue below, the Chinese in fact were anything but confident at the time, and sought to draw lessons from the Soviet collapse to help them avoid the same fate as their comrades in Moscow.

Mention should also be made of some outstanding works on Sino-Russian relations which highlight the importance of mutual perceptions between the Communist giants. Lukin's *The Bear Watches the Dragon* is an impressive tome that documents Russia's image of China from the time of early contacts to the present day, though it makes no attempt to illustrate the ways in which this image may have affected Russia's view of itself.[20] Likewise, Dittmer's *Sino-Soviet Normalization and its International Implications*, though focusing on the changing patterns of relations between the Soviet Union and the PRC during the latter half of the twentieth century, includes some excellent analysis of China's perception of the Soviet Union and provides an impressive amount of evidence to illustrate the ways in which Communist China sought to distinguish itself from the shadow of its Soviet *laodage* (revered older brother).[21]

There is also a small but significant body of literature that contributes to research on the interdependence of Communist reform by focusing on the effects of external factors on the reform process. Important contributions in this area include work by Tucker and Lukin on the impact of events in China on the course of events in the Soviet Union and the work by Halperin and Tubilewicz on Chinese lesson-drawing from the East European economic experience.[22] While these works consider the impact of external events and ideas on policy choice, by focusing on only Russia or China and narrow policy areas during a brief period of time, it is not possible to reach broad conclusions regarding the interdependent nature of Communist reform in a way that becomes possible with a broad and detailed analysis of the reform experiences in both countries over an extended period.

While all of these studies certainly elucidate the Soviet and Chinese transitions from Communist rule, we are still lacking a complete picture of the interdependent nature of Communist reform, one that highlights the role of interaction effects and lesson-drawing and can be used as a basis for refining social science theory. Why does almost all work in comparative politics fail to consider the impact of such factors? The reason is that we are guided by theories that do not account for such variables. While it seems strange for us to ask how events in one country affect events in another, we know intuitively that the way we view an event of one order affects the way we view other events of the same or similar order. This heuristic device is useful for understanding events and, indeed, is perhaps the underlying principle of comparative politics, but it traps our thinking into a box from which it is difficult to escape, for we fail to recognize that the policymakers we are studying are also thinking in the same way. If we are to develop comprehensive explanations for political events, we must develop a rigorous theoretical model that can account for these factors.

The emphasis here on the interdependent nature of Communist reform is not meant to discount the significance of other factors, such as structural conditions, institutions, political culture, or social mobilization. All of these factors play significant roles in political transitions and were certainly at work in the Soviet Union and China. Most analyses, however, have overlooked the interdependent nature of the reform process and the importance of the specific policy choices made by the leaders of both countries. Any complete analysis of Communist reform must include in the equation the objectives, intentions, and understanding of the policymakers and leaders that directed the reform processes and the interdependent nature of politics on the world stage. While interaction effects and lesson-drawing might not be any more important than other contributing factors, can we neglect any significant factor? If we know a factor impacts the transition process and political processes in general, can we continue to operate under the assumption that it does not? Neglecting such factors leads to incomplete explanations and inaccurate assessments of political phenomena, and eventually contributes to incorrect policy advice and strained relations between nations.

Research Design and Structure of the Study

This study focuses on three sets of questions. The first set of questions relates to the decision to reform the Soviet and Chinese Communist systems and the initial paths taken, which in both cases resulted in systemic crisis. What led these states to seek such sweeping reforms, and how did attempts to improve these systems result in crisis? How were these crises dealt with, and why did one state collapse as a result, while the other is seemingly stable? The second set of questions focuses on the development paths taken in post-Soviet Russia and post-Tiananmen China after the crises, focusing on Russia's attempt to make a transition to democracy and the free market and China's attempt to chart a different course to reform, one that bypasses the traumatic events of a systemic collapse but still lands safely upon the shores of prosperity. Finally, the last set of questions centers on the impact interaction effects and lesson-drawing had on the reform paths taken in both countries, building upon the base of knowledge developed in the previous sections. Switching between cases in such a staggered-chronological manner permits these sets of questions to be considered separately, with everything being tied together in the conclusion. It also allows the details of the two reform paths to be laid out before investigating the role of interaction effects and lesson-drawing.

Following this introduction, I begin in chapter 2 with a review and critique of the major assumptions of the transitology literature, the main body of theory that informs this study. I then review the methodology of comparative political analysis and discuss some of the difficulties associated with this method, including its inefficiency in dealing with causal factors that transgress state borders, particularly interaction effects and lesson-drawing. After considering how such factors have been dealt with in the field, I attempt to incorporate some of the theoretical advances made in these areas in the field of policy studies into the study of comparative politics. Using the insights gleaned from this body of research, I am then prepared to compare the reform processes in the Soviet Union and China with an eye to the potential impact of such factors.

In chapter 3, I compare the Chinese and Soviet experiences with reform from their initiation to systemic crisis. I begin by examining China's reform initiative launched in 1978 and its effects. After examining the way in which the system evolved throughout the 1980s, I examine the events that led up to the Tiananmen Square incident of 1989, when Chinese leaders used force to quell student protests rather than initiating a dialogue that may have led to a negotiated transition from Communist rule. Throughout the analysis I pay particular attention to the impact perestroika and glasnost had on China's reform agenda, especially on the attitudes and objectives of student leaders. I also discuss what role force played in keeping the CCP in power. Finally, I explore the impact Gorbachev had on the events in China due to his visit to Beijing in May 1989.

In the second half of chapter 3, the analysis switches over to the Soviet case, beginning with an examination of the state of Soviet society on the eve of Gorbachev's reforms and concluding with an analysis of the factors that led to the destruction of the Soviet Union itself. Of course, Gorbachev's reforms were not created in a vacuum, and he was very aware of the fact that China had initiated its own restructuring nearly a decade earlier. Gorbachev's understanding of these reforms, however, was largely shaped by the information he received from Soviet think-tanks specializing in China, which at the time still had very negative views on the prospects for change in the Middle Kingdom. It should not come as a surprise, therefore, that Gorbachev was explicit in his refusal to learn any lessons from Beijing, instead reaching the conclusion that, rather than pursuing economic reform alone, the Soviet Union should embark upon rapid and simultaneous economic and political liberalization. Particular attention is devoted to the effect the Tiananmen incident had on Gorbachev and the Russian people, and the impact this had on the direction of reform between 1989-1991 and on the eventual collapse of the Soviet Union. Finally, I explore the underlying reasons for the Soviet collapse.

In chapter 4, the analysis focuses on the path of reform in China following the Tiananmen incident and developments in Post-Soviet Russia. I begin by exploring whether or not the Chinese Communist system was on the verge of collapse in 1989 and argue that most predictions about a Chinese collapse are the result of simple analogous reasoning, not serious analysis of China's contemporary situation. The remainder of the section surveys the reforms undertaken throughout the 1990s and the country's current political, economic, and social conditions, before finally considering the chances that China might yet suffer a Soviet-style collapse. The analysis then turns its focus to post-Soviet Russia and the process of post-Communist economic and political development. I begin by showing that the transition from Communist rule in Russia has been plagued with difficulties, and that rather than developing "democracy from scratch," Russia has had to build democracy and the free market from under the ashes and ruble of a dysfunctional Soviet system, legacies of which exist even today. Finally, I show that, more than a decade after the Soviet collapse, a significant proportion of Russians regret this event, and I explore how the Communist Party remained the most popular party in Russia at the end of the millennium, winning a larger share of legislative votes than any other party in every election except for the initial post-Communist election of 1993, when it was banned from participating and thus campaigning until the very last moment.

In chapters 5 and 6, the focus turns to the issue of lesson-drawing as I seek to explain the reform paths identified in the previous two chapters. In gathering evidence in support of my hypotheses, I examine an eclectic mix of sources, including public statements made by political figures, scholarly research in each of the countries, unofficial documents, public opinion data (where available), and interviews with party insiders and political figures. Given the nature of these regimes both in the past and presently, the evidence that I am able to gather is necessarily different for the two cases and for different periods of time. For example, during periods of staunch Communist censorship, the only available data are from public statements and scholarly research. While this can be supplemented with memoirs in the Russian case, no such sources are available (or reliable) for China. Likewise, while I can refer to public opinion data for post-Soviet Russia, there is no comparable data for contemporary China (due to the sensitivity of the issues involved). While such a variety of sources would make it impossible to trace the evolution of attitudes or beliefs across time, it is adequate to the task at hand, which is to uncover evidence of lesson-drawing and how it may have affected the course of reform in Russia and China.

In chapter 5, after examining the available evidence, I suggest that one reason China has yet to collapse is that Chinese leaders have sought to learn from the collapse of Communism in Eastern Europe and the Soviet Union and have sought to adjust their policies to buttress their political power. I also examine some of the lessons the Chinese have drawn from the New Russia, focusing on Russia's troubled economic transition and diminished international stature. Finally, I examine how Chinese view the situation in Russia today and how they feel vindicated for following the path they have rather than pursuing a rapid transition.

Similarly, in chapter 6 I consider some of the lessons that Moscow could have learned from Beijing in terms of the transition from state planning, only to find that Russian leaders—despite the calls of some policy advisors and intellectuals—refuse to learn from the Chinese experience, and only draw negative lessons from the Chinese reform path, with Gorbachev in particular looking upon many aspects of China's reforms as precisely what *not* to do. I then explore several explanations for these phenomena, concluding that although the success of China's reform agenda is acknowledged and commended by some, political leaders in Russia either consider that they have nothing to learn from a developing country such as China, or they fear what might happen if Russians today were to begin to question the course of reform followed up to this point.

In the conclusion, I consider the drastic differences between the reform of Communism in Russia and China, and their current locations on the paths of reform. While it is clear that Communist reform has been a process that has transcended state boundaries, with a high level of interaction and the opportunity to draw lessons from the experience of other countries, it is just as apparent that the lessons that have been drawn have tended to be negative ones. And while the opportunity for lesson-drawing certainly existed on both sides, moreover, Russia has consistently failed to draw lessons from China's successful economic reforms while China has been very adept at learning from both the successes and failures of the Soviet Union and later Russia. I then explore the role culture may play in explaining such behavior, concluding that culture may in fact explain why Communism was less amenable to reform in the Soviet Union than in China and the way leaders went about reforming their systems. Finally, I bring this study to a close with a discussion of the future of Russia and China, including the likelihood of an eventual Chinese collapse and of democracy taking root in Russia.

Unparalleled Reforms

Setting aside the Cold War and the proxy conflicts between the West and the "Communist bloc," Communist regimes perpetrated some of the most horrific crimes the world has ever known against their own people. While we will never know for sure, solid estimates put Stalin's and Mao's victims somewhere in the vicinity of 60 million. But in the end, it was not external aggression or domestic rebellion but a new generation of leaders who sought to change direction and embark upon the problematic path of Communist reform. Although China began the process first, its reforms have largely remained limited to the economic sphere, and today it continues to play a balancing act with the forces of modernization and democratization, with the outcome far from certain.

Despite the lead China had by initiating reforms earlier, the Soviet Union was not far behind, and once new blood took over in the Kremlin, Gorbachev moved fast and implemented wide-sweeping reforms. The effects of these reforms were just as rapid, and by the spring of 1989 revolt was spreading throughout Eastern Europe. By year's end the Soviet Empire in Eastern Europe had collapsed, to be followed within a brief two years by the USSR itself. While the collapse of Soviet rule in Eastern Europe may have been a liberation, the Soviet Union's reforms were in actuality a tragic failure, with the country going from reform to collapse in less than 5 years, while even today the successor states continue to struggle with issues of identity, liberty, and economic adjustment. Indeed, the success of the Rose, Orange, and Tulip Revolutions in Georgia, Ukraine, and Kyrgyzstan, respectively, attest to the fact that the transitions in 1991, while transitions *from* Communism, were not necessarily transitions *to* democracy.

While the jury is still out on whether or not democracy is in the future for Russia and China, what can be stated without fear of exaggeration is that the reforms of the Soviet and Chinese Communist systems over the past quarter century have been unparalleled—never before in history have such radical changes been attempted by two governments which together ruled nearly two billion people comprising almost two hundred nationalities living on a territory stretching halfway around the planet. The reforms attempted by Moscow and Beijing are unparalleled in another sense as well—the reform agendas pursued in the USSR and the PRC have followed different trajectories and differed substantially in terms of sequencing, speed, and substance. It remains to be seen, of course, whether or not they will remain dissimilar in their outcomes, as the PRC does its best not to follow the Soviet Union into the "dustbin of history." The purpose of this book is to offer the reader a sophisticated understanding of the reform processes in both countries that can serve as the basis for an accurate assessment of the future of both societies and its implications for the rest of the world.

Notes

1. Quoted in Lu Nanquan and Jiang Changbing, eds., *Sulian jubian shencengci yuanyin yanjiu* (Beijing: Zhongguo shehui kexue chubanshe, 1999), 3.

2. "Hu Jintao sizhong quanhui neibu jianghua," *Kaifang zazhi* 12 (2004).

3. Jack Snyder, *From Voting to Violence: Democratization and Nationalist Conflict* (New York: W. W. Norton, 2000).

4. Gilbert Rozman, ed., *Dismantling Communism: Common Causes and Regional Variations* (Washington, DC, and Baltimore: Woodrow Wilson Center Press and Johns Hopkins University Press, 1992), 16.

5. Bruce Dickson, "Unsettled Succession: China's Critical Moment," *The National Interest* (Fall 1997): 64-72. As of the summer of 2002, Dickson continued to hold such a view (personal correspondence with the author).

6. Nicholas Kristof, "China's Hero of Democracy: Gorbachev," *New York Times,* May 14, 1989, A10.

7. Bill Keller, "Soviets and China Resuming Normal Ties After 30 Years," *New York Times,* May 17, 1989, A1; Sheryl WuDunn, "Students in China Flood Main Square," *New York Times,* May 15, 1989, A8; and "300,000 Flowers Bloom in China," *New York Times,* May 17, 1989, A26.

8. Quoted in Keller, "Soviets and China Resuming Normal Ties After 30 Years."

9. Nancy Bernkopf Tucker, "China as a Factor in the Collapse of the Soviet Union," *Political Science Quarterly* 110, no. 4 (1995-96): 518.

10. Alexander Lukin, "The Initial Soviet Reaction to the Events in China in 1989 and the Prospects for Sino-Soviet Relations," *The China Quarterly* 125 (March 1991), 119-136.

11. Lukin, "The Initial Soviet Reaction to the Events in China in 1989 and the Prospects for Sino-Soviet Relations," 129.

12. Bill Keller, "Gorbachev Visits Beijing for Start of Summit Talks," *New York Times,* May 15, 1989, A1.

13. Timothy Garton Ash, "The Revolution of the Magic Lantern," *New York Review of Books,* January 18, 1990.

14. Samuel Huntington, *The Third Wave: Democratization in the Late Twentieth Century* (Norman, OK: University of Oklahoma Press, 1991), 100-106.

15. Gilbert Rozman, *A Mirror for Socialism: Soviet Criticisms of China* (Princeton: Princeton University Press, 1985), and *The Chinese Debate about Soviet Socialism, 1978-1985* (Princeton: Princeton University Press, 1987).

16. Rozman, *Dismantling Communism*; Gilbert Rozman, "Sino-Russian Relations: Mutual Assessments and Predictions," in Sherman Garnett, ed., *Rapprochement or Rivalry: Russia-China Relations in a Changing World* (Washington, DC: Carnegie Endowment for International Peace, 2000), 147-174; Gilbert Rozman, "Sino-Russian Relations in the 1990s: A Balance Sheet," *Post-Soviet Affairs* 14, no. 2 (April-June 1998): 93-113; and Gilbert Rozman, "Chinese Studies in Russia and their Impact, 1985-1992," *Asian Research Trends* 5 (1994): 143-160.

17. Zbigniew Brzezinski, *The Grand Failure: The Birth and Death of Communism in the Twentieth Century* (New York: Charles Scribners, 1989), 147. The date cited here, 1988, while not the date of publication, is the date at which he completed his manuscript.

18. Minxin Pei, *From Reform to Revolution: The Demise of Communism in China and the Soviet Union* (Cambridge, MA: Harvard University Press, 1994).

19. Peter Nolan, *China's Rise, Russia's Fall: Politics, Economics and Planning in the Transition from Stalinism* (New York: St. Martin's Press, 1995), 5.

20. Alexander Lukin, *The Bear Watches the Dragon: Russia's Perception of China and the Evolution of Russian-Chinese Relations Since the Eighteenth Century* (Armonk, NY: M.E. Sharpe, 2003).

21. Lowell Dittmer, *Sino-Soviet Normalization and its International Implications, 1945-1990* (Seattle: University of Washington Press, 1992).

22. Tucker, "China as a Factor in the Collapse of the Soviet Union"; Lukin, "The Initial Soviet Reaction to the Events in China in 1989 and the Prospects for Sino-Soviet Relations"; Nina Halpern, "Learning From Abroad: Chinese Views of the East European Economic Experience, January 1977-June 1981," *Modern China* 11, no. 1 (January 1985): 77-109, and Czeslaw Tubilewicz, "Chinese Press Coverage of Political and Economic Restructuring of East Central Europe," *Asian Survey* 37, no. 10 (October 1997): 927-943.

Chapter 2

Transitions, Interaction Effects, and Lesson-Drawing

Never be content with looking at states purely from within; always remember that they have another aspect which is wholly different, their relation to foreign states. . . . We have an inveterate habit of regarding our own history as self-contained, and of assuming that whatever has happened in England can be explained by English causes. So much so, that I think the English history still remains to be written which shall do anything like justice to foreign or continental influences which have contributed to determine the course of English affairs.
–John Robert Seeley (1886)[1]

THEORY and methodology both directly impact a study's findings, since it is theory which determines what facts are considered important and thus selected for inclusion in any analysis. Likewise, methodology determines what facts are available for observation and how they are measured and categorized. Theoretical and methodological choices thus both significantly impact a study's conclusions, since they guide the processes of data collection, measurement, and analysis. Before we can turn to an examination of the reform paths pursued by Russia and China, therefore, in this chapter we consider the theoretical and methodological bases that guide the subsequent analyses.

The theoretical literature that informs this study is a somewhat amorphous conglomeration of work that can be grouped under the label of transitology and which examines the processes of reform and transition with the goal of identifying common causes and outcomes. While debates continue to rage over whether or not transitions from authoritarian rule are similar enough to transitions from Communism to merit comparison, all appear to be in agreement that transitions from Communism are comparable, that is, comparing the reform processes of various Communist countries in order to identify trends and patterns can be a fruitful exercise. While focusing solely on transitions from Communism allows me to avoid the problem of "conceptual stretching,"[2] or inappropriately applying a label to an overly-broad class of phenomena, I find that conceptual constriction, i.e., seeking to force-fit cases into a predetermined theoretical framework, is a problem that has remained overlooked in the study of post-Communist transitions and must be avoided.

While myriad factors were at work in often unique combinations in the dozens of societies that sought to exit from Communism in the late 1980s and early 1990s, the reform of Communism was not separate processes operating independently of each other, but rather part of a single, global phenomenon. In order to reach a proper understanding of this phenomenon, therefore, we must use an appropriate methodology, one that does more than simply juxtapose the cases as if they were isolated and independent of one another. Although a straightforward comparative analysis such as this will form the basis of this study, the interdependent nature of Communist reform forces us to look beyond the borders of each country to other potentially significant factors, and will be taken up in chapters 5 and 6.

Comparative politics as a field focuses almost exclusively on domestic sources of politics, often neglecting potentially significant factors that may emanate from the international system. Two such factors that played important roles in the Soviet and Chinese transitions from Communism are interaction and lesson-drawing. Analysis of such factors is not entirely absent in the field of comparative politics, but they are often overlooked and rarely considered in a methodologically rigorous manner. The reason for this is that comparative research is guided by theories that do not adequately account for such variables. In fact, it even seems strange for a comparativist to ask how events in one country are affected by events in another, since the preoccupation in the field is with comparing cases to identify differences and similarities between the units under analysis, often working under the dubious assumption that the cases are independent of each other.

In addition to considering the implications of the theories that inform and the methodologies that guide this study, in this chapter I also argue that the fields of international relations, comparative politics, and policy studies have each drifted apart from one another to the detriment of all. While the development of these "separate tables"[3] in the field may seem fairly innocuous, the fact that there is virtually no dialogue among these research traditions means that advances made in one body of literature are rarely incorporated into analyses grounded in one of the other traditions, even though we often analyze the same or similar phenomena. I therefore attempt to reach beyond the traditional bounds of comparative politics in this study and to combine insights from all three research traditions.

This chapter begins with a review and critique of the major assumptions of the transitology literature, the main body of theory that informs this study. Next, I review the methodology of comparative political analysis and discuss some of the traps associated with using this method, including its inefficiency in dealing with causal factors that transgress state borders, particularly interaction effects and lesson-drawing. After considering how such factors have been dealt with in the field, I attempt to incorporate some of the theoretical advances made in these areas in the field of policy studies into the study of comparative politics. Finally, this prepares us to heed the call of John Robert Seeley, in the quote that opens this chapter, to be aware of the fact that the processes we are studying do not have solely domestic sources.

The Comparative Study of Transitions

"However unique," argued Russell Bova in the Soviet Union's final days, transitions from Communism can "be usefully viewed as a subcategory of a more generic phenomenon of transition from authoritarian rule."[4] Thus was drawn a connection between the collapse of Communism in Eastern Europe and the transitions from authoritarian rule in Southern Europe and Latin America. The reason for this extension of the comparative study of transitions was the idea that similar processes and dynamics were at work in both the transitions from authoritarianism in the 1970s and 1980s and the transitions from Communism in the late 1980s and early 1990s. As Bova further argued, Spain's transition was more similar to the processes underway in the Soviet Union than they were to its Iberian neighbor.[5] If similar processes were at work, then it made perfect sense to study countries undergoing transition as a group, both to seek out common factors and to use the extensive experience of studying the former to illuminate the latter.

The birth of the comparative study of transitions is most often traced back to the seminal 1970 article on "Transitions to Democracy" by Dankwart Rustow.[6] While Rustow's main point was that there was no set of social and economic conditions required for a society to make a successful transition to democracy, thus offering a critique of the then-dominant paradigm of modernization theory, the true impact of Rustow's study was that it gave birth to a new subfield of comparative politics—transitology. While the body of work that would eventually grow out of this loosely-defined "field" would differ on numerous points—not the least of which would be the actual existence of such a field—the term itself has provided a useful rubric under which seemingly disparate research has come to be categorized, whether or not the authors of such work even agree to such a labeling.

If it was Rustow's article that gave birth to transitology, then it was with the Transitions Project and the subsequent publication of *Transitions from Authoritarian Rule* that the fledgling field reached the point of maturity.[7] The findings of this impressive examination of the collapse of authoritarian rule in Southern Europe and Latin America conducted by prominent scholars in the field resulted in a key set of assumptions that would come to form the core of the field of transitology. Although not disagreeing with Rustow's assertion that democratic regimes were possible in any country that exhibited national unity, O'Donnell and Schimitter, in the concluding chapter, posited that democracy was more or less

likely in a society given certain structural contexts. Most significantly, they focused their attention on individual-level behavior, concentrating on the interaction among elites and their bargaining tactics. By analyzing how leaders of the
ancien regimes negotiated with members of the opposition, O'Donnell and
Schmitter concluded that patterns of elite interaction themselves significantly
impacted the transition and affected its outcome. Subsequent research in the
field more often than not worked within this newly articulated paradigm, resulting in an impressive body of scholarship by the time that the Communist regimes of the world began to enter their crisis phase between 1989-1991.

The field of Communist Studies was ill-prepared to deal with the tumult and
change of 1989. Contrary to those who seek to blame the field for its lack of
academic rigor, to the contrary Communist Studies was a very impressive field
of inquiry given the closed nature of the societies it sought to study. It was the
secrecy, isolation, and subterfuge of the Communist regimes that forced scholars
who devoted their careers to this field to develop new and innovative methods
and unique theories to explain the phenomena they studied. The collapse of
Communist rule in Eastern Europe, however, and the seeming similarity between what was occurring in Prague and Berlin at that moment with what had
occurred in Lisbon and Brasilia years before led a few Communist Studies
scholars to look for new approaches.[8] The most significant shift, however, was
among the new generation of scholars coming up through the ranks of the academy who themselves began to turn to this body of literature. These scholars
were then able to conduct research the way their colleagues in Latin American,
European, and African studies had for years, with extensive field experience,
close interaction with political and community leaders, and armed with a literature and body of theory that could seemingly explain it all, and which begged to
be applied to these new cases. Finally, there were those transitologists who had
been working on Latin America and Southern Europe who sought to "travel" to
the East and to test the theories of the prevailing paradigm—with Philippe
Schmitter himself offering his encouragement.[9]

Despite its seeming appeal, the "travel of the transitologists" to Eastern
Europe was accompanied by a heated debate in the literature over the appropri-
ateness of "stretching" the concepts developed in studying transitions from authoritarian rule to fit the cases of the post-Communist world. The call to
"ground" these transitologists was more than a mere turf war—there are many
valid reasons why transitions from Communism are distinct from transitions
from authoritarianism.[10] As Bunce argued in direct response to Schmitter and
Karl's call to move eastward, the nature of Communist rule differed sharply
from authoritarianism in terms of "its social structure, its ideology and ideological spectrum, its political economy, its configuration of political and economic
elites, its patterns of civil-military relations and its position in the international
hierarchy of power and privilege."[11] If these differences themselves did not in-
validate all attempts to compare the East and the South, there were also dis-
tinctly different modes of transition, with regime change coming to Eastern
Europe only with the nod of approval from Moscow—something without paral-

lel in the transitions from authoritarian rule. This is why the collapse of Communism in Eastern Europe must be seen as a much as a national liberation as a regime change.

Bunce raises some very interesting and accurate points in her strident critique of Schmitter and Karl. There are many very significant differences between the transitions in Latin America and Southern Europe and those of the Communist world. One of the most important was the very real difference between authoritarianism and the totalitarian nature of Communist societies, as Bunce briefly mentioned. As harsh as authoritarian rule may be, totalitarianism appears to have a lasting impact on a society, inflicting a poison into a society's social fabric that can be washed but perhaps not removed. As Kovács has phrased it, "there is an awful lot of handwriting on the allegedly blank sheet of postcommunist culture—handwriting that is extremely hard to erase."[12]

Additionally, the transitions from Communism were "dual-transitions," since they were as much about building market economies as they were about democratization, a factor that has greatly complicated the process of post-Communist democratization. Finally, societies in Eastern Europe and the former Soviet Union have had to deal with the very factor that Rustow pointed out years ago as the one requisite of democracy—national unity. The existence of such ethnic conflicts along the borders of the post-Communist states, such as Bosnia, Kosovo, Chechnya, and Abkhazia, make this part of the world quite distinct from Latin America and Southern Europe, where the cases of the Basque Country and Catalonia represent the exception rather than the rule.

While the differences between transitions from authoritarian and Communist rule are very real, the fact of the matter is that the higher up the ladder of abstraction any scholar goes, the fewer will be the similarities among the cases included. Likewise, moving down the ladder of abstraction allows for more similarity while necessarily reducing both the number of cases available for observation and the generalizability of the study's findings. All in all, a scholar's choice of level of abstraction is a rather silly thing to argue about, since research at all levels is useful and helps build cumulative knowledge. It is also interesting to point out that no similar debate seems to be directed against an even higher level of analysis, that of democratization, which is the highest level of abstraction possible for studying transitions to democracy. Analyses by scholars such as Vanhanen and Huntington, which group such transitions together as those of the United States and the United Kingdom with Spain and the Soviet Union, actually find their strength in the great variation among the historical, cultural, and social contexts of the cases included in their analyses, which also makes the resulting findings generalizable and conducive to theory building. Such studies are considered some of the most influential and significant works in the field, and purportedly include every possible case, irrespective of time and space.[13]

This is exactly the point Carothers makes in his call to lay the transition paradigm to rest, where he argues that the changes that swept the world in the last quarter of the twentieth century shared a dominant characteristic— "simultaneous movement . . . away from dictatorial rule toward more liberal and often more democratic governance."[14] In dispelling the myth of democracy being the likely outcome of transitions, Carothers suggests that the majority of societies in transition actually enter the gray zone, where they either suffer under the condition of feckless pluralism, with democracy remaining shallow and troubled, or they become characterized by dominant-power politics, with one political group dominating the system. While Carothers effectively puts an end to the transition paradigm that sees democracy as the teleological endpoint of all transition states,[15] he simultaneously provides the best justification yet for the comparative study of transitions, making his new categories applicable to all cases.

Transitions from Communism

While the debate over transitology is an important one, it is not crucial to the present study, as I am here dealing only with countries that are on the path away from Communism, which, as Bunce proposes, is "the most logical comparison to be made."[16] Of course, the major difference between the former Soviet Union and China is that the former is a post-Communist society while the latter is still "Communist," insofar as the country is controlled by the Chinese Communist Party. I am not, however, working from the a priori assumption that both are moving in the same direction or will arrive at the same end point, only assuming that they are moving away from comparable positions, i.e., Stalinist regimes.

One could even question whether or not the analysis conducted here can even be classified as transitology. After all, I do not attempt to compare a case of transition from authoritarian rule with a case of transition from Communism, nor do I employ many of the theoretical innovations or methodological techniques developed in the study of transitions from authoritarianism. I still place my analysis under the rubric of transitology, however, since I am in fact analyzing the *transition* process in these societies. Despite employing the term, my work is in many ways no different from the majority of analyses of post-Communist transitions that, as Gans-Morse points out, spend more time critiquing transitology than actually applying any transitological approach to their own work.[17] I still believe that the label transitology is a useful one, as it connotes analysis that approaches the study of societies in transition with the assumption that transitions are comparable and that conclusions reached can be used to illuminate other cases of transition. Such an understanding of transition is perhaps what the founders of the British publication *The Journal of Communist Studies and Transition Politics* had in mind when naming their journal.

One issue that is conspicuously absent from the transitology debate is that transitions from Communism are themselves quite distinct. Bova, of course, recognized this from the very beginning, observing that "there appears to be as much variability in the transition process on each side of the communist/non-communist divide as there is across it."[18] From Yugoslavia to Vietnam, and from Poland to North Korea, the reform of Communist systems takes myriad forms and the world's Communist countries are currently at almost every conceivable stage in the process of transition, from the pre-reform phase (Cuba and North Korea) to consolidated democracy (Czech Republic, Poland, and Hungary). This is where the case for "grounding the transitologists" is its weakest, since the fact is that Poland's transition to democracy is more compatible with that of Spain than it is with North Korea.[19] Likewise, Cuba's eventual transition will be infinitely more comparable to that of Argentina or Chile than the USSR.

TABLE 2.1.
Typology of Communist Transitions.

Type	Objective	Examples
Indigenous Abandonment	While original objective is to improve the system, in later phase this changes to abandonment of the Communist system itself	Russia
Independence by Default	Ranges from strong desire for national independence (Ukraine, Georgia) to regret over the broken ties between the republics (Belarus)	The Newly Independent States
National Liberation	Liberation from Soviet domination	Poland, Czechoslovakia, Hungary, Lithuania, Latvia, Estonia
Indigenous Reform	Improve the system while retaining control	China, Vietnam
Personal Dictatorship	Retain control at all costs	Cuba, North Korea

As a group, however, the cases of transition from Communism can be placed into five more or less distinct categories (see table 2.1). The Soviet Union itself actually presents two cases—the reform movement and processes as initiated in Moscow and the Russian Republic, and the fracturing of the Soviet state and the transition processes among the successor republics. The reform agenda launched by Moscow, insofar as it was a restructuring by Russians and for Russians, was indigenous and had as its goal the improvement of Soviet society. In the midst of reforming the system, however, the leadership broke into factions fighting over competing visions of the future of the country, providing an opening for secessionist calls in the republics. The Newly Independent States are thus in a class by themselves, as they entered the Soviet Union by way of the Russian Empire, and achieved independence by taking advantage of its disintegration. This is only half true for the Baltics, whose period under Soviet rule and process of incorporation are similar to that of Poland and other East European societies. Although constituent republics of the USSR, however, secessionist calls in the Baltics were significantly triggered by events in Eastern Europe and had as their goal national liberation and freedom from Soviet domination.

Despite the fact that their Communist regimes had all been installed by Moscow and survived for roughly the same length of time, Eastern Europe remains a somewhat distinct category from that of the Baltics, since these societies were part of the extended Soviet empire, not an integral part of the system itself. These societies conducted periodic "tests" of the Kremlin's resolve, attempting to wiggle out from under Moscow's hold every few years or so, beginning in East Berlin in June 1953 (immediately testing the limits of Stalin's successors) all the way to the tearing down of the wall in 1989. It was a matter of course that Communism in Eastern Europe would be overthrown the second Moscow showed that it no longer had the resolve to shed the requisite level of blood to keep the Soviet empire in Eastern Europe intact. The exceptional cases here, however, are Yugoslavia and Albania, whose Communist revolutions were indigenous and which remained free from Soviet control. Although they embarked upon transitions at roughly the same time as their neighbors, these factors make the process itself significantly distinct and force us to put them in the next category.

Much like Yugoslavia and Albania, the People's Republic of China and Vietnam adopted Communism as a means of throwing off imperial yokes, and did so in a way that combined Communism with nationalism from the start. China and Vietnam remain distinct, however, not only due to their cultural similarities but because both are also attempting to transform their societies through reform, rather than simply abandoning Communist rule outright.

Our fifth and final group is comprised of North Korea and Cuba. Although these countries differ in the means by which Communist rule was installed, with an authentic revolution in Cuba and Communism coming to North Korea through Soviet tutelage, these two regimes fall into their own category. This is not simply due to the fact that neither has yet sought to transition away from Communism, but because they represent special cases as systems that are personal dictatorships which long ago ceased any serious attempt to put Marxist-Leninist thought into practice.

Given the depth of analysis required to explicate the process of Communist reform from the initiation of reform to the present while attempting to account for as many of the myriad factors at work as possible, this study must remain limited to only two cases. For a number of reasons, I focus my study on the cases of the Soviet Union and China. If it were not enough that they represent the two most populous Communist states, in both cases Communist rule was the result of an authentic revolution, genuine attempts were made to put Marxist-Leninist principles into action, and the decisions to reform the systems were internal. Moreover, both the Soviet Union and China were regional powers that influenced their neighbors more than they were influenced by them. Finally, given the great cultural distinctions between them, the divergent paths to reform each has pursued, and their different stages in the reform process, these two cases offer sufficient variation to allow us to gauge the impact of factors such as culture, sequencing, and history in the reform process.

The distinct characteristics of the Soviet Union make any comparison with it problematic. First and foremost, as the world's first successful Communist state, the Soviet Union always held a special position among the world's other Communist states—regardless of whether or not they were under Moscow's tutelage. It was the example *par excellence* of a successful revolution, the state built by Lenin himself, and of course it was a superpower rivaled only by the United States. These facts made it natural for other states to be influenced, both directly and indirectly, by the Soviet Union to an extent without parallel among the Communist world. But of all the Communist states in the world, China is perhaps the only one that is similar enough that it can be compared to the USSR. In addition to the factors enumerated above, China also specifically modeled itself after the Soviet Union, including its party and state structure, education, military, and economy. Its most significant attempt to diverge from the Soviet example, however, regards its attempt to follow a path to reform that does not result in a Soviet-style collapse.

Comparative Politics

The theoretical body of literature devoted to the comparative study of transitions is a field largely defined by its method, that of the comparative method. And as with transitology, one of the most contentious issues in comparative politics concerns the level of abstraction. For a field defined by a methodological approach, research in the field of comparative politics is quite diverse, ranging from cross-national studies that include hundreds of cases all the way down to in-depth analysis of a single case. As Rose points out, however, what ties the field together is the idea that comparative research is *comparable,* that is, that scholars in the field use concepts and theories that have been or potentially can be applied to other cases. As Rose phrases it, "the use of concepts makes a case study of interest outside its geographic boundaries, just as the absence of concepts makes it impossible to compare evidence from two different countries."[20] This is, of course, a general characteristic of all social science, since the goal of the scientific method is to categorize and seek generalizations across classes of phenomena.

While the field of comparative politics is not as large as the whole of social science, it is perhaps as varied as the entire field of political science. Consider the fact that what falls under the rubric of comparative politics includes all of the other subfields of political science whenever they are applied to cases other than the United States. Whether it be judicial politics, elections, legislative process, or state and local government, all of these areas are topics of comparative research when conducted in a foreign context. The irony is that this is largely an American phenomenon, since the study of the United States becomes comparative politics when conducted by foreign scholars.

A further problem with comparative politics is its underlying epistemology. Perhaps as a result of its central focus on comparison, there is a tendency in the field to assume that like processes will have like results. When scholars begin to develop models based on extant cases, there is a propensity to conclude that other, seemingly similar cases that are at earlier stages of progression will inevitably come to the same end as that of the earlier cases. A different outcome is seen as not possible, or at least as deviant. There is a major reason why this sort of theory building is problematic in the social sciences. In the social world, analytical models are almost always developed before all possible iterations have occurred, for instance, as is the case with a phenomenon such as revolutions. But consider for a moment the fact that many theories may be developed before even a sufficient number of cases have even occurred (as was the case with transitions from authoritarian rule). It is possible, in fact, that even the most defining cases may occur at a later stage, as is the case with the Bolshevik Revolution. By developing theories from a limited number of observations or early in the development of a phenomenon, observers may incorrectly view certain cases as deviant, when in fact they define a new paradigm. Those who resist the paradigm shift will thus continue to view deviant cases as exceptions, or perhaps wait for an eventual change, rather than reconsidering the basis for the theory itself.

While in the hard sciences it is usually a safe assumption to predict that later events will follow a path similar to that of earlier ones, in the social world this is a teleological fallacy based on reasoning by analogy. As scholars who employ a comparative approach, we tend not only to construct a comparative analysis, but actually to be drawn into the comparison, sometimes to the point that we fail to recognize that we are the ones constructing the analogy. This may be a natural result of the comparative method, since we are trying to create order out of chaos. It is a dangerous mistake, however, for two reasons. First, there is more than one path away from a given destination, just as there are an endless number of paths down from a mountain. Secondly, in the complex social world, no two cases are really sufficiently similar to guarantee a similar outcome, that is, no two cases are actually beginning from the same point. While it is tempting to assume that where similar processes are followed similar outcomes will result, this is simplistic and misleading. This does not, however, undermine the whole enterprise of comparative politics or force us down a slippery slope that ends in conceding that all events are unique and therefore ultimately incomparable. Rather, I am simply trying to illustrate the point that in the complex social world other factors can intervene and change the course of events. Two such factors that tend to escape the purview of scholars working in comparative politics are interaction effects and lesson-drawing. In this regard, the biggest problem facing comparative politics is not what it considers, but what it often fails to consider.

Interaction Effects and Lesson-Drawing

The focus of comparative politics is of course on domestic politics, but now more than ever domestic issues are affected by what happens across a state's borders. The states of the world exist within an international system, and they are not isolated from events occurring in other parts of the world. For example, in the wake of September 11, is there any way that the changes that are taking place in American politics, including discrimination against Muslim Americans, the creation of the Department of Homeland Security, or even airport security procedures, can be explained without considering the role of the international system? This is an extreme example, and while the impact may be less pronounced in other cases, it is not necessarily absent or irrelevant.

If realist scholars of international relations are sometimes criticized for viewing states as black boxes when in fact they are complex social structures, comparativists often fall short in their own right by failing to take into account the fact that the societies they study exist within a larger system, not as isolated cases within a vacuum. This error may be even more egregious, for systemic realists are well aware that domestic factors are at work, only working on the assumption that causality emanates from the system and that such factors are more significant than events in the domestic realm. Comparativists, however, tend to focus solely on what goes on inside the black box while neglecting the international system in which it is located. By working under the assumption that there is little to no interaction between the cases under study, or that such interaction is insignificant, comparativistis often neglect the systemic forces that impact domestic politics.

In surveying several major instructional texts on comparative politics, the issue of interaction effects is virtually absent. Landman and Lane make no mention of any related concepts,[21] while Ragin only briefly considers system-level variables, and mostly as a means of determining what he feels is *not* truly comparative, i.e., cross-national research.[22] Zahariadis, who provides great detail on case selection and degrees of freedom, also makes no mention of interaction effects or systemic factors, despite the fact that he includes one of the most articulate discussions of the topic (by Rose, see below) in his volume.[23]

Although rare, discussion of systemic factors does exist in the literature. Dogan and Pelassy, for example, in what is considered the definitive account on comparative research strategies, have a quite excellent discussion of interaction effects, contagion, and policy diffusion. They do so, however, only in a section devoted to "comparing to escape from ethnocentrism," never visiting the issue again.[24] Of all of the major instructional texts in comparative politics, it is Hague, Harrop, and Breslin who offer perhaps the best discussion of such factors in their consideration of the independence and interdependence of cases. As they point out, "countries learn from, copy, compete with, influence and even invade each other in a constant process of interaction."[25] In such an environment, "it is clear that any comparative study which assumes that cases are independent . . . must seek to justify a dubious starting point."[26]

As the quote that opens this chapter makes clear, the significance of external forces and the potential of interdependence among cases is not something only recently discovered. In fact, as White, Korotayev, and Khaltourina point out, this phenomenon was first identified by Sir Francis Galton (who, incidentally, was the cousin of Charles Darwin). At a meeting of the Anthropological Institute of Great Britain and Ireland in 1888, Galton made a remark with respect to a paper that had been delivered in which he suggested that the cultural attribute being compared might not be independent, but rather that each culture may have derived them from the same source, "so that they were duplicate copies of the same original."[27] As Hague, Harrop, and Breslin explain, today we refer to Galton's problem as the difficulty in determining whether similarities are the result of parallel but independent development or diffusion.[28]

Perhaps the best treatment of the subject in comparative politics comes from Rose in a 1991 article on comparative method from *Political Studies*. As Rose points out, "the idea of states operating independently in parallel is being eroded by changes in the international system."[29] From policymakers who seek to learn from the experience of others to the impact of changes in the international system on domestic institutions, interaction effects are everywhere. Two areas in which their impact is most apparent is in "the movement of ideas about public policy" and "the interaction arising from interdependence."[30]

Despite its lack of a central place in the conceptual toolbox of comparative politics, there is a long tradition of scholarship that takes these variables into account.[31] In fact, many of the leading scholars in the field repeatedly identify such factors in their analyses. Charles Tilly has perhaps gone the farthest in showing that revolutions and social movements have significant causes and factors that emanate from outside the borders of the nation-state,[32] an issue that Skocpol also identified in her work on social revolutions. Skocpol was clear in stating that the revolutions she was comparing were not independent of one another.[33] And as she also pointed out, it is international leaders who often transmit international forces into domestic politics.[34] Other scholars, such as Gourevitch, Putnam, and Huntington, have also attributed significant causal power to variables emanating from the international system.[35]

More than a quarter of a century ago, Almond surveyed the field for examples of international interaction, known at that time as the national-international connection. He concluded that there is not only "a record of substantial accomplishment" in the area of interaction, but one of "greater promise," and he called for greater work in the area, predicting that "we are at the beginning of significant curricular adaptations which will . . . enable us to deal more effectively with the interaction of the domestic society, the international environment, and the political system."[36] Unfortunately, a generation later, this promise remains unfulfilled, despite some excellent examples of how international interaction can be incorporated into comparative research.

Despite the existence of a long tradition of research into international interaction, it has never taken its rightful place in the discipline. While many studies do point to such factors as significant, they are certainly the exception, not the rule. Of course, given the topic, interaction effects may be insignificant, but unless we regularly consider the impact of external factors we run the risk of not identifying them in cases when they may be highly significant.

The existence of interaction effects allows forces external to the state to impact domestic politics through the processes of lesson-drawing and learning. In fact, the greater the degree of interaction, the greater the possibility that lesson-drawing and learning will occur. Actors can draw lessons from the experience of others, leading them to change their behavior accordingly. Much like Galton's problem, similar outcomes might then be due not to similar processes, but to a conscious decision to emulate a particular behavior, policy, or strategy. Skocpol found this in regards to revolutions, arguing that actors in later revolutions were influenced by earlier ones.[37] It is this sort of process, moreover, that is responsible for revolutions picking up steam as they spread, a phenomenon which Huntington has labeled snowballing.[38] Similar phenomena have been identified with respect to ethnic conflict and separatism. As Olson points out, minorities, who are "made to feel alien and unwelcome by ruling authorities," are often "influenced by what they can see happening in other countries," and thus search for "their own desire and voice for separateness."[39] An excellent example of this is the former Yugoslavia, where the Kosovo Liberation Army drew important lessons from the war in Bosnia.[40] Outside of comparative politics, in the field of policy studies a growing body of literature is documenting the myriad ways in which external factors affect domestic politics, primarily in the form of the diffusion of specific policies and laws.[41]

This process also works in the reverse, however. As Skocpol also identified in her research, the impact of revolutions might be in the other direction, with actors seeking to learn a negative lesson. As she points out, "revolutions affect not only those abroad who would like to imitate them. They also affect those in other countries who oppose revolutionary ideals but are compelled to respond to the challenges."[42] The idea that actors may draw a negative lesson from another country's experience is what Raffe and Rumberger call negative borrowing. As they describe it, negative borrowing is a "type of learning [that] can take place when increased self-awareness helps a country recognize features of its own system that are dysfunctional, or which obstruct other policy aims."[43]

The field of policy studies has certainly progressed the farthest in the systematic study of lesson-drawing and learning, although it remains focused on issues related to public policy, such as healthcare, education, and economics. The implications of this research, however, reach far beyond administrative policies all the way to national development strategies. Perhaps the best example in this regard is the American Founding Fathers, particularly James Madison, who studied the major governments of the world for positive examples, while also examining the British system in an attempt to learn how to avoid its faults.[44] As Rose explains, this phenomenon continues to this day:

> Policymakers who live in small countries subject to the influence of larger neighbors recognize that many decisions influencing them are taken elsewhere. Hence, the Canadian government watches what is done in Washington, and smaller European countries such as the Netherlands and Belgium watch what is done in Germany and France. Japan, a big country that has had a small-country complex, regularly sends domestic policy officials abroad in order to learn from the experience of Western nations.[45]

Are we to assume that this process is somehow different in Communist societies? From whom are they likely to learn? The obvious answer would seem to be from other Communist and transition societies, but we cannot a priori discount the impact events in the Western world might have in such places as well. In seeking to uncover the factors that influenced the reform processes in the Soviet Union and China, therefore, we must be aware of the potential impact played by lesson-drawing and learning. Likewise, studies that view the reform process in isolation or without an eye to interaction effects and lesson-drawing might be missing a significant part of the picture.

Interaction Effects and Lesson-Drawing in the Soviet and Chinese Transitions from Communism

Comparativists often remain blind to the impact international factors have on domestic politics. Events such as regime transitions do not take place within a vacuum, however, but within an international system that has become much closer and intimate based on the rise of communications technology, the ease of world travel, and the presence of the media. In today's world, events in one part of the globe are immediately known across the planet, presenting greater opportunities for lesson-drawing than at any other point in history. This has led to the increased importance of a factor that remains relatively unexamined in the study of transitions—the process of learning between and among political systems.

When countries are highly interdependent, whether due to close cooperation, geographic proximity, or simply keen interest on the part of policymakers and citizens, events in one country may significantly affect events in the other in myriad ways. This is, of course, the case with Russia and China, two states that have gravitated between close cooperation and conflict throughout their history, and with the level of curiosity in the other always relatively high. These facts make a straightforward comparative analysis inappropriate, as simply juxtaposing these two cases in side-by-side analyses would ignore the interdependent nature of Communist reform and discount the importance of interaction and lesson-drawing in that process.

In the pages that follow, therefore, I not only compare the reform processes in both countries, which is the focus of chapters 3 and 4, but I also seek to determine the influence lesson-drawing had on the reform strategies chosen and their results. By first comparing the transition experiences of both states I am able to establish a base level of knowledge of the cases under examination before turning to the issues of interaction effects and lesson-drawing as a means of generating insight into why the specific reform paths were chosen.

Notes

1. John Robert Seeley, *An Introduction to Political Science* (London: Macmillan, 1886), 133.

2. Giovanni Sartori, "Concept Misformation in Comparative Politics," *American Political Science Review* 64, no. 4 (December 1970): 1040-1041. For the pitfalls of conceptual stretching in regards to transitology, see Russell Bova, "Political Dynamics of the Post-Communist Transition: A Comparative Perspective," *World Politics* 44, no. 1 (October 1991): 113-138.

3. Gabriel Almond, *A Discipline Divided: Schools and Sects in Political Science* (Thousand Oaks, CA: Sage, 1990).

4. Bova, "Political Dynamics of the Post-Communist Transition," 113.

5. Bova, "Political Dynamics of the Post-Communist Transition," 115.

6. Dankwart Rustow, "Transitions to Democracy: Toward a Dynamic Model," *Comparative Politics* 2, no. 3 (April 1970): 337-363.

7. Guillermo O'Donnell, Philippe C. Schmitter, and Laurence Whitehead, eds., *Transitions from Authoritarian Rule: Prospects for Democracy* (Baltimore: Johns Hopkins University Press, 1986).

8. An excellent example is Rudolf Tökés, a longtime Communist Studies scholar who later applied the negotiated pact approach to transitions to the study of Hungary. Rudolf Tökés, *Hungary's Negotiated Revolution: Economic Reform, Social Change and Political Succession* (Cambridge, UK: Cambridge University Press, 1996). Timothy Colton is another excellent example of a Kremlinologist who developed into a scholar of transition politics employing sophisticated research methodologies; Timothy Colton, *Transitional Citizens: Voters and What Influences them in the New Russia* (Cambridge, MA: Harvard University Press, 2000).

9. Philippe C. Schmitter with Terry Lynn Karl, "The Conceptual Travels of Transitologists and Consolidologists: How Far to the East Should they Attempt to Go?" *Slavic Review* 53, no. 1 (Spring 1994): 173-185.

10. Valerie Bunce, "Should Transitologists be Grounded?" *Slavic Review* 54, no. 1 (Spring 1995): 111-127.

11. Bunce, "Should Transitologists be Grounded?" 120.

12. János Mátyás Kovács, "Rival Temptations and Passive Resistance: Cultural Globalization in Hungary," in Peter Berger and Samuel Huntington, eds., *Many Globalizations: Cultural Diversity in the Contemporary World* (Oxford: Oxford University Press, 2002), 146.

13. Tatu Vanhanen, *Prospects of Democracy: A Study of 172 Countries* (London: Routledge, 1997), and Huntington, *The Third Wave*.

14. Thomas Carothers, "The End of the Transition Paradigm," *Journal of Democracy* 13, no. 1 (Spring 2002): 5.

15. Guillermo O'Donnell, for example, explicitly argues that the whole concept of democratic consolidation is teleological. See his "Illusions About Consolidation," *Journal of Democracy* 7, no. 1 (April 1996): 34-51. A rejoinder is offered by Richard Gunther, P. Nikiforos Diamandouros, and Hans-Jurgen Puhle, "O'Donnell's 'Illusions': A Rejoinder," *Journal of Democracy* 7, no. 3 (October 1996): 151-59.

16. Valerie Bunce, "Comparing East and South," *Journal of Democracy* 6, no. 3 (Fall 1994): 95.

17. Jordan Gans-Morse, "Searching for Transitologists: Contemporary Theories of Post-Communist Transitions and the Myth of a Dominant Paradigm," *Post-Soviet Affairs* 20, no. 4 (2004): 328.

18. Bova, "Political Dynamics of the Post-Communist Transition," 115.

19. Excellent evidence in support of this proposition is Jose Casanova, "Church, State, Nation and Civil Society in Spain and Poland," in Said Arjomand, ed., *The Political Dimensions of Religion* (Albany, NY: SUNY Press), 1993.

20. Richard Rose, "Comparing Forms of Comparative Analysis," *Political Studies* 39, no. 3 (1991): 446.

21. Todd Landman, *Issues and Methods in Comparative Politics: An Introduction* (London: Routledge, 2000); Ruth Lane, *The Art of Comparative Politics* (Needham Heights, MA: Allyn and Bacon, 1997).

22. Charles Ragin, *The Comparative Method: Moving Beyond Qualitative and Quantitative Strategies* (Berkeley: University of California Press, 1987), 4.

23. Nikolaos Zahariadis, *Theory, Case, and Method in Comparative Politics* (Ft. Worth: Harcourt Brace, 1997).

24. Mattei Dogan and Dominique Pelassy, *How to Compare Nations: Strategies in Comparative Politics* (Chatham, NJ: Chatham House, 1990), 6-8.

25. Rod Hague, Martin Harrop, and Shaun Breslin, *Political Science: A Comparative Introduction* (New York: Worth, 1998), 275.

26. Hague, Harrop, and Breslin, *Political Science*, 275.

27. Douglas R. White, Andrey Korotayev, and Daria Khaltourina, *Using SPSS: Analysis and Comparison in the Social Sciences* (draft manuscript, 2004), chapter 8. Available online at: http://eclectic.ss.uci.edu/~drwhite/xc/book.htm.

28. Hague, Harrop, and Breslin, *Political Science*, 275.

29. Rose, "Comparing Forms of Comparative Analysis," 458.

30. Rose, "Comparing Forms of Comparative Analysis," 458.

31. Although closely related to the second-image and second-image reversed literature in international relations, which has developed an impressive body of literature in the area, I am here looking at research on the topic coming out of the field of comparative politics.

32. Charles Tilly, ed. *Formation of National States in Western Europe* (Princeton: Princeton University Press, 1975).

33. Theda Skocpol, *States and Social Revolutions* (Cambridge, MA: Harvard University Press, 1979), 38.

34. Skocpol, *States and Social Revolutions*, 24.

35. Peter Gourevitch, *Politics in Hard Times: Comparative Responses to International Economic Crises* (Ithaca, NY: Cornell University Press, 1986); Robert D. Putnam, "Diplomacy and Domestic Politics: The Logic of Two-Level Games," *International Organization* 42, no. 3 (Summer 1988): 427-460; and Huntington, *The Third Wave*.

36. Gabriel Almond, "National Politics and International Politics," in Albert Lepawsky, Edward Buehrig, and Harold Lasswell, eds., *The Search for World Order* (New York: Appleton-Century-Crofts, 1971), 284-285. Cited in Gabriel Almond, "The International-National Connection," in Gabriel Almond, *A Discipline Divided: Schools and Sects in Political Science* (Thousand Oaks, CA: Sage, 1990), 267.

37. Skocpol, *States and Social Revolutions,* 23.

38. Huntington, *The Third Wave,* 100-106.

39. William J. Olson, "A New World, a New Challenge," in Max Manwaring and William J. Olson, eds., *Managing Contemporary Conflict: Pillars of Success* (Boulder, CO: Westview, 1996), 6.

40. Christopher Marsh and Mark Heppner, "When Weak Nations Use Strong States: The Unintended Consequences of Intervention in Kosovo," *Nationalities Papers* 31, no. 3 (September 2003): 281-293.

41. Some of the major works in this area include: David Collier and Richard Messick, "Prerequisites versus Diffusion: Testing Alternative Explanations for Social Security Adoption," *American Political Science Review* 69, no. 4 (December 1975): 1299-1315; Robert Eyestone, "Confusion, Diffusion, and Innovation," *American Political Science Review* 71, no. 2 (June 1977): 441-447; Virginia Gray, "Innovation in the States: A Diffusion Study," *American Political Science Review* 67, no. 4 (December 1973): 1174-1185; James Lutz, "Emulation and Policy Adoptions in the Canadian Provinces," *Canadian Journal of Political Science* 22, no. 1 (July 1989): 147-154; Richard Rose, *Lesson-drawing in Public Policy: A Guide to Learning across Time and Space* (Chatham, NJ: Chatham House, 1993); Robert Savage, "Diffusion Research Traditions and the Spread of Policy Innovation in a Federal System," *Publius: The Journal of Federalism* 15, no. 4 (Fall 1985): 1-27; Jack Walker, "The Diffusion of Innovations Among the American States," *American Political Science Review* 63, no. 3 (1969): 880-899; Jerold Waltman, *Copying Other Nations' Policies: Two American Case Studies* (Cambridge, MA: Schenkman, 1980).

42. Skocpol, *States and Social Revolutions,* 4.

43. David Raffe and Russell Rumberger, "Education and Training for 16-18 Year Olds in the UK and USA," *Oxford Studies in Comparative Education* 2, no. 2 (1992): 135-157.

44. A similar point is made by Rose, *Lesson-drawing in Public Policy,* x.

45. Rose, *Lesson-drawing in Public Policy,* 6.

Chapter 3

From Reform to Crisis

In sum, there is no such thing as socialism, and the Soviet Union built it.
                                                              —Martin Malia[1]

T
HE year 1989 has been described as *annus mirabilis*, the year of miracles, a time when even "the most quixotic optimists proved too cautious."[2] In April of that year, thousands of students began to gather in Tiananmen Square in Beijing to call upon the Chinese government to implement democratic reforms. By mid-May, their numbers had swelled to over a quarter of a million. Similar demonstrations were also underway throughout Eastern Europe, and by late August East Germans picnicking along the Austrian border began to cross over to freedom in the West. When East Berlin caught on and prevented others from taking similar picnics, East German vacationers headed for Prague where they made their way to the West German and American embassies and eventually to the West. Within weeks, the Berlin Wall was pulled down, followed quickly by student demonstrations in Prague in Wenceslas Square and culminating in the execution of Romanian Communist leader Nicolae Ceausescu on Christmas day. By the end of the year, the Communist regimes of Eastern Europe had fallen, and the winds of change were blowing east into the Soviet Union itself. As British Prime Minister Margaret Thatcher summarized the events, "What a fantastic year this has been for freedom! 1989 will be remembered for decades to come as the year when the people of half our continent began to throw off their chains."[3]

While the year 1989 may have appeared as a "year of miracles" to opposition forces in the Communist world and observers in the West, it was a year of catastrophe for Communist leaders in Moscow and Beijing. Systemic crisis is not what Soviet and Chinese Communist leaders had envisioned when they chose to embark upon fundamental reforms of their political and economic systems years earlier. Rather than increasing support for Communist Party rule, however, economic reforms and political liberalization actually resulted in calls for the removal from power of the very leaders who launched the reforms. The

irony of the situation, therefore, is that while leaders both in Moscow and Beijing attempted to improve their systems, in both cases the results were crises that
shook these Communist giants to their very foundations.

In this chapter I examine the reform paths taken in the Soviet Union and
China from the initiation of reforms to the systemic crises that brought these
regimes to the brink of collapse—and in the Soviet case, over the edge and into
the abyss. I begin with an analysis of the Chinese reassessment of socialism and
the decision to abandon the Soviet model, tracing events from Mao's attempt to
adapt the Soviet model to China's circumstances through the decision to launch
economic reform following his death and to the uprising at Tiananmen Square in
1989. Moving on to the Soviet case, I trace the rapid and simultaneous reforms
pursued as part of Gorbachev's perestroika from inception through to the collapse of the Soviet Union itself, concluding with an assessment of the causes of
the Soviet collapse. Finally, I discuss the "unparalleled" nature of the Soviet and
Chinese attempts to reform their Communist systems and what lessons can be
gleaned from what was clearly one of the most significant events of the twentieth century, the failure of the Communist experiment.

From Reform to Revolt:
Crossing the Turbulent River of Reform

In sharp contrast to most of Eastern Europe, Communist rule was brought to
China through a genuine Communist revolution, not one exported from Moscow.[4] Nevertheless, Chinese Communist leaders voluntarily adopted the Soviet
model immediately upon assuming the reins of power in October 1949. Indeed,
by late June 1949 Mao Zedong had already made the decision to "lean to one
side" and pursue cooperation and friendship with the world's first Communist
state, and immediately following China's Liberation he made an extended visit
to Moscow to meet with Stalin. When Mao returned to Beijing in February
1950, he had in hand a Sino-Soviet Treaty of Friendship, Alliance and Mutual
Assistance, a pledge of Soviet aid amounting to U.S. $300 million, and a de-
tailed framework on how to structure China's socialist society. Over the next
few years, scores of Soviet advisors and technicians flooded the country and
helped the Chinese establish the world's most populous Communist state. In the
process, China not only laid the foundation of its Soviet-style command economy and Leninist political system, the Soviet model was also adopted in industry, science, and education and research.

The decision to adopt the Soviet model was not one simply based upon material incentives. Mao apparently believed at the time that adopting the Soviet
model would facilitate China's rapid economic development, as it had in the
USSR. Such an idea was conveyed by his statement, which later became a very
popular slogan, that "the Soviet Union's today will be our tomorrow." The
choice also made pragmatic sense to a group of Communist revolutionaries who

had little experience governing and who had just seized control of a state comprising one-fifth the world's population. As Mao later explained, "In the early stages of Liberation, we had no experience of managing the economy of the entire nation . . . so . . . we could do no more than copy the Soviet Union's methods." As he also commented, however, "we never felt altogether satisfied about it."[5] Indeed, not long after adopting the Soviet model Mao began attempts to adapt it to China's particular conditions. Such an adaptation of the Soviet model was not revisionist from a Marxist point of view, since the Soviet model was really nothing more than the Stalinist model, not a blueprint designed by Marx or even Lenin, but rather the result of a particular set of historical circumstances and an interpretation of (vague) Marxist prescriptions. Moreover, as early as 1947 the Soviets themselves had already begun to abandon certain aspects of the specific Stalinist model the Chinese were adopting because it had proven too disruptive of working patterns.[6]

In April 1956 Mao began to question publicly the applicability of the Soviet model for China, suggesting that some of China's problems "had been exacerbated by slavishly following the Soviet Union."[7] Mao's initial attempt to depart from the Soviet model was his May 1956 call to "let a hundred flowers bloom, a hundred schools of thought contend," which quickly concluded with those who had spoken out being labeled as "poisonous weeds." Before long, however, Mao's critique of the Soviet model began to take shape. His criticism was partly aimed at the model's theoretical foundations, particularly the Soviet doctrine of "primitive socialist accumulation," the theory of productive forces, and the Stalinist conception of leadership.[8] Mao's criticism was more than just theoretical calisthenics, however, as he also criticized the Soviets for the way they had translated such theories into practice. In particular, Mao expressed great dissatisfaction with the Soviet Union's lopsided stress on heavy industry at the expense of agriculture and light industry, suggesting that China needed to "walk on two feet," i.e., to develop both industry and agriculture together. He was also critical of the USSR's extreme centralization, and while he acknowledged that some central planning was necessary, Mao argued that complete domination of the economy was not. Not only did such a policy exclude the masses from playing a role in the country's development, it also favored experts over the Party.

In an attempt to develop a distinctive Chinese model of socialism, Mao began to chart a new course. Besides his "hundred flowers bloom" campaign, Mao attempted some minor reforms, including decentralization in healthcare, education, and welfare.[9] As Dittmer points out, however, "The Maoist attempt to articulate a coherent positive alternative to command planning was most fully realized in practice during the Great Leap Forward."[10] As the devastating effects of the Great Leap quickly became clear, however, it was immediately abandoned and almost all of its policies reversed. With Mao's initial attempt to strike out on a distinctive Chinese path failing so utterly, the focus shifted away from abandoning the Soviet model toward simply salvaging the economy and recovering from a devastating famine. And as the country descended into turmoil during the Cultural Revolution, issues of economic development and performance became much less important than mere survival. As Dittmer further points out, Mao's "ideological antipathy to capitalism" had led him "to reject reliance on the market as an alternative to central planning;"[11] it would thus be up to Mao's successors to find a path that included market reform.

The Chinese Reassessment of Socialism

That the post-Mao era would come to be one characterized by dramatic economic reforms and a break with the excesses of the Cultural Revolution was not a foregone conclusion upon the death of China's first Communist leader. Reformers and moderates had to join together to prevent the radical Gang of Four from consolidating its grip on power following Mao's death in September 1976. Led by Mao's wife Jiang Qing, the Gang of Four had been penetrating ever deeper into the party's inner circle since 1973, and in Mao's final years they had been moving to consolidate their power and position themselves to take the helm of the Middle Kingdom upon Mao's eventual death (he had been diagnosed with cancer in 1972). Their fate had been all but sealed in early 1976, however, with Hua Guofeng appointed acting Premier of the State Council in February following Zhou Enlai's death, and then Mao seemingly selecting Hua as his heir apparent in April by remarking to him that "with you in charge I am at ease."[12] In June at a meeting with Hua and other party leaders, Mao stated his intentions for China's leadership upon his death, announcing that "a tripartite leadership of old, middle-aged, and young cadres" should govern collectively, while the decision about whether or not Jiang Qing should be included was left up to the politburo.[13] Hua decided on a different fate for Jiang Qing and the Gang of Four; less than one month after Mao's death they were removed from their positions and arrested. The Cultural Revolution was thus finally brought to a close, but China's future course was still not determined.

With the radical alternative eliminated, two distinct camps on the future direction of the country began to emerge.[14] The first came to be known as the "whateverists," taking their name and line of thinking from a speech given by Hua Guofeng in January 1977. Hua, who only days after the Gang of Four's arrest had been elevated to the positions of chairman of the Central Committee and head of the Military Affairs Commission, had stated that "Whatever policies Mao has made we will resolutely safeguard and whatever instructions Mao has given we will forever follow."[15] Hua's remarks, which were quickly published in *Renmin ribao*, *Hongqi*, and *Jiefangjun bao*, came to define the whateverists' stance. The essential position undergirding the "two whatevers" was that Maoist thought should continue to guide the PRC, and such principles should continue to be followed as avoiding the "capitalist road," "continue the revolution," and class struggle as the "key link," referring to a quotation from Mao that identified the "gradual resolution of the contradiction between socialism and capitalism" as the "key link" of the party's work during socialist construction.[16]

The line of thinking that eventually came to be counterposed to the two whatevers first began to be articulated by Deng Xiaoping between March and July 1977. Rather than following whatever policies or instructions Mao had left, Deng and his supporters, including Hu Yaobang, argued that Mao Zedong thought should be treated "accurately and comprehensively as a scientific system."[17] He also argued that there must be a distinction drawn between those aspects of Mao's thought that are of fundamental significance (or essential elements) and specific content (or nonessential elements), the applicability of which is limited by time, space, and subject. As later articulated by other members of this camp, the "truth seekers" argued that "practice is the sole criterion of truth," suggesting that the correctness of the party's policies should be assessed based upon practice, not theory alone.

Throughout 1977-1978, the battle between the two camps played itself out in the form of a public debate over the correct way to uphold Mao Zedong thought. In public speeches, newspaper and journal articles, and at party and state conferences the two groups further articulated their positions and debated back and forth. The whateverists attempted to show that deviation from Mao's policies was revisionism, and that the theory of practice was two-sided, since theory also guides practice. At an All-Army Conference on Political Work on June 2, 1978, however, Deng leveled what was perhaps the lethal blow, arguing that there are two kinds of fidelity to Mao's thought, one that remains true to his fundamental thought, and the other that simply seeks to uphold "whatever" he had said.[18] Deng declared that "What we should uphold and use as a guide to action are the fundamental principles of Marxism-Leninism-Mao Zedong Thought, in other words, the scientific system consisting of these fundamental principles. As to the specific conclusions, neither Marx, Lenin, nor Mao could avoid making this or that error."[19] The senselessness of the whateverist's position was made even more clear when a 1964 speech of Mao's, in which he confessed to errors he had made during the Great Leap Forward, was republished prominently on July 1.[20] That Mao himself had even admitted that he had made mistakes fatally undermined the whateverist's position, for it implied that wrong policies could be continued simply because Mao had enacted them.

The Third Plenum of the Eleventh Central Committee of the Chinese Communist Party in December 1978 was a decisive victory for Deng's views. The Party publicly rejected the Maoist principle of class struggle as the key determinant of policy and opened the way for a more pragmatic approach to reform, one that would eventually come to include market principles. Victory in the ideological battle also determined the outcome to the power struggle that had ensued between Deng and Hua. While Hua would continue to maintain a high profile in the press and at formal functions and retain his post as Party leader, Deng was already officially in control. The transfer of power was made complete at the Sixth Plenum of the Central Committee in June 1981 when Hua tendered his resignation, with Deng taking over as head of the Military Affairs Commission and Hu Yaobang becoming chairman of the Central Committee. The past was simultaneously put to rest with the passing of a resolution on the Party's history, which concluded, *inter alia*, that Mao's achievements had been "70 percent good, 30 percent bad."[21] While Mao's accomplishments had liberated China and led it on the path to socialism, it would take a more pragmatic approach to modernize the country and to develop "socialism with Chinese characteristics."

Socialism with Chinese Characteristics

Even before the ideological debate had been concluded and the power struggle was over, Deng and the other reformers had begun to implement economic reforms. At the Third Plenum of the Eleventh Central Committee back in December 1978, at which Deng's views on the interpretation of Mao's thought had emerged victorious, Deng had declared the country's economic development a priority and restated the goal of the Four Modernizations. Originally conceived of by Zhou Enlai and declared by Deng at the Fourth National People's Congress in 1975 prior to his second purge, the Four Modernizations called for the all-round modernization of agriculture, industry, national defense, and science and technology, so that by the end of the century, "China will have a new look and will stand unshakably in the East as a modern, powerful socialist country."[22] The economic reforms that began to be implemented in 1978 focused primarily on rural agriculture, but before long they would expand to virtually every sector of the economy.

While Deng's reforms were based on a solid ideological reassessment of socialism, they were not a systematic and coherent reform package. Rather, while clearly a movement away from the Soviet model of socialism and the extremism and tumult characterized by Mao's leadership, the reforms that would fundamentally transform China over the coming decades were an eclectic and pragmatic combination of measures introduced from above and arising spontaneously from below. They were a clear departure from the past in many ways, and while the ultimate goal of prosperity and stability was known, how to accomplish this was not. This situation was popularized by the idea of crossing a river by grasping for stones (*mozhe shitou guo he*), meaning that, while the objective is clear (the other side of the river), the path to get there is not, and a combination of trial and error would be necessary to succeed.[23]

As originally conceived, Deng's reforms were not a disguised transition to a market economy. Rather, they were understood as the development of a "socialist commodity economy" that was meant to supplement the existing socialist economy.[24] It is for this reason that privatization of state assets was not pursued, since the reforms were meant to improve the socialist economy, not supplant it. Indeed, even with the Sixth Five-Year Plan (1981-1986), the economy was to remain centrally planned and managed, with room only being made for entrepreneurial activity and market forces. Material incentives and merit pay did begin to replace egalitarianism, but this was also understood as compatible with a socialist economy, since "distribution according to labor" was a socialist tenet, albeit one that needed to be resurrected and employed to mobilize the work-force.[25]

As a primarily agricultural society, it made sense that initial reform efforts were focused on the rural sector. With the Maoist communal agricultural system abandoned in 1978, the basic agricultural unit was to be changed from the bri-gade to groups of peasants who were to be responsible for making all decisions regarding planting, cultivation, and the scheduling of their labor on state-held land which they were contracted to manage. These peasants were permitted to retain any production in excess of their quotas, and they could consume or sell their excess production at rural collective markets, which were now also allowed to function legally. While the responsibility system did dramatically increase agricultural productivity, it did not quite work out the way Party leaders had planned. Rather than developing into a "group" responsibility system, what eventually emerged was a "household" responsibility system, as work units be-gan to form along family lines. Moreover, the system was meant to be experi-mented with only in certain provinces and villages. It began to spread almost spontaneously, however, due to a combination of peasant initiative and permis-siveness. While finally authorized for the entire country in 1982, by this time it had already spread across most of the country. In fact, by 1983 just over 97 per-cent of communes had already converted to the responsibility system.[26]

Both agricultural and industrial reforms were experimented with in a similar way, with reform initiatives being field tested prior to making any determination on their effectiveness or attempting to implement them on a national scale.[27] By allowing a certain amount of autonomy and innovation in experimenting with market reforms, the central leadership was able to take a wait-and-see approach, and to allow successful practices to spread while abandoning unsuccessful ones. This approach to dealing with the emerging private sector came to be known as the three "no's"—no official promotion, no propaganda campaign, and no crackdown. Allowing the private sphere to function in this way had the added benefit of shielding the central leadership from any responsibility for policy failures as well as preventing miscalculations from disturbing the national econ-omy. While villages in several regions experimented with reforms in this way, Sichuan province was particularly active and innovative. The home to Deng Xiaoping, Sichuan was headed by Zhao Ziyang during the key years of experi-mental reforms, from 1975-1979, prior to Deng bringing him to Beijing and into the party's inner circle, eventually replacing Hua Guofeng as premier in 1980.

Though initially much less emphasis was placed upon the industrial sector, by 1979 reforms in industry began to be implemented. The initial goal of the industrial reforms was to transform state enterprises into more effective produc-ers, not to replace the state sector with a new private sector. Thus, just as agri-cultural reforms began by relegating responsibility over production decisions to individual work groups, industrial reforms proceeded in a similar manner with state-owned enterprises (SOEs) and township and village enterprises (TVEs) being given greater managerial autonomy and responsibility.[28] Factories were to produce quotas at fixed prices and were permitted to sell surplus production on the open market, using the profits as they saw fit, either to be reinvested or distributed to workers in wages and bonuses. As Pei points out, rather than pursuing "privatization of ownership," therefore, a policy of "privatization of management" was begun,[29] whereby control over state industrial assets were leased and contracted out to private groups. With the introduction of the contract system, management was given a short-term lease to run a factory autonomously, giving enterprise managers decision making authority over production, allocation of resources, and labor. In some cases, managers even switched to manufacturing different commodities. While leases were initially short-term, before long they were permitted for up to 15 years, and by 1987, lease contracts could even be bought and sold. Meanwhile, private enterprise had begun to emerge, with some TVEs being in actuality private firms, only registering in this way as a means of disguise.[30] It was not until 1988, however, that the State Council finally legalized private firms.

External resources also figured prominently in Deng's reform strategy, hoping to follow the model of the NICs, which had relied upon an export-led growth strategy to transform their economies over a period of decades. By "using foreign things to serve China," international trade, foreign direct investment, and Western technology could be used to help China modernize. A key reform initiative in this area was the development in 1979 of Special Economic Zones (SEZs). Originally only permitted in four cities along the southern Chinese coast (Xiamen, Shenzhen, Zhuhai, Shantou), by 1984 similar benefits were being extended to the island province of Hainan and fourteen coastal cities. By 1988, a total of 288 counties in eleven provinces had been opened to the global economy in this way. Using China's cheap labor force and the world's largest consumer market to attract foreign capital, trade, and technology, foreign investment began to pour in, tripling from 1983 to 1985 alone, at which point foreign direct investment (FDI) reached $6.3 billion, and almost doubling again by 1992.[31]

TABLE 3.1.
Average Annual Growth Rates for China and Select Post-Communist Economies, 1980-1993.

Country	GDP	Per capita GNP	Agriculture	Industry	Services
China	9.6	8.2	5.3	11.5	11.1
Hungary	-0.1	0.7	-0.8	-1.6	1.5
Poland	0.7	0.4	-0.5	-3.2	2.7
Russia	-0.5	-1.0	-0.9	0.2	2.0

Source: Compiled from data in Justin Yifu Lin, Fang Cai, and Zhou Li, *The China Miracle: Development Strategy and Economic Reform* (Hong Kong: Chinese University Press, 1996), 3-5.

China's economic reforms begun in 1978 had a near immediate effect on all sectors of the economy. Peasant income doubled between 1978 and 1984 alone, while grain production increased by 4.9 percent annually over the same period.[32] Throughout the 1980s, the economy grew steadily and at an amazing rate. Between 1980 and 1993, per capita gross national product (GNP) grew at an annual rate of 8.2 percent, while gross domestic product (GDP) grew 9.6 percent annually (see table 3.1). The engine of China's economic growth, moreover, was the private and quasi-private sectors, with rapid expansion of TVEs and, in the late 1980s, private firms. Whereas the state sector contributed 73.4 percent of gross industrial output in 1983, by 1989 its share had fallen to 56.1 percent, and continued to give way to the emerging private sector.[33]

Weiji: Danger and Opportunity

Economic reforms transformed not only the economy, but the people themselves and the way they viewed their relationship to the state. Such an outcome is by no means unique; from at least Aristotle onward observers of political life have identified a strong correlation between economic development and the growth of political efficacy. In this sense, economic development presents danger as well as opportunity, for if the people's calls for greater political participation are not met, a crisis is likely to ensue. Political liberalization itself is also a dangerous game, as it tests a regime's commitment to reform and the people's allegiance to the regime. It is perhaps no coincidence that the Chinese word for crisis, *weiji*, is made up of two component characters meaning danger and opportunity. Nevertheless, China's reform leaders attempted to pursue fundamental economic reforms while only permitting limited political liberalization. Although the economic reforms were quite successful at meeting the people's material wants, the political reforms did not keep pace with their political aspirations. The result was demonstrations and protests that developed into several small crises, before finally culminating in a crisis of titanic proportion that brought the Middle Kingdom to the brink of collapse barely a decade into the reform process.

The political expectations of China's citizens began to rise almost simultaneously with the initiation of economic reforms. On November 19, 1978, the first of many big-character posters (*dazibao*) appeared on what became known as Democracy Wall. Located in central Beijing, Democracy Wall became an outlet for young workers and students to express their opinions on political matters freely and frankly. At its height, the Democracy Wall movement involved some 30,000 people in Beijing, and led to similar expressions in Shanghai, Guangzhou, and Hangzhou. Initially, the criticism displayed on the posters was leveled against the Cultural Revolution and the Gang of Four, particularly Mao Zedong and Jiang Qing, while praising Deng Xiaoping. In fact, early posters were so praiseful of Deng that some suspect he may have even masterminded the event.[34] Nevertheless, the support expressed for Deng in the early days of the Democracy Wall was certainly beneficial to him and helped him with the drive toward reform.

Before long, however, criticism began to shift to the Party leadership and Deng himself, while calls also began for democracy and human rights.[35] In the language of reform, Wei Jingsheng put up a poster on December 5 calling for the "fifth modernization," that of democratization. Wei, an electrician at the Beijing Zoo, argued that democratization was the only way to achieve the four modernizations, and he called for the right of the people to choose their own representatives, thus throwing the CCP's rule into question. It was at this point that Deng decided that the Democracy Wall had gone too far, and steps began to be taken to curtail freedom of expression and assembly, and eventually to shut it down. Wei was arrested and sentenced to 15 years in prison, and a constitutional amendment and accompanying legislation were passed which revoked and curtailed several liberties, such as the right of publication, demonstration, and to post big-character posters.[36]

Deng soon made it clear that the behavior exhibited as part of the Democracy Wall movement would not be tolerated. In a public speech given in March 1979, Deng established the Four Cardinal Principles as the parameters within which China's reform and liberalization would have to take place, declaring that China must keep to the socialist road, uphold the dictatorship of the proletariat, as well as the leadership of the CCP, and uphold Marxism-Leninism and Mao Zedong Thought. Having clearly established these parameters, Deng launched a program of controlled liberalization and political reform that continued throughout the 1980s. Not only was the Cultural Revolution brought to a definite close and class struggle abandoned, greater "rule by law" was introduced into the Chinese political system with the introduction of a new legal code and administrative reforms. In fact, even the trial of the Gang of Four was conducted in an uncharacteristically procedural fashion.

There were also several reforms and developments that were launched during this time that would eventually come to hold great significance, although their effects would take quite some time to become clear. As part of the process of breaking up the rural communes, government administration was separated from economic management with the political functions of the communes being transferred to township and village governments.[37] Elections to township councils were also introduced, a process that would eventually lead to competitive village elections on a national scale.[38] Finally, by late the 1980s, the NPC had ceased to be the rubber stamp Leninist parliament it once was and had begun to exert greater legislative autonomy, a process that would continue throughout the 1990s.[39]

By the mid 1980s a debate had begun over the nature, scope, and speed of reform, with two camps emerging. The first camp, headed by Chen Yun and Peng Zhen, argued that modernization would lead inexorably to capitalism. The second, more liberal camp, was headed by Hu Yaobang and Zhao Ziyang, and supported not only continuing with economic reforms, but expanding the reform agenda to include political and social reforms. Although Deng Xiaoping, who was no fan of political reform, failed to align with either group, he allowed reforms to continue and retained an unstated right to intervene as crises of varying scales rose.

Political reforms appeared to pick up renewed momentum in the summer of 1986, when Hu Yaobang and Deng Xiaoping began to express their intention to initiate further political reforms. Throughout the summer the people's expectations again began to rise in anticipation of the upcoming meeting of the CCP. Their hopes were dashed in September at the 12th Central Committee meeting, however, when along with a reassertion of the Four Cardinal Principles (particularly the leading role of the Party), party members were called upon to defend against "bourgeois liberalization," meaning complete Westernization and the development of a Western-style democracy. While mention was made of democracy, legality, and freedom in the arts, the people had hoped for more. In fact, some—particularly students—had found the very ideas that had just been classified as bourgeois liberalization appealing. While they certainly also admired the capitalist economies of East Asia, many were enamored with American democracy to the point that they refused to believe that modern American society faced any social or political difficulties.

With the Party having failed to address their political aspirations, by late fall some members of the Chinese intelligentsia began to speak out. In November, Lin Binyan, a well-known investigative reporter, denounced the oppressive nature of the Four Cardinal Principles in a public speech.[40] Not long thereafter Fang Lizhi, Vice President of the Chinese University of Science and Technology in Hefei, publicly challenged the CCP's conception of democracy, arguing that democracy does not consist of the Party "allowing" the masses to speak, something that is a natural human right.[41] The spark that set off the large-scale student protests, however, was a public speech delivered by Fang in which he encouraged students to fight for democracy, exclaiming to them that "democracy is not granted from the top, it is won by individuals."[42] With the students thus mobilized, the largest demonstrations in China since the Cultural Revolution began to develop over the next few weeks, eventually spreading across the country to seventeen cities.

The demonstrations in Shanghai escalated in late December, swelling to 50,000-70,000 people between December 19-21.[43] While espousing the ideals of democracy and political reform, students began clashing with authorities, even breaking through police barriers. Finally, the demonstrations came to a head on New Year's Day when thousands of students assembled in Tiananmen Square, despite a ban on protests. Then on January 16, 1987, Hu Yaobang, who had been asked three times to resign his post, was ousted from the position of general secretary of the CCP for not being able to manage the student protests. Hu, who had been suspected of using the protests as a means of promoting liberalization and his own career, admitted in his confession that his "ideological laxity had fostered spiritual pollution and bourgeois liberalization, thereby bringing on student turmoil."[44] Hu's removal resulted in an abrupt end to the protests, and the situation was thus contained, though only for a brief moment.

The Tiananmen Crisis of 1989

Throughout the winter of 1988-1989, the issue of political reform began to be raised once again. In addition to discussions among intellectuals for human rights (which ironically coincided with the proclamation of martial law in Tibet), calls also began for the release of Democracy Wall demonstrator Wei Jingsheng. Hu Yaobang even seemed poised to launch a comeback, reportedly delivering an emboldened speech at an enlarged politburo meeting on April 8.[45] Hu suffered a heart attack in the middle of the meeting, however, and later passed away after a second heart attack on April 15. Within days, students took up Hu as a hero for not having taken harsh action against them during the 1986-1987 protests. Thousands of students began to gather in Tiananmen Square to pay their respects to the former CCP general secretary and to express demands for political reform. Eventually, the students' platform developed into calls for democracy and civil liberties, along with a "correct evaluation" of Hu's actions during the demonstrations of 1986-1987.

The confrontation between students and the regime took a decisive turn on April 26, when an editorial in *Renmin ribao* referred to the demonstrations as "turmoil" (*dongluan*) organized by a small group of people and suggested that force would be used if necessary. In an open expression of defiance, as many as 100,000 students marched through the streets of Beijing the following day, breaking through a police cordon and swarming onto Tiananmen Square. Upon his return from a brief trip to North Korea, where he had been when the April 26 editorial had been published, Zhao Ziyang took a conciliatory stance toward the students and opened a dialogue with the students while refraining from any attempt to crack down with force. Zhao believed at the time that the demonstrations were well-intentioned and patriotic—indeed he maintained this position even after his ouster and the crackdown that followed.[46] For their part, the students added to their list of demands for liberalization of speech and the press a reversal of the position stated in the April 26 editorial that referred to the demonstrations as "turmoil." While the demonstrations seemed to be under control in early May, the visit of Soviet leader Mikhail Gorbachev later in the month added fuel to the fire as students took advantage of the media attention that accompanied the Soviet reformer. During Gorbachev's historic visit, the number of demonstrators in Tiananmen Square swelled to over a quarter of a million. It was at this point that the decision was made to invoke martial law on May 19, the day following Gorbachev's departure.

When PLA troops hit the streets of Beijing on May 20, the outpouring of support for the students was so strong that it prevented the troops from resorting to violence, though it is by no means certain that the forces called in at that time would have done so. On June 3 and into the morning hours of June 4, however, troops from the 27th Army stormed the city and reestablished order, not only in Tiananmen Square, but also along the surrounding boulevards where opposition had grown considerably strong. While we will perhaps never know the true cost in human life, with various estimates putting the number of casualties at around

1,000 killed and 10,000 injured, we now know from *The Tiananmen Papers* that the decision to use force was not consensual or easily arrived at.[47] From the same source we also know that it was Li Peng who convinced Deng Xiaoping that the movement was counterrevolutionary, as Li attempted to use the opportunity to move up the party ranks and get rid of his political rival Zhao Ziyang. It was Jiang Zemin, however, at that time a Shanghai Party leader who had shown his skills at handling such situations during the 1986-1987 demonstrations, who was chosen to replace Zhao.

The economic reforms that had been launched more than a decade earlier had brought prosperity to the Middle Kingdom, but the limited political liberalization allowed by the regime could not keep pace with the aspirations of the people, particularly students and intellectuals. Meanwhile, across the globe, reforms that were still in their infancy were already blossoming into freedom and democracy, with the first free elections in Poland being held on the same day as the crackdown in Tiananmen Square. By the end of the year, however, every Communist regime in Eastern Europe would have to face fatal crises of their own, as would the Soviet Union itself within another two years.

From Reform to Collapse:
Perestroika and the End of the Soviet System

Just as the roots of reform in China are found in the death of Mao, in the Soviet Union they can be traced back to Stalin's passing in 1953.[48] Long before Gorbachev conceived of perestroika, other Soviet leaders had recognized that the USSR needed economic and political reform. Lenin had attempted to rebuild the war-torn economy with his New Economic Policy, while Stalin even allowed limited political liberalization in certain spheres following World War II. It was Khrushchev and later Andropov, however, who attempted to implement significant changes. Following his denunciation of the crimes of the Stalin era in his 20th Party Congress speech of 1956, Nikita Khrushchev launched the process of de-Stalinization and attempted to re-legitimize the Soviet political system, which had strayed from its initial objectives under Stalin. He set to work to rebuild the status of the Communist Party, rebuild the economy, and to liberalize the totalitarian state that Stalin had built (and which he himself had faithfully served).

In Eastern Europe, de-Stalinization had a stimulating but also destabilizing effect. Khrushchev's denunciation of Stalin, and the openness which his reforms brought, were seen by the people of Eastern Europe as a signal to introduce similar reforms and to stand up and demand the removal of their own "Stalinist" leaders. Strikes quickly broke out in Poland, creating a confrontation between hard-liners and reformers, while in Hungary a reformist faction led by Imre Nagy stirred up expectations for democratic elections, freedom of speech, the elimination of censorship, and independence from Moscow. The limits of Khrushchev's reforms were clearly illustrated by Soviet tanks rolling into Budapest in October 1956 to quell the public disturbances and to remove the Nagy government.

Khrushchev later attempted other reforms, unveiling a new Party Program at the Twenty-second Party Congress in October 1961 which proclaimed that within twenty years the Soviet economy would catch up to and surpass that of the United States. Khrushchev's overzealous program was an attempt to put the Soviet Union back on the road to communism, and to launch a period of "full-scale communist construction." Shortly thereafter, Khrushchev launched a series of reforms within the Communist Party, including the introduction of the principle of rotation of offices within the party and setting term limits for the Presidium, Central Committee, and regional and local party committees. He also conducted a purge of local and regional party secretaries in order to install those loyal to him. These maneuvers effectively eliminated political "job security" in the Party, and in so doing wiped out much of Khrushchev's support base.

Khrushchev's "thaw" brought a much needed rapprochement between the regime and society. The people were given more freedom and a better quality of life in exchange for their passivity in politics. Khrushchev's rule, however, created such political instability and resentment among high-ranking officials that he was eventually ousted and sent into retirement. While his efforts to de-Stalinize the Soviet Union were by and large successful, his "hare-brained" attempts to implement political and economic reform were certainly less so.

At the Central Committee meeting in which Khrushchev was removed, Leonid Brezhnev was already sitting in the chair of the Party First Secretary. Although Brezhnev's leadership was not characterized by attempts to reform Soviet society radically, rather seeking to introduce a period of relative stability, limited economic innovations were attempted at the plant and locality level.[49] In 1965, limited economic decentralization was even briefly experimented with under the direction of Soviet Premier Aleksei Kosygin, who had been in that position during Khrushchev's period as General Secretary. During the Brezhnev era the economy grew slowly but steadily, however, based primarily on the exhaustion of Soviet energy and other natural resources. Agricultural output increased at an average annual rate of around three percent, while industrial production also saw significant growth. In the political realm, the regime not only left in place many of the limited liberties introduced by Khrushchev, further freedoms were allowed in such areas as religion, private production of food, and communication with relatives and friends outside the USSR was relaxed.[50] By the mid-1970s, the Soviet economy had lost what little dynamism it had and the country entered a period of stagnation, with growth provided by the expansion of the economy but with no reforms being implemented.

Further reforms were attempted by Brezhnev's successor, Yuri Andropov, who had begun to play an increasingly significant role in running state affairs in the final days of Brezhnev's life. Andropov was chosen by the Politburo as the new Party General Secretary in November 1982, and although he was to be in power for only a short time, he attempted some much needed reforms, the most audacious of which was a crackdown on the special privileges of the elite, which turned out to be largely unsuccessful and led to great animosity against him. Andropov also advocated economic reforms such as greater autonomy for factories, enterprises, and collective farms. With the able assistance of a young Mikhail Gorbachev, Andropov also mobilized a massive crackdown on absenteeism, alcoholism, and shoddy work. Andropov's modest reform agenda accomplished little, however, mostly due to his short period of time in power and his failing health while in office.

Reform initiatives were again abandoned under Konstantin Chernenko, a long-time Brezhnev protégé, who was chosen to succeed Andropov in February 1984, although apparently Andropov himself had wanted Gorbachev to be his successor.[51] Chernenko's brief tenure in power was a return to the stability of the Brezhnev era, with few policy initiatives. Chernenko remained in office until his death on March 11, 1985, though his health had begun to fail in the fall of 1984, at which point Mikhail Gorbachev began to play an increasingly visible role. Finally, Gorbachev succeeded Chernenko on the same day that the latter's death was made public.

Gorbachev and Perestroika

Before leaving for the meeting at which he was to be selected as the new General Secretary of the CPSU, Mikhail Gorbachev said to his wife "life can't be lived like this any longer."[52] Indeed, shortly after assuming the party's leading office, Gorbachev began a reform initiative that would fundamentally alter the bases of Soviet society, and in the opinion of some, undermine its very existence.

A supporter of Andropov's reforms, Gorbachev immediately set to work to renew similar efforts. He attacked corruption by launching criminal investigations of suspect officials, with those found guilty dismissed from their posts. Gorbachev went after the ruling elite in other ways as well, making personnel changes that eclipsed those of previous leaders. In his first year in office alone, Gorbachev managed to obtain the replacement of 47 out of 121 regional party secretaries and more than half of the CPSU Central Committee. These were no mere personnel changes, moreover, as Gorbachev replaced old-time party members with younger, better-educated personnel. He soon found, however, that the Soviet Union's ills could not be cured with disciplinary measures or new personnel, no matter how progressive they were. Comprehensive reform was necessary.

After the end of his first year in power, Gorbachev announced his intention to introduce sweeping reform into the Soviet system. Within two years, glasnost and perestroika would become household words the world over. His reform agenda initially centered on three components, that of *glasnost*, new political thinking, and *perestroika*. *Perestroika* was not a set of policies or even a general agenda. Rather, as conceived by Gorbachev, it was a new approach to politics, economics, and society. On the economic front, the main goal was the invigoration of the Soviet economy, or as Gorbachev himself frequently expressed it, acceleration. Economic reforms initially centered on disciplinary measures intended to bring about greater accountability and on converting the Soviet economy from an extensive mode of production, under which greater resources were funneled into the economy in order to increase outputs, to intensive production, in which production was increased through efficiency, technology, and quality. Before long, however, individual enterprises and business cooperatives were legalized and the development of the private sector was encouraged.

The policy of new political thinking pertained mostly to foreign policy and relations with the West. The rhetoric of an "unavoidable confrontation with the capitalist world" was abandoned and Gorbachev sought to reduce the tensions of the Cold War confrontation, making his intentions clear as early as the October 1986 Reykjavik Summit with U.S. President Ronald Reagan. New political thinking also entailed a new approach toward the Soviet bloc states of Eastern Europe, which were now allowed to find their "own paths toward socialism." These actions increased Gorbachev's popularity abroad, although decreasing it at home. Resistance developed particularly among those in the military-industrial sector, who along with nationalists and conservatives, had felt comfortable with the Soviet Union's role in the world and wished to preserve the glory of the empire and the country's superpower status. To such groups, Gorbachev's moves seemed to be a mistake.

Gorbachev attempted to make party and state leaders more responsive to the people's needs through the policy of *glasnost,* or openness. Glasnost provided greater access to information and legitimized the articulation of individual and group interests. Glasnost also made leaders more accountable by opening them up for criticism, with public officials even having to appear on radio and television programs to answer citizen complaints. More openness was permitted in political discourse as well and there was the opportunity to comment on issues with greater frankness in the media. In short, glasnost allowed a dialogue to be opened between the government and the people, and as a result voluntary sociopolitical organizations began to flourish and strengthen the country's nascent civil society.[53]

Perhaps the aspect of perestroika that was most celebrated in the West was *demokratizatsiya*, or democratization. While perestroika had initially begun as an economic reform initiative, by late 1986 Gorbachev was paying increased attention to the importance of political reform. At an address to the plenum of the CPSU Central Committee in January 1987, Gorbachev discussed the seriousness of the social problems which the Soviet Union faced, such as crowded housing, low-quality health care, corruption, and alcoholism, and placed the blame for these conditions on the leading organs of the state and the party. To remedy the situation he proposed democratizing the political system by instituting multiple-candidate elections for certain posts and allowing greater involvement in government by nonparty members. Coupled with the expansion of private economic activity, Gorbachev was attempting nothing short of nearly simultaneous reform of the USSR's economic and political life, the very basis of the Soviet system itself.

Economic Reforms

Gorbachev initially tried to revitalize the Soviet economy through disciplinary measures, launching a massive crackdown on absenteeism, alcoholism, and shoddy work soon after taking office. An official quality control inspectorate, *Gospriemka*, was established with instructions to reject shoddy products and to dock the pay of those responsible, introducing greater worker accountability into the Soviet economy. Absenteeism was attacked by sending police out to bars, liquor stores, and movie theaters to check people's working papers, with those supposed to be at work being sent back after imposing fines upon them. Finally, Gorbachev launched a very unpopular anti-alcohol campaign, which included decreases in alcohol production, an increase in prices, reduced access (due to a reduction in the number of liquor stores and restaurants allowed to serve alcohol), and fines for public drunkenness.[54]

Additionally, Gorbachev's policies attempted to bring about higher quality and greater efficiency in production by retooling industry and employing advanced technology, all of which would contribute to the economy's transition from extensive growth to intensive growth. Together, these measures were an attempt to reinvigorate the Soviet economy through the use of disciplinary measures, incentives, accountability, and technology infusion, not by changing the fundamental nature of the economy. These reforms had little impact, however, other than leading to an increase in illegal brewing and distilling and to a stall in economic output due to the high number of goods being rejected by *Gospriemka*, including the very machinery that was to be used to retool industry.[55]

Initially Gorbachev had not considered implementing market reforms, actually viewing private economic activity as part of the problem, as it was seen as encroaching upon the efficiency of the state sector.[56] Prior to 1987, therefore, Gorbachev had only sought to "clarify" the role of private economic activity. This began to change, however, as reform measures were soon pursued which aimed at developing a form of "market socialism," with increased economic autonomy for enterprises and individuals, albeit within an economy still dominated by state ownership and central planning.

The first clear step in the direction of a free market was taken with the Law on Individual Labor Activity, which went into effect in May 1987. The Law did little more than make aspects of the Soviet shadow economy legal and was only intended to specify more clearly the circumstances under which legitimate private enterprises could operate. Private enterprises would be required to be licensed and registered, and housewives, the unemployed, and moonlighting workers would be allowed to participate in the economy legally. The Law made it very clear, moreover, that private economic activity was in no way meant to supplant employment in the state sector, especially for moonlighting workers already working for state enterprises, who could engage in private economic activity only on a part-time basis. Although this policy did not open up the state economy to competition from the private sector, it was an important first move toward recognizing the significance of private economic activity.

A further step toward market development was taken with the Law on State Enterprises of July 1987, which introduced market reforms into the state sector itself. By allowing state enterprises to contract directly with their suppliers and customers, enterprises were given greater freedom over decisions concerning investment and the use of profits.[57] Later, in 1988, they were also given greater latitude with their self-financing activities as a result of monetary reforms. With administrative control over enterprise deposits lifted, state enterprises were able to use them as they saw fit and to take advantage of market opportunities.

It was the Law on Cooperatives of May 1988, however, that finally put private enterprises on par with state-owned enterprises (SOEs). Cooperatives, which could range from a three-person family unit all the way to a large collective farm, were allowed to engage in a broad range of activities, including the leasing of property, subcontracting work to other cooperatives or individuals, hiring labor, and raising capital through the issue of shares.[58] This policy shift indicates that the government recognized the fact that the private sector that had been developing since the early reforms had been initiated was one centered mostly on informal cooperatives, not on individual labor activities. In fact, although there were only 15,000 individuals employed in cooperatives in January 1987, by April 1988 (the eve of the Law on Cooperatives) that number had grown to 245,700.[59] The Law further encouraged this trend, and by October 1990 there were some 215,000 cooperatives in the Soviet Union employing 5.2 million people, more than 3.5 percent of the country's total workforce.[60] Conversely, by June 1990 there were only 200,000 persons engaged in individual labor activities in the Soviet Union.[61]

The development of cooperatives was only meant to supplement the state sector, not replace it, but state authorities saw the cooperatives for what they were—competitors. This resulted in problems with registration, as state authorities would sometimes reject a cooperative's registration application, or erect administrative barriers to registration. For example, authorities sometimes refused to register cooperatives lacking an independent business address, although none was required under the law. In certain republics and regions, cooperatives were also prohibited from engaging in specific economic activities, while only being allowed to engage in other activities under contract with a state enterprise; both acts that were in direct violation of the Law on Cooperatives. In October 1989, the Supreme Soviet even passed a resolution permitting local Soviets to set maximum prices for cooperative products and forbidding cooperatives from selling products for more than state stores sold comparable goods.[62] While this policy was reversed as early as spring 1990, those cooperatives that chose to sell their goods above state-set prices were required to pay between three and five times the official prices for their raw materials.[63]

Aside from permitting private economic activity to develop alongside the state sector, the May 1989 Decree on Leasing began the process of transferring control of enterprises from the state into private hands. Although only a form of "semi-privatization," this policy permitted private economic entities, including cooperatives, to lease state-owned enterprises. While the initial projection was that over a period of six years about 20 percent of SOEs would be leased, on the eve of the disintegration of the Soviet Union some 9 million workers in various sectors were employed in leased enterprises.[64] It was not until the summer of 1990, however, that the Soviet government finally turned to genuine privatization and began to allow the sale of state-owned assets to private individuals and economic entities. Privatization began to pick up momentum throughout 1991, particularly after the Law on the Basic Principles of Destatization and Privatization of Enterprises was passed in the summer of that year. By year-end, however, 92 percent of productive forces remained in state hands.[65]

TABLE 3.2.
Change in Economic Performance under Perestroika (in percent).

	1986-1990	1990	1991
Gross Industrial Output	2.5	-1.2	-7.8
Agricultural Production	1.1	-2.3	-7.0

Source: Keith Bush, "The Disastrous Last Year of the USSR," *RFE/RL/RR* 1, no. 12 (March 20, 1992), 40.

Perestroika's economic reforms fundamentally altered the Soviet socialist economy, allowing private economic activity and privatizing state enterprises and property. As Pei points out, however, "unlike Chinese reforms, the early Soviet reforms failed to create favorable conditions for the rapid emergence of the private sector."[66] Not only did these reforms not reinvigorate the Soviet economy, they actually brought it to its knees. While Soviet gross industrial output had grown 2.5 percent between 1986 and 1990, it fell 1.2 percent in 1990 before plunging 7.8 percent in 1991. Agricultural production fared no better, having grown only 1.1 percent between 1986 and 1990 before dropping 2.3 percent in 1990 and 7 percent in the Soviet Union's final year.[67] Perhaps if the more radical market reforms of 1990-1991 had been implemented earlier things would have turned out differently. As it turned out, the reforms were too little, too late for the Soviet economy, the fate of which was tied inextricably to the political life of the country, which itself was in a tailspin as a result of *demokratizatsiya*.

Demokratizatsiya and Political Reform

In the political realm, Gorbachev had initially called for the establishment of a law governed order, in which state power would be subordinate to the law and arbitrary application of Soviet law would be brought to an end. By replacing "socialist legality" with a "socialist legal state," the individual, "rather than the collective or the abstract interest of the class, state or Communism, as interpreted by the party, was thus made the fundamental unit of society."[68] As part of the development of a law governed state (*pravovoe gosudarstvo*), a series of legal reforms were initiated, many of which were eventually enacted. The constitutional amendments passed by the Supreme Soviet in December 1988, *inter alia*, restricted the powers of the state and gave institutional force to the separation of powers between the legislative and executive branches, and enhanced the independence of the judiciary. Members of the executive, for example, were now prohibited from serving as parliamentary deputies, and judges were to apply the law strictly according to the constitution. In addition to establishing a commission to draft a new constitution, new laws were also passed on press freedom and religious belief, while a new criminal code was drafted which reduced prison sentences, restricted the death penalty, and abolished external exile.[69]

Gorbachev did not see legal reform as separate from democratization. As he explained, democracy "cannot exist and develop without the rule of law, because law is designed to protect society from abuses of power and guarantee citizens and their organizations and work collectives their rights and freedoms."[70] Gorbachev also realized, however, that the rule of law was not enough, and that true democracy cannot exist without free and competitive elections. Although the Soviet Union had held elections since the country's inception, they were noncompetitive and far from free and fair. Instead, they served a system-legitimizing function, although they also drew the ire and contempt of many who longed for truly democratic elections.[71] This would all change with Gorbachev's policy of *demokratizatsiya*. Party and state officials would be held personally accountable for policies and have to stand for competitive elections. Beginning in 1987, positions within the Communist Party, trade unions, and Komsomol (Communist Youth Organization) began to be filled through competitive, secret, and direct elections. In June 1987 a limited experiment was conducted in local soviet elections, with 5 percent of the deputies elected in multi-member districts in competitive elections. Gorbachev's motivations for such measures of democratization were also pragmatic, as he expected that the new democratic procedures would increase his chances of defeating his conservative, anti-reformist colleagues. Nevertheless, once the reforms were implemented they took on a life of their own.

The amendments to the Soviet constitution enacted in December 1988 by the Supreme Soviet also created a new legislative body, known as the Congress of People's Deputies (CPD), which was to be composed of 2,250 deputies. Once the Congress convened, it would then elect from among its own ranks the members of the Supreme Soviet, which was to be the supreme legislative body and would be responsible for managing the daily affairs of the legislature. Of the

2,250 deputies in the CPD, 1,500 were to be chosen in national elections, while the remaining 750 were to be chosen by social organizations, including the Communist Party, trade unions, and Komsomol, which were each given a set number of seats. While this latter provision prevented the legislature from being fully democratic, the vast majority of representatives were to be chosen in democratic and contested elections.

Ironically, with the democratic changes implemented, a larger share of seats went to members of the Communist Party in the initial CPD elections in March 1989 than in previous Soviet elections. Although in the past 71.5 percent of seats customarily went to members of the Communist Party, with a balance between party and nonparty members meant to provide the illusion that the party did not monopolize politics, in the 1989 CPD elections 87 percent of the seats went to party members. Despite the high percentage of Communist Party members winning election, 88 percent of the new deputies had been elected for the first time. The CPD would have a strong Communist Party representation, therefore, but it was not to be dominated by the old guard. When the new Congress of People's Deputies met for the first time in late May, it elected from among its own ranks the 542 members who would compose the new Supreme Soviet. The Supreme Soviet, in turn, then elected Mikhail Gorbachev as its chairman.

Although the initial stages of demokratizatsiya seemed to have gone off without a hitch, within one year things would change drastically. It would soon become clear that glasnost and civil society's ability to place collective demands upon the state had begun to outpace the progress of reform. In the summer of 1989 striking miners in Kuzbas, Donbass, and Vorkuta began to voice radical political and economic demands, including calling for the abolition of Article 6 of the Soviet constitution, which guaranteed a political monopoly for the Communist Party. Dissident scientist Andrei Sakharov and others then staged a "strike" at the second convocation of the CPD in December of that year calling for the elimination of Article 6. Then in February 1990, the Supreme Soviet finally voted in favor of amending Article 6, thus opening up the political realm. At its next session in March, the CPD ratified this decision and brought the Communist Party's monopoly on power to an end. The following day, the CPD elected Gorbachev the first president of the Soviet Union in an uncontested and indirect election, which, as Sakwa describes it, meant a shift from "party-guided perestroika . . . to presidential perestroika."[72] The legalization of alternative political parties and the creation of a Soviet presidency were to have profound effects on the future course of reform in the Soviet Union.

The Collapse of the Soviet Union

While the creation of a popularly elected legislature was a tremendous step forward in the democratization of the Soviet Union, Gorbachev's failure to put himself before the Soviet electorate greatly diminished his democratic credentials. Democratization had already begun to trickle down to the republic level, however, with several republics and localities holding elections to regional legislatures in late winter 1990, prior to Gorbachev's selection as Soviet president in mid March. It was at this point that it became clear that grassroots democracy had begun to outpace perestroika and Gorbachev's "reform from above." Before long, it would overtake the reform process and lead to a series of crises that would test the limits of perestroika and Gorbachev's resolve.

Perhaps the most significant republic elections to take place in late winter 1990 were those in the Baltic republics, where the fall of the Berlin Wall and the collapse of Communism in Eastern Europe had led these East Europeans—who had joined the Communist camp at roughly the same time as the satellite states of Eastern Europe and to whom Soviet rule was perhaps just as alien—to dream of their own independence. Nowhere were the calls for independence greater than in Lithuania, where several groups had begun to emerge from within civil society demanding reforms and greater freedom, the most important of which was the Lithuanian Movement for Restructuring (*Lietuvos Persitvarkymo Sajudis*), or simply *Sajudis* (the movement).

In Lithuania's elections to the Congress of People's Deputies in February 1990, *Sajudis* won 80 percent of the seats it contested. With Vytautas Landsbergis as its chairman, the Lithuanian Supreme Council quickly declared Lithuania's independence on March 11, 1990, announcing that "The Lithuanian nation has an old and strong tradition of statehood that it has never renounced of its own free will; it therefore has the natural and inalienable right to reestablish independent Lithuania."[73] This declaration of independence only resulted in an economic embargo against Lithuania, however, which Moscow later lifted once Lithuanian leaders agreed to suspend its declaration.[74] In the final days of 1990, however, and into the beginning of the new year, the situation in Lithuania became increasingly unstable, and by January 11, 1991, Soviet troops were being employed to quell the situation. Then on January 13, taking advantage of the West's engagement in the Persian Gulf, Soviet forces attempted to reestablish control of the rebel republic, resulting in the death of fourteen civilians.

Lithuania was not the only republic seeking exit from the USSR by this time; Estonia and Latvia quickly followed Lithuania's example, while Ukraine joined the list in July. Although perhaps too late, Gorbachev began to recognize the degree of discontent felt by many in the republics, and he began to propose a new form of union among the republics, one that would give greater autonomy and sovereignty to the republics while preserving the union. On March 17, 1991, Gorbachev put the issue to the people in a national referendum, asking Soviet citizens, "Do you consider necessary the preservation of the Union of Soviet Socialist Republics as a renewed federation of equal sovereign republics, in which the rights and freedoms of the individual of any nationality will be fully guaranteed?" More than 75 percent of voters responded favorably to the question, although Armenia, Georgia, Moldova, and the Baltic republics boycotted the vote, their opinions perhaps already known clearly enough.

Despite the clear expression of the will of Russia's citizens in the referendum, 71 percent of whom supported preserving the union, the Russian Parliament declared its sovereignty in June 1991, placing the weight of its own decisions above those of the USSR. This move was more an expression of Boris Yeltsin's own political ambitions, however, rather than an expression of the people's will. Yeltsin, who had been chosen as chairman of the Russian Congress of People's Deputies the year before, had used his position to tack a question on the creation of a presidency for the Russian Republic on to the March 17, 1991, referendum. With the item approved, Yeltsin was elected the new president of the Russian Republic in June.

The creation of a Russian presidency and Yeltsin's election to the post put the Soviet Union in a precarious position. Although Gorbachev continued to search for solutions to the Soviet Union's many ills, the Russian presidency provided an alternative power structure, which Yeltsin used to continue his call for the sovereignty of Russia over the Soviet Union while encouraging the leaders of the other republics to "take all the sovereignty they could swallow." As if the situation were not perilous enough, a group of Communist hardliners staged an attempted coup d'etat on August 19, 1991, on the eve of the signing of a new Union Treaty that would have led to a looser union among the Soviet Union's republics and perhaps pacified the nationalist aspirations of the secession-minded republics. Once the coup attempt had been put down by Yeltsin and other liberal forces, the torch seemed to pass to Yeltsin, who had stood up against the hardliners and who could claim a popular mandate based upon his electoral victory.

The following months saw Yeltsin "swallow" as much sovereignty as he could, as he attempted to take over for Russia as many of the functions of the Soviet state as possible, including the Ministry of Foreign Affairs, the Ministry of Finance, and even the KGB. Meanwhile, Gorbachev stood by apparently unwilling or unable to do anything to prevent Yeltsin and the other republican leaders from dismantling the bankrupt and quickly disintegrating Soviet state, continuing in his attempt to hold the union together with a new union treaty. These hopes seemed to fade as well when on November 25, Gorbachev stood publicly humiliated as Yeltsin refused to sign the new treaty. Then, on December 7, the leaders of Ukraine and Belarus joined Yeltsin in Minsk to discuss the future of the Soviet Union, quickly declaring the founding of a Commonwealth of Independent States. As Hough describes, the three leaders "were overthrowing the [Soviet] president, the government, and the state more surely than had the organizers of the August coup."[75]

Following Yeltsin's return to Moscow, the Supreme Soviet declared Russia's formal independence, thus following the Baltics and Ukraine, which had already abandoned ship. Finally, on December 25, 1991, Gorbachev resigned his post as president of the Soviet Union, thus relegating the world's first Communist state to the dustbin of history.

The Causes of the Soviet Denouement

It was not Gorbachev's intent to collapse the Soviet Union, but rather to breathe new life into the decrepit Soviet system. The forces he unleashed to carry out that task, however, led eventually to the system's collapse. Insofar as the system Gorbachev had meant to revitalize collapsed, perestroika had failed. In looking back on the situation some years later, however, Gorbachev sees perestroika's many successes rather than its failure:

> What specifically did we accomplish as a result of the stormy years of perestroika? The foundations of the totalitarian system were eliminated. Profound democratic changes were begun. Free general elections were held for the first time, allowing real choice. Freedom of the press and a multiparty system were guaranteed. Representative bodies of government were established, and the first steps toward a separation of powers were taken. Human rights . . . now became an unassailable principle. And freedom of conscience was also established.[76]

Indeed, these were great accomplishments, but the fact remains that the collapse of the Soviet state meant that these accomplishments could later be reversed by the regimes that inherited the vestiges of Soviet power, most notably being the post-Soviet regimes of Belarus and Tajikistan, though others struggle with similar problems to lesser degrees, such as Ukraine, Uzbekistan, etc. Russia itself continues to wrestle with these issues as well, as we will discuss in the following chapter.

Gorbachev's longtime friend, Zdenek Mlynar, defends the last Soviet leader's course of action, saying, "when there were arguments about your policies I frequently defended your point of view, that you could not have done anything differently if you did not want to use force on a massive scale. And I see it as being to your credit that you did not."[77] Of course, it is to Gorbachev's credit that, in the final instance, force was not used to keep the flailing union together. But the collapse of the Soviet Union cannot be seen simply as the result of Gorbachev's failure to use force to keep it together. The roots of the collapse go back much deeper than this, the only question is how deep. While some scholars suggest that the roots of the system's demise actually coincide with the system's founding, arguing that Communism as a system was simply not workable,[78] the direct causes of the collapse are clearly found in perestroika itself. Indeed, one of the reasons the collapse of the Soviet Union was not predicted by Western social scientists is that it was not inevitable or even likely until very late in the process of reform.

Policy decisions such as the elimination of Article 6, the level at which democratic elections were introduced, the primacy given to democratic reforms over economic reforms, and even Gorbachev's failure to stand for democratic elections all had long-term consequences for the way perestroika unfolded and the collapse came about. Each of these policy choices and others carried the Soviet Union down a very specific course, one which only ended with the collapse. It is possible that another selection and sequencing of policies would have led the country down a different path, and although this path, too, may have arrived at some form of democracy and free market, it may have done so without the tumultuous effects of a regime collapse and the complete disintegration of the USSR and the tremors of further dissolution in several of the successor states themselves.

While the collapse of the Soviet Union was not inevitable prior to the launching of perestroika, it became increasingly likely as events unfolded and decisions were made about how to proceed. The first real phase of the collapse began between March and December 1989, from the initial elections to the Congress of People's Deputies through the Tiananmen uprising to the collapse of Communist rule in Eastern Europe. During this phase, a collapse went from being a remote possibility to being a potential outcome of reform. By this time perestroika had run into an impasse, and Gorbachev attempted to reinvigorate his reform agenda by pushing ahead with democratization. But in so doing, Gorbachev gave electoral ballots to a population largely in need of food stamps, and gave free expression to a people bottled up with resentment over past mistreatment and facing one of the most daunting economic transformations the world has ever known.

During the second phase of the collapse, from approximately January 1990 to August 1991, a systemic collapse became an ever increasingly possible outcome. The competitive elections to the republican Congresses of People's Deputies in late winter 1990 was shortly followed by declarations of sovereignty and even independence, while Yeltsin's meteoric rise to power in Russia, and his call to the other republics to swallow as much sovereignty as they could handle, was a lethal blow to Soviet statehood, one which the March 1991 referendum did little to heal. Indeed, by August the situation was so severe that the coup plotters attempted to do what Gorbachev himself would not—reclaim the reins of power with force. The failure of the coup led the country into the third and final phase of collapse, which saw the union crumble piece by piece throughout the fall of 1991. Throughout this phase the collapse was all but inevitable, and while perhaps something could have been done to preserve a rump state of former republics, it is unlikely that force alone would have been able to do so; nevertheless, it would certainly have taken more than a new union treaty to slow the centrifugal forces of disintegration.

The topic of the Soviet collapse has not gone without serious scholarly attention, and researchers have taken various approaches to explaining the collapse, focusing on such factors as ideology, nationalism, and socio-structural conditions.[79] One scholar has argued that the underlying reason why the Soviet Union ultimately failed in its attempt to reform, and instead collapsed in the process, was that the Soviet system was in many ways alien to Russia and incongruent with the country's cultural heritage and traditional values. As Petro cogently explains, Bolshevism was never deeply rooted in Russian political culture but was "rather a particular ideology whose popularity was directly tied to the fortunes of the Communist Party." Moreover, "despite decades of trying, the Soviet regime ultimately failed in its effort to legitimize the rule of the Communist Party."[80] This is indeed true, and once the ideology of Marxism-Leninism was discredited even among the elites, there was very little left to hold the empire together. One fact that certainly complicated the Soviet regime's attempt to legitimize its rule may be that, while it espoused democracy and marched its citizenry out on a regular basis to participate in staged elections, it never allowed the people any real role in the political process. Its support for the "forms" of democracy, moreover, perhaps legitimized genuine elections and eventually led to calls from the people for true democracy.[81]

Another significant factor in the Soviet Union's collapse was the country's tremendous ethnic diversity, which roughly corresponded with internal territorial boundaries, which quickly became the fracture lines along which the union broke apart.[82] Once the potential for nationalist-based political unrest was enabled by *glasnost*, moreover, nationalist aspirations seemed to grow in direct proportion to the discrediting of Soviet ideology and the regime's loss of legitimacy. And as the façade of Soviet ideology faded, nationalism was the first identifying factor people began to look toward. Politicians were quick to react and play the nationalist card to great success, as reawakened Lithuanians, Georgians, and even Tatars and Russians began to use their newly-won electoral rights to vote for nations rather than policies.

Glasnost unleashed not only nationalist aspirations, but communal and interest-based groups of all sorts, with ethnicity and nationalism only being the most visible.[83] While Russian civil society was unable to take the lead in democratization efforts due to its relative weakness, important groups did side with liberalizing forces in the battle against anti-reformists and hardliners, culminating in the collapse of the Soviet Union. Although civil society most certainly played an important role in the process of Soviet democratization, it would be an exaggeration to conclude that it wrested the reins of power from the Soviet regime, as the fact is that the Soviet state relaxed its grip on society as time went on, finally liberalizing under Gorbachev and his policies of glasnost and perestroika.[84]

This is not an exhaustive list, of course, as myriad factors played roles of varying significance in the Soviet denouement. Perhaps the most complete and succinct account of the collapse of Soviet Communism is that offered by Martin Malia, who focuses on the country's socio-structural failures and economic situation:

> The most fundamental cause was the economic decline and its repercussions for the Soviet Union's superpower status. It is this crisis of performance that moved Gorbachev to launch *perestroika* in the first place; and this restructuring soon led him to attack the Party, and so run what turned out to be the suicidal risks of *glasnost* and then of democratization. Finally, the economic decline discredited the claims of the ideology, and *glasnost* made it possible to proclaim this fact, thereby delegitimizing the system and, ultimately, depriving it of the will to coerce. And this circumstance in turn made possible the revolt of the minority nationalities and the collapse of the people's democracies.[85]

While Malia's description nicely weaves together the most critical factors involved in the Soviet collapse, he assigns the greatest causal weight to the failure of the centrally-planned economy, only adding as an aside that "we may include in the chain of causation various tactical errors of Gorbachev, such as pushing democratization faster than economic liberalization, or, at the end, surrounding himself with conservative enemies of his own reforms."[86] Lest his position is not yet clear enough, Malia explicitly states that the "proximate" causes of Communism's "collapse are not discrete or adventitious phenomena," but rather "they are parts of a pattern arising from the nature of that system itself."[87]

In this regard he is quite in agreement with Kornai, who has argued that, "In spite of generating a whole series of favorable changes, reform is doomed to fail: the socialist system is unable to renew itself internally so as to prove viable in the long run."[88] As Kornai further explains toward the end of his study of the political economy of Communism, "the incoherence, internal contradictions, and lack of stability in the reform socialist system suggest that it is not lastingly viable. The process of reform yields a heteromorphic formation that contains the seeds of its own destruction: inner tensions that build up until it bursts."[89]

Such accounts of the failure of perestroika and the collapse of Communism place all blame on the system itself, and like Mlynar, leave Gorbachev and his policy decisions unscathed. Malia even argues explicitly that "the great crash of 1989-1991" should have settled the question over the claim that "the Soviet collapse was produced by accidents and errors" once and for all, concluding that Leninist systems are irreformable and will inevitably collapse under the weight of reform.[90] The question over the reformability of Communism is not simply pedantic, however, for the fate of the world's largest Communist state hangs in the balance. If scholars such as Malia and Kornai are right, then attempts to reform Chinese Communism are doomed to failure as well, and the torpidity with which Chinese leaders have pursued reform is only postponing a Chinese collapse, not ultimately avoiding the same fate that befell the Soviet Union.

While structural conditions certainly contributed to the failure of Communism, the Soviet collapse was also due in great measure to the policy choices made by Gorbachev and the reformist camp, particularly regarding the pace and scope of reform. And while the reformers were constrained by the country's social, economic, political, and cultural conditions, the specific policies employed to restructure Soviet society were causative.

Unparalleled Reforms

Communist reform in the Soviet Union and China was similar in a few respects, particularly regarding the underlying wish to abandon the traditional Soviet model that had prevailed in both societies. The reforms carried out, however, were actually quite dissimilar in most aspects. For one, the circumstances under which the reforms were launched and carried out were quite different. China launched its reform effort almost immediately following the death of its first Communist leader, and the reforms were initiated and implemented by many leaders who had actually brought Communism to China, including Deng Xiaoping himself. The circumstances in the Soviet Union were quite different altogether, as perestroika was attempted by a leader and his supporters who had not even been born before the Bolshevik Revolution, and in fact whose formative years had coincided with Khrushchev's thaw and own reassessment of the Stalinist model. While the fact that China began to reform its system at an earlier stage of evolution meant that the system was less ossified and its leaders had more legitimacy to speak on behalf of Communist rule, it also imposed constraints. The fact that many reformers had actually helped erect the Chinese Communist system meant that they would be less inclined to abandon some of the fundamental principles of the system, a system which they believed still had considerable potential. While this resulted in greater stability and less drastic reforms, it also meant that reform would come much more slowly and not keep pace with the desires of the younger and better-educated segments of society.

The reforms in the Soviet Union and China also had very different ideological bases, partly as a result of the characteristics of the leaders who initiated the reforms. Deng and his colleagues sought to soften the totalitarian state that Mao had constructed, and under which Deng himself had twice suffered, and to improve the economic situation in the country. The measures that were employed in these tasks, moreover, were rationalized with the writings of Marx, Lenin, and Mao, meaning that Chinese socialism was being "reassessed," not necessarily abandoned. This strategy was not coincidental; Chinese leaders, particularly the whateverists, were afraid that any ideological revision would encourage the people to "doubt everything" and question the Party's leadership role.[91] On the contrary, in the Soviet Union it was quite clear to all that Gorbachev was abandoning many of the tenets of socialism in rapid succession, with little or no consideration given to the effects this might have on a population that had been indoctrinated with Marxist-Leninist thought for generations. Liberalization and economic development, moreover, were clearly modeled on Western forms, making very clear how sharp was the intended break with the prescriptions of Marxism-Leninism.

Finally, the actual reforms themselves were initiated and carried out in quite different ways. While China began with economic reforms, only later slowly introducing political liberalization, the Soviet Union launched both market reforms and democratization nearly simultaneously. There were similar differences regarding the speed with which the reforms were implemented, with China introducing market reforms over a period of years (indeed, more than two decades later the economy is still not entirely free of state control), while the Soviet economy went from allowing private economic activity to carrying out the world's largest privatization effort in a period of only a few years. Reforms were also received in quite different terms in both countries, being not only welcomed in China but actually assisted with a significant degree of local and grassroots initiative, while reforms in the USSR were met with a tepid response and bureaucratic obstruction.

The level on which the reforms were focused also differed drastically. While the bulk of reforms in China were experimented with first on the local level, such as the household responsibility system and even village elections, in the Soviet Union entire industries were privatized and infused with foreign investment before small enterprises (which could have created capital to purchase and invest in large-scale enterprises, not to mention the development of human capital and entrepreneurial skills) even had a chance to develop. Likewise, national legislative and executive leaders in the Soviet Union were being freely elected well before Soviet citizens even had the chance to learn democratic practices through local democracy. Indeed, as we will see in the next chapter, this remains one of Russia's greatest challenges even today.

There were also significant commonalities in the results of the Soviet and Chinese attempts to reform Communism. In both countries the reforms had the effect of spurring on the development of a middle class and led to divisions between different ideological camps, i.e., reformers, moderates, and conservatives. In China, a power struggle preceded reforms, which gave Deng and his supporters the ability to proceed with reforms with only minor resistance. In the Soviet Union, however, it was a power struggle between Gorbachev and the leaders in the republics that helped turn a crisis into a collapse.

Most significantly, however, was the concomitant rise of civil society in both countries. By the late 1980s, civil society in China had only begun to stir, and the demonstrations at Tiananmen Square in April-June 1989 were their clearest and most powerful manifestation. In the Soviet Union, however, the greater liberties granted to the Soviet people virtually overnight and the relative strength of the middle class and elite meant that civil society developed and organized there quickly. These facts, coupled with the country's particular multiethnic makeup and the existence of a foreign multinational empire in Eastern Europe, meant that events unfolded in a somewhat different manner, with powerful calls for national sovereignty and independence, calls that would generate a crisis on a monumental scale. While the processes that eventually led to the collapse of the Soviet Union were not initiated by civil society, it was groups of dissatisfied citizens organized along political and ethnic lines that pulled it down.

Both systems also ran into crisis as a result of their reforms. Crisis moments can occur in all regime types, of course, including democracies. As it turned out, the crisis the Soviet Union faced between 1989-1991 was much more severe and fatal than the one faced by China. It is not just that China resorted to the use of force and that this action prevented a Soviet-style collapse in the Middle Kingdom; had the circumstances in China been more similar to those in the Soviet Union, such a use of force would not have been sufficient to hold the country together. China faced a crisis of a smaller scale, however, one that could be contained with a level of force that the regime was willing and able to exert. To see this difference clearly one must be careful not to view the Soviet and Chinese crises of Communism between 1989-1992 as an analogy, which could lead one to expect that, since Communist rule in Eastern Europe and the Soviet Union collapsed, a similar collapse is likely to occur in China in the near future. Not only is such an analogy false, it fails to acknowledge the progress China has made over the past decade in carrying out a transformation.

Notes

1. Martin Malia, *The Soviet Tragedy: A History of Socialism in Russia, 1917-1991* (New York: Free Press, 1994), 496.

2. *Economist*, November 18, 1989, 13.

3. Cited in Jeremy Bransten, "The East: Ten Years After 1989—The Revolutions That Brought Down Communism," *Radio Free Europe/Radio Liberty*, October 8, 1999.

4. The exceptions here are Yugoslavia and Albania, whose Communist revolutions were "genuine" as opposed to "exported" and were led by local revolutionaries rather than having Communism imposed from Moscow.

5. Mao Zedong, "Reading Notes on the Soviet Text *Political Economy*," in Mao Zedong, *A Critique of Soviet Economics* (New York: Monthly Review Press, 1977), 122. As cited in Dittmer, *Sino-Soviet Normalization*, 26.

6. D. A. Kaple, *Dream of a Red Factory* (Oxford: Oxford University Press, 1994), viii-ix.

7. Alan Lawrance, *China Under Communism* (London: Routledge, 1998), 38.

8. Dittmer, *Sino-Soviet Normalization*, 26-28.

9. Dittmer, *Sino-Soviet Normalization*, 28.

10. Dittmer, *Sino-Soviet Normalization*, 29.

11. Dittmer, *Sino-Soviet Normalization*.

12. Lawrance, *China Under Communism*, 97.

13. Lawrance, *China Under Communism*.

14. The line of argument in this section relies heavily upon the research of Yan Sun, who has conducted the most thorough analysis of the ideological debates of this period and the importance of the theoretical reassessment that undergirds China's reform policies. Yan Sun, *The Chinese Reassessment of Socialism, 1976-1992* (Princeton: Princeton University Press, 1995). Cf. Kalpana Misra, *From Post-Maoism to Post-Marxism* (New York: Routledge, 1998).

15. Sun, *The Chinese Reassessment of Socialism*, 23.

16. Sun, *The Chinese Reassessment of Socialism*.

17. Sun, *The Chinese Reassessment of Socialism*, 24.

18. Sun, *The Chinese Reassessment of Socialism*, 29.

19. Sun, *The Chinese Reassessment of Socialism*, 36.

20. Lawrance, *China Under Communism*, 101.

21. Debra Soled, ed., *China: A Nation in Transition* (Washington, DC: CQ Press, 1995), 91.

22. Deng Xiaoping, "The Four Modernizations," in Molly Joel Coye and Jon Livingston, eds., *China Yesterday and Today*, Second Ed. (New York: Bantam Books, 1979), 510-12.

23. A somewhat different take on the meaning of this phrase is offered in Justin Yifu Lin, Fang Cai, and Zhou Li, *The China Miracle: Development Strategy and Economic Reform* (Hong Kong: Chinese University Press, 1996), 166.

24. Sun, *The Chinese Reassessment of Socialism,* 76-91.

25. Sun, *The Chinese Reassessment of Socialism*, 26.

26. Pei, *From Reform to Revolution*, 95-96.

27. Lin, Cai, and Li, *The China Miracle,* 273-274.

28. Jean Oi, "The Fate of the Collective after the Commune," in Debora Davis and Ezra Vogel, eds., *Chinese Society on the Eve of Tiananmen: The Impact of Reform* (Cambridge, MA: Council on East Asian Studies, Harvard University, 1990), 15-36.

29. Pei, *From Reform to Revolution*, 85-86.

30. Pei, *From Reform to Revolution*, 88.

31. Soled, *China,* 100.

32. Dittmer, *Sino-Soviet Normalization*, 48.

33. Pei, *From Reform to Revolution*, 92-94.

34. Colin Mackerras, Pradeep Taneja, and Graham Young, *China Since 1978: Reform, Modernisation and "Socialism with Chinese Characteristics"* (New York: St. Martin's Press, 1994), 16.

35. Merle Goldman, "The Reassertion of Political Citizenship in the Post-Mao Era: The Democracy Wall Movement," in Merle Goldman and Elizabeth Perry, *Changing Meanings of Citizenship in Modern China* (Cambridge, MA: Harvard University Press, 2002), 159-186.

36. Lowell Dittmer, *China Under Reform* (Boulder, CO: Westview, 1994), 137-138.

37. Tyrene White, "Political Reform and Rural Government," in Davis and Vogel, *Chinese Society on the Eve of Tiananmen,* 37-60.

38. Kevin J. O'Brien, "Villagers, Elections, and Citizenship," in Goldman and Perry, *Changing Meanings of Citizenship in Modern China,* 212-231. See also: David Zweig, *Democratic Values, Political Structures, and Alternative Politics in Greater China.* Peaceworks no. 44 (Washington, DC: United States Institute of Peace, July 2002).

39. Murray Scot Tanner, "The National People's Congress," in Merle Goldman and Roderick MacFarquhar, *The Paradox of China's Post-Mao Reforms* (Cambridge, MA: Harvard University Press, 1999), 100-128, and Michael William Dowdle, "Constructing Citizenship: The NPC as Catalyst for Political Participation," in Goldman and Perry, *Changing Meanings of Citizenship in Modern China,* 330-352.

40. Dittmer, *China Under Reform*, 142

41. Dittmer, *China Under Reform*, 141.

42. Mackerras, Taneja, and Young, *China Since 1978*, 36.

43. Dittmer, *China Under Reform*, 143.

44. Lawrance, *China Under Communism,* 117.

45. Dittmer, *China Under Reform*, 146.

46. Dittmer, *China Under Reform*, 151.

47. *The Tiananmen Papers: The Chinese Leadership's Decision to Use Force Against Their Own People—In Their Own Words*, compiled by Zhang Liang and edited by Andrew Nathan and Perry Link (New York: Public Affairs, 2001).

48. While I do not wish to ascribe any causal nature to this fact, I do think that it holds some significance. Kornai, however, argues that the initiation of reforms in Communist regimes shows "no conspicuous regularity." Janos Kornai, *The Socialist System: The Political Economy of Communism* (Princeton: Princeton University Press, 1992), 394.

49. Timothy Colton, *The Dilemma of Reform in the Soviet Union* (New York: Council on Foreign Relations, 1986), 19-22.

50. Colton, *The Dilemma of Reform in the Soviet Union*, 23.

51. Mikhail Gorbachev, *Zhizn' i Reform*, vol. 1 (Moscow: Novosti, 1995), 248.

52. Gorbachev, *Zhizn' i Reform*, 265.

53. Nicolai Petro, "Perestroika from Below: Voluntary Socio-Political Associations in the RSFSR," in Alfred Rieber and Alvin Rubinstein, eds., *Perestroika at the Crossroads* (Armonk, NY: M. E. Sharpe, 1991), 102-135.

54. Stephen White, *Russia Goes Dry: Alcohol, State and Society* (Cambridge, UK: Cambridge University Press, 1996).

55. International Monetary Fund, The World Bank, Organisation for Economic Cooperation and Development, and European Bank for Reconstruction and Development, *A Study of the Soviet Economy*, vol. 1 (Paris: OECD, 1991), 22-23.

56. International Monetary Fund, et al., *A Study of the Soviet Economy*, 21.

57. International Monetary Fund, et al., *A Study of the Soviet Economy*, 26.

58. International Monetary Fund, et al., *A Study of the Soviet Economy*, 29.

59. Kornai, *The Socialist System*, 440.

60. International Monetary Fund, et al., *A Study of the Soviet Economy*, 30.

61. See Pei, *From Reform to Revolution*, 120.

62. International Monetary Fund, et al., *A Study of the Soviet Economy*, 30.

63. International Monetary Fund, et al., *A Study of the Soviet Economy*.

64. Pei, *From Reform to Revolution*, 124.

65. Sergei Shatolov, "Ownership Changes in the Soviet Union—Opinion from Moscow," *Transition* 2, no. 4 (April 1991): 4.

66. Pei, *From Reform to Revolution*, 133.

67. Statistics from Keith Bush, "The Disastrous Last Year of the USSR," *RFE/RL/RR* 1, no. 12 (March 20, 1992): 40.

68. Richard Sakwa, *Gorbachev and His Reforms, 1985-1990* (Englewood Cliffs, NJ: Prentice Hall, 1990), 128.

69. Sakwa, *Gorbachev and His Reforms, 1985-1990*, 128-132.

70. *Pravda*, October 24, 1988, 2. Cited in Stephen White, Richard Rose, and Ian McAllister, *How Russia Votes* (Chatham, NJ: Chatham House, 1997), 23.

71. Theodore Friedgut, *Political Participation in the USSR* (Princeton: Princeton University Press, 1979), 75.

72. Sakwa, *Gorbachev and His Reforms, 1985-1990*, 162.

73. V. Stanley Vardys and Judith Sedaitis, *Lithuania: The Rebel Nation* (Boulder, CO: Westview Press, 1997), 143.

74. Christopher Marsh, "Power Capabilities, External Recognition, and Sovereignty: The Case of Lithuanian Independence," *East European Quarterly* 35, no. 1 (March 2001): 75-92.

75. Jerry Hough, *Democratization and Revolution in the USSR, 1985-1991* (Washington, DC: Brookings Institution Press, 1997), 481.

76. Mikhail Gorbachev, *Gorbachev: On My Country and the World* (New York: Columbia University Press, 2000), 57.

77. Mikhail Gorbachev and Zdenek Mlynar, *Conversations with Gorbachev: On Perestroika, the Prague Spring, and the Crossroads of Socialism* (New York: Columbia University Press, 2002), 70.

78. Brzezinski, *The Grand Failure*; Malia, *The Soviet Tragedy*; Kornai, *The Socialist System*.

79. An excellent survey of the myriad causes is offered in a special issue on "The Strange Death of Soviet Communism," in *The National Interest* 31 (November 1993).

80. Nicolai Petro, *The Rebirth of Russian Democracy: An Interpretation of Political Culture* (Cambridge, MA: Harvard University Press, 1995), 59.

81. Christopher Marsh, *Russia at the Polls: Voters, Elections, and Democratization* (Washington, DC: CQ Press, 2002).

82. Rogers Brubaker, "Nationhood and the National Question in the Soviet Union and Post-Soviet Eurasia: An Institutionalist Account," *Theory and Society* 23, no. 1 (Feb. 1994): 47-78; Stephen White, *Gorbachev and After* (Cambridge, UK: Cambridge University Press, 1993); Helene Carrere D'Encausse, *The End of the Soviet Empire: The Triumph of the Nations* (New York: Harper Collins, 1993); Valery Tishkov, *Ethnicity, Nationalism, and Conflict in and after the Soviet Union: The Mind Aflame* (Thousand Oaks, CA: Sage, 1997); Gregory Gleason, "National Self-Determination and Soviet Denouement," *Nationalities Papers* 20, no. 2 (March 1992): 1-8.

83. Mary Buckley, *Redefining Russian Society and Polity* (Boulder, CO: Westview Press, 1993).

84. Christopher Marsh, "The Challenge of Civil Society," in Stephen Wegren, ed., *Russia's Policy Challenges: Security, Stability, and Development* (Armonk, NY: M. E. Sharpe, 2003), 141-158.

85. Malia, *The Soviet Tragedy*, 492-493.

86. Malia, *The Soviet Tragedy*, 493.

87. Malia, *The Soviet Tragedy*.

88. Kornai, *The Socialist System*, xxv.

89. Kornai, *The Socialist System*, 574.

90. Malia, *The Soviet Tragedy*, 492.

91. Sun, *The Chinese Reassessment of Socialism,* 29.

Chapter 4

Transition or Transformation?

The Chinese do not, of course, have an interest in a lightning-speed disintegration of our country, and they made tactful hints to that effect. In assessing what is happening, they are looking into a mirror more than through a window. We are neighbors, and present generations can remember more than one instance in which we have influenced each other. And they see a danger in our example.

–Vladimir Lukin[1]

THE crisis of Communism that played itself out between 1989 and 1991 turned out to be a critical juncture in the history of the world's Communist regimes. Whereas Communism had been expanding since World War II, the fall of the Berlin Wall and the subsequent collapse of Communism in Eastern Europe signaled the first clear reversal of that process. For the first time since their inception, Communist regimes across the globe appeared to be on the retreat. Indeed, it seemed that the remaining Communist systems would quickly follow their comrades into the "dustbin of history," leading to an ironic twist on Marx's fateful prediction. More than a decade later, however, the PRC stands as a testament to the resilience of Communist rule and the ability of Communist systems to carry through reforms sufficient to prolong their existence. Whether or not such regimes will ultimately be able to avoid the same fate as Communist regimes in Eastern Europe, however, remains to be seen. Meanwhile, post-Communist development in Eastern Europe and the former Soviet Union has proven to be a much more problematic and lengthy process than most had assumed. A decade of reform in Russia, for instance, has seen as much success as it has setbacks, and progress in market reform and democratization has been slow and uneven. Indeed, it is also too soon to conclude whether or not the Russian polity will be able to maintain the freedoms that, long only an unattainable dream, seemed to be within reach during the heady days of perestroika, glasnost, and demokratizatsiya.[2]

In an attempt to explore these issues and reach some preliminary conclusions, the analysis in this chapter focuses on the reform path in China following the Tiananmen incident and the transition to democracy and the free market in post-Soviet Russia. I begin by surveying the progress China has made over the past decade in carrying out further economic reforms and political liberalization, leading the Middle Kingdom down the path of transformation rather than abrupt transition. I continue by considering the nature of regime stability in contemporary China and whether or not it is truly transforming, or simply postponing an inevitable Soviet-style collapse. After examining the current situation in China in the areas that played key roles in the disintegration of the Soviet Union, I conclude that, while an eventual collapse cannot be ruled out, the chances of a regime collapse in China today are much less than they were a decade ago, and for that matter, less than they had been in the Soviet Union in its final days. I then argue that predictions about a Chinese collapse only surfaced after the disintegration of the Soviet Union, and that most predictions about a Chinese collapse are simply based upon analogous reasoning, not factual understanding of the events that led to the Soviet denouement or accurate assessments of contemporary China.

The analysis then turns its focus to post-Soviet Russia and the process of post-Communist economic and political development. I begin by showing that the transition from Communist rule in Russia has been plagued with difficulties, and that rather than developing "democracy from scratch," Russia has had to build democracy and a free market from under the ashes and ruble of a dysfunctional Soviet system, legacies of which exist even today. The primary focus here is on developments in the areas of economic and democratic reform, which has proceeded in fits and spurts, and the outcome of which remains uncertain. I then consider the road ahead, and the likelihood that Russia's citizens will yet attain the goals of perestroika, such as prosperity and freedom. Finally, I show that more than a decade after the Soviet collapse, a significant proportion of Russians regret the demise of the USSR, and I explore the continuing nostalgia for socialism and the popularity of the Communist Party, which remained one of the most widely-supported parties in post-Soviet Russia for more than a decade after the Soviet collapse.

China after Tiananmen:
Evolution or Revolution?

The crackdown in Tiananmen Square in June 1989 brought reform to a screeching halt and forced Party leaders to turn away from reform and toward entrenchment. It also resulted in a significant leadership shuffle that seemingly made the cleansing of liberal reformers from the Party's inner circle complete. Instead of Hu Yaobang and Zhao Ziyang occupying the highest positions of the state and the Party, conservative Li Peng seemed to be on the rise, while Jiang Zemin, who had proven himself adept at dealing with the "turmoil" in Shanghai, had been brought in as the new general secretary. Rather than continuing the decade-long reform initiative, the Party's central leadership concentrated its efforts on restoring order and stability to the Middle Kingdom. Within a brief two years, however, the situation would again shift abruptly and economic reform would be pursued with renewed vigor.

Although Deng and Jiang were certainly in agreement with the other members of the politburo that their first concern should be with maintaining order, Deng and his protégé both felt that reform itself was necessary to sustain stability through the long term, although Jiang himself apparently placed even more concern on stability than the elder statesman.[3] In the fall of 1991, with Jiang's support, Deng began to make moves against party conservatives and to prepare for a new wave of economic reforms. The decisive move came in January 1992, when Deng embarked upon an impromptu trip to China's southern provinces. During his "southern tour," Deng met with local party leaders and visited joint-ventures and factories, where he repeatedly voiced his call to be "more daring in opening and reform," and "to accelerate reforms." Meanwhile, back in Beijing, Jiang was simultaneously raising the banner of reform. Conservative elements were attempting to hold back the new wave of reform, however, and it took more than one month for Deng's tour to be made public. Jiang attempted to support the reform initiative by circulating a compilation of Deng's speeches among the members of the politburo, who then passed them down the party chain of command. Within weeks, the media was forced to break its silence and word of the "southern tour" began to spread throughout the country, where it was met with great enthusiasm.

Deng's 1992 call for economic reform was more than just the launching of another wave of reform. This time, Deng addressed head-on some of the most difficult questions involved in the reassessment of socialism and the embracing of market reforms. For example, to those who feared that increased foreign investment in China would mean more capitalism, Deng replied: "These firms make profits in accordance with our laws. And besides, we levy taxes, our workers are paid, and we learn new technology and management. What's wrong with that?"[4] Deng also clarified the relationship between capitalism, socialism, and the market by declaring that "the fundamental difference between socialism and capitalism does not lie in the degree of planning or the market present in an economy," thereby opening the way for an increased role of the market in China's "socialist" economy.[5] The use of the term "planned commodity economy" to describe the country's economic system, which was being used by Li Peng and other conservatives, was then replaced by the term "socialist market economy" at the 14th Central Committee meeting of the CCP in the fall of 1992. For the first time in post-Mao China, therefore, it was acceptable to refer to China's economic system as a market economy.[6] Throughout the decade and into the new millennium, the Chinese economy would develop at a fantastic rate. In the political realm, however, change would be less substantial, though by all means not absent.

The Chinese Economy Takes Off

In the wake of the Tiananmen Incident and the international sanctions that followed, foreign investment in China significantly slowed, as did Chinese economic growth in general. Whereas the economy had grown at a rate of nearly 10
percent each year since 1978, GDP grew only 3.8 percent in 1990. Modest im-
provements were already apparent by 1991, however, with growth exceeding 9
percent once again. It would soon take off, surpassing 14 percent in 1992 and
remaining above 10 percent each year through 1995, and hovering just below 10
percent ever since (see table 4.1).[7] This more moderate rate of economic expansion has also been coupled with a reduction in inflation, down to around 7 percent in 1996 compared with 25 percent in 1994. Deng's southern tour of 1992
was just the impetus that was needed to get the economy back on the path of
reform. The economy did not grow on its own, however, but as a result of several concrete policy measures employed during the 1990s.

TABLE 4.1.
Average Annual Growth Rates for the Chinese Economy, 1989-1999.

	GDP	Primary Industry	Secondary Industry	Services	Investment Rate
1989	4.1	3.1	3.8	-8.3	26.1
1990	3.8	7.4	3.2	-4.8	24.4
1991	9.2	2.4	13.9	4.5	25.9
1992	14.2	4.7	21.1	13.1	30.3
1993	13.5	4.7	19.9	6.6	37.3
1994	12.7	4.0	18.4	7.7	36.4
1995	10.5	5.0	13.9	5.9	34.2
1996	9.6	5.1	12.0	5.4	33.4
1997	9.5	3.5	10.8	8.5	33.4
1998	9.7	3.2	9.2	8.5	35.8
1999	9.7	3.5	10.2	8.5	37.9

Source: Compiled from data in Liu Guoguang, Wang Luolin, Li Jingwen, Liu Shucheng, and Wang Tongsan, eds., *Economics Blue Book of the People's Republic of China, 1999: Analysis and Forecast* (Armonk, NY: M. E. Sharpe, 1999),
509-511.

One of the first substantive policy moves made in the post-Tiananmen period was the demand by the central government that state-owned enterprises
begin to operate more efficiently and compete more effectively in the emerging
market economy. In 1992, the State Council enacted a set of regulations calling
for the "transformation" of the country's SOEs. State-owned enterprises could
now do many of the things that private enterprises could, including establish
prices on their products, hire and fire employees under a contract system, set
wages, and essentially become independent producers and managers.[8] A further

step was taken in March 1997 at the Fifth Plenum of the Eighth NPC, at which Li Peng offered up a set of guidelines for the reorganization of SOEs. State-owned enterprises would receive bank credits and financial support and simultaneously be able to raise their own funds through the issuance of stocks and bonds. Emphasis was also placed on increasing the quality of products and the utilization of technology in production. Finally, reorganization was encouraged, whether through mergers, the establishment of joint-stock partnerships, or the selling off of enterprises.[9] Later in the year, at the Fifteenth Congress of the CCP, the use of the shareholding system to convert small and medium-sized enterprises was also introduced.[10] Taken together, these policies had two seemingly contradictory goals. The first was to keep the SOEs afloat, since their failure would mean large-scale economic dislocation, particularly for the 108 million industrial workers employed by more than 100,000 large and medium-sized state-owned enterprises. Secondly, these policies were meant to help the SOEs compete more effectively in the market economy and reorganize into more efficient forms of ownership.

These reforms not only progressed slowly, they also had unanticipated negative consequences. First, the initial efforts to convert state-owned enterprises into shareholding companies resulted in serious "irregularities," as many SOE managers and local officials took advantage of various techniques to divest their enterprises in ways that made themselves rich while pushing debts onto state banks, resulting in Beijing issuing calls to curb the process.[11] Secondly, state-owned enterprises were reluctant to lay off redundant workers, and once Zhu Rongji called for massive layoffs to enhance efficiency, many SOEs continued to maintain some sort of connection with their former employees, including paying them a basic allowance and providing insurance benefits. Additionally, it is reported that in 1998 some 800 labor protests, most related to labor restructuring, were being held in various parts of the country each day.[12]

The Party's answer was a new Resolution on State Enterprise Reform passed during the Fourth Plenum of the Fifteenth Central Committee in September 1999. This Resolution attempted another two-pronged approach to enterprise reform, focusing on debt restructuring and the raising of new capital, a seeming contradiction aptly summarized by the phrase "advance and retreat simultaneously."[13] The debt restructuring strategy centered on debt-equity swaps, under which select state-owned enterprises would have their long-term debts converted into shares to be controlled by asset-management corporations, themselves under the state banks. Simultaneously, new capital could be raised by allowing state-owned enterprises to transform into shareholding corporations. Unfortunately, as Ma, Mok, and Cheung argue, the East European experience suggests that such measures may not improve economic performance in the long term.[14]

While the Party was attempting to "plan" a market economy through the reform of state-owned enterprises, the collective and private sectors of the economy were expanding and overtaking the state sector. By 1993, state-owned enterprises accounted for only 53 percent of total economic activity, down from 78 percent just a decade earlier. Collective and private production, meanwhile, al-

ready accounted for 36 percent of production, with the private sector alone contributing 11 percent.[15] By 1999, the share of industrial output contributed by
state-owned enterprises had plummeted to 28 percent.[16] Between 1990 and
1997, the state sector increasingly gave way to private enterprise, with the number of SOEs dropping from 54.6 percent in 1990 to 26.5 percent by 1997, with
the remainder taken up approximately evenly by the collective and private sectors. This shift was due in large measure to the rates of growth in the private
sector, which grew at a rate of 44 percent between 1990 and 1997, followed by
the collectives, which grew at a respectable 21.1 percent per year. State-owned
enterprises, meanwhile, only grew at a modest rate of 6.8 percent.[17]

The 1990s, therefore, witnessed the explosive growth of the private economy. As Fewsmith points out, the number of registered private enterprises doubled between 1991 and 1993, from the year prior to Deng's southern tour to after the Fourteenth Party Congress, at which different forms of enterprise
ownership were permitted.[18] While private enterprises numbered only 90,000 in
1989, by 1999 the number had skyrocketed to 1.23 million, accounting for 90
percent of new employment and 80 percent of economic growth.[19] Even these
figures, however, grossly underestimate the size of the private economy, perhaps
by as much as half, since many private enterprises are not registered. Additionally, some maintain that the majority of township and village enterprises either
function as private enterprises or are in fact private enterprises, though at this
point they fail to register as such. Although Oi argues that it is too simplistic to
generalize in this way, in her own work she compellingly argues that TVEs nevertheless more closely approximate private forms of ownership by utilizing such
managerial arrangements as leasing and shareholding.[20]

Over the past 25 years, the Chinese economy has grown at the amazing rate
of almost 10 percent per year, although this pace began to slow in the early years
of the new millennium as GDP growth hovered around 8 percent per an-
num.[21] Even at this rate, the size of China's already enormous economy will
quadruple in less than twenty years. With approximately $110 billion in hard
currency reserves and $140 billion in foreign direct investment, China ranks
second in the world in both areas.[22] While the country's per capita GNP of only
$540 ranks it among the world's developing economies, the shear size of the
economy itself is staggering. The fact that China has a population that exceeds
1.2 billion also masks the diversity of wealth within the economy, for alongside
poor, rural villages there exist bustling and wealthy metropolises such as Shanghai. Finally, China has emerged as a major trading nation and important trading
partner of the United States, which recently extended to the PRC permanent
most-favored-nation trade status. Coupled with its membership in the World
Trade Organization, China is in a position to experience continued economic
growth and further integration into the global economy in the twenty-first century.

Controlled Political Liberalization

While China has progressed far in transferring economic power from state to private hands, political power remains firmly in the hands of the CCP. Nevertheless, post-Tiananmen China has experienced significant political reform, including a transformation of the party itself. From the institutionalization of political power to media liberalization, China has transformed itself from the police state that characterized the Cultural Revolution into a freer and more open society. Significant progress has been made in several areas, including the introduction of competitive elections at the village level, the rise of institutional pluralism in the National People's Congress, and the strides made in legal reform. While any direct movement toward democracy was thwarted in 1989, the crackdown in Tiananmen Square should not be taken to mean that the Chinese leadership is opposed to any substantive political reform, only that it desires to keep the process under control and within certain limits. With the emergence of a nascent civil society and the development of public attitudes favorably disposed toward civic life and democracy, moreover, it appears that this process is certainly underway. The question of whether or not leaders in Beijing will be able to keep it under control, however, remains unanswered.

One of the most significant political developments of the 1990s actually went into effect in 1988, that of the 1987 Organic Law of Villagers' Committees. As CCP leaders determined that they were losing control in the countryside, they also concluded that they had little to lose by experimenting with democratic reforms in the country's villages. They thus established village committees to serve as organs of self-government to manage local affairs, and empowered them with limited but real autonomy, particularly in the economic sphere. The committees were to be comprised of 5 to 7 elected members and run by an elected director and vice-director. Although slow in getting started due to the political turmoil of 1989 and confusion over what the vaguely-stated law actually meant, thus far some 900 million villagers have participated in elections, and in some villages residents have taken part in as many as four elections.[23] Moreover, in about 40 percent of village elections voting is done by secret ballot and with multiple candidates.

As envisioned by Peng Zhen, the law's architect, the idea behind village elections was to inculcate villagers with democratic ways of thinking and to give them experience governing, which later could be extended upwards to other levels, such as the township and county level.[24] According to research by scholars such as Zweig, the policy seems to be having the desired effect. For example, over 80 percent of villagers surveyed believed they had the right to defer to higher level officials if they were unsatisfied with local policies. In addition, Zweig found that many villagers engage in political discussions and are interested in political affairs. Finally, after analyzing the respondents' answers to a series of questions, Zweig was able to conclude that over 40 percent "had strong prodemocratic values."[25]

Value change has occurred among China's urban population as well. Research by Shi on Beijing residents indicates that individual political interest and knowledge has in some cases changed dramatically since the 1980s. While those stating that they are interested in politics only increased from 76.5 percent in 1988 to 81.3 percent in 1996, their level of political knowledge has in actuality increased significantly greater over the past decade. Likewise, across a range of measures, including letter writing to government officials, lodging complaints through formal channels, and persuading others to attend campaign meetings, Beijing residents have significantly increased their level of political engagement.[26]

Chinese are also increasingly likely to channel their political involvement through established institutions. One of the most significant developments in this area has been the drastically growing tendency for citizens to lodge complaints and pursue legal action through the courts. As Shi also documents, in 1996 Beijing residents were almost four times more likely to bring a case to court as they were in 1988.[27] Pei has pointed out that between 1986 and 2000 the growth of litigation in China skyrocketed, from 989,409 civil cases filed in 1986 to 3,412,259 in 2000. As he argues, these "rising litigation rates suggest that courts are increasingly viewed by the Chinese people and economic actors as institutions where social and commercial disputes may be resolved according to acceptable procedures."[28]

While significant in their own right, increased levels of political participation and efficacy will be of little value if grievances fall upon deaf ears or complaints land in the laps of bureaucrats uninterested or unwilling to address the issues. Here again change seems to be evident in the Chinese system, as bureaucrats and party leaders become more responsive to citizens and public opinion. One of the areas where this process has progressed the farthest is probably the National People's Congress, where the "rubber stamp" nature characteristic of Leninist legislatures has given way to increased policymaking influence. As Tanner has shown, draft legislation with the blessing of the Politburo and State Council rarely passes through the NPC today without substantial review, delay, or revision.[29] The NPC has not only developed an "established capacity for sustained, significant influence" in the policy making process, the changes in the legislature are also noteworthy for its "accessibility, representativeness, participation, and relatively effective accountability to an ever-widening share of the population."[30]

As Tanner points out, NPC leaders are still CCP members and the legislature has not become an institutional rival of the party. Rather, increasingly vague notions of "party discipline" and the increased autonomy of individual party members has resulted in a "loosening" of the system, with deputies now acting more assertively and reconsidering whom they represent.[31] While the party is still very much in control, it is transforming itself. Not only has it evolved from "red" to "expert," the party's ranks are increasingly being filled by professionals and members of the new elite, including businessmen. The party is also actively recruiting college students who are eager to join the CCP, only today's young recruits are doing so for pragmatic purposes such as career paths and social mobility, not any commitment to Marxism-Leninism-Mao Zedong thought.[32] Meanwhile, radical and leftist voices are being increasingly marginalized within the party.

Finally, the changes that have taken place in Chinese society over the past decade and more have not only altered the party and government organs, but the public sphere as well. As mentioned above, Chinese are becoming increasingly politically-minded and civically-engaged. Although some of this activity is directed against the state, such as demonstrations over wages or working conditions, the state is allowing the public a greater sphere of autonomy within which to exercise legitimate political participation. The outer bounds of this sphere are being constantly tested, and the state has not hesitated to use force against such groups as the Falun Gong who try to push beyond the acceptable limits. Nevertheless, the past decade has seen significant liberalization in areas such as media freedom and religious belief (for recognized religious groups participating in sanctioned activities). While it is perhaps too soon to declare the establishment of a civil society in China, an independent and autonomous sphere is most certainly developing.[33]

Staving off a Chinese Collapse

As Communism was falling in the Soviet Union and Eastern Europe between 1989 and 1991, Chinese Communism appeared poised to follow a similar path in the "dustbin of history." Now more than a decade after its regime crisis, China has made substantial progress in economic reform and political liberalization and enjoys relative stability. In fact, the country has not yet again witnessed the kind of large-scale demonstrations it did in 1986-1987 and 1989. More significantly, this is not due to extreme political suppression or a reintroduction of totalitarian rule; in fact, in almost all regards China is freer today than it was between 1989-1991 (see chapter 7 below). While the Tiananmen crackdown certainly established the fact that the Communist regime is willing to use force to prevent a revolution, it does not mean that the PRC leadership is against all change. Rather than allowing an abrupt transition to democracy, China's leaders are attempting to pursue controlled political liberalization, slowly transforming into a stable modern state, perhaps along the lines of South Korea or Taiwan, both of which evolved from authoritarian regimes into Asian democracies, but without the attendant trauma of a Soviet-style collapse. The question that remains, however, is whether or not it can accomplish this objective without eventually suffering the same fate as the Soviet Union.

Many China watchers are dubious of China's chances in this regard, pointing to such sources of regime instability that could contribute to a potential collapse as leadership succession, disparities in economic growth, the loss of party legitimacy, and the bankruptcy of the Chinese economy. Given the potential for a leadership succession to lead to instability, some had pointed to the eventual death of Deng Xiaoping as the spark that would ignite such a collapse. Surely China would collapse amidst the ensuing power vacuum. As Dickson pointed out, however, before his death Deng had given up every formal position of power he had held, so there was in fact no power vacuum when he eventually died in February 1997.[34] In a similar fashion, the transition from Jiang Zemin's leadership to his successor was also identified as a potential factor that could spark a revolution and regime transition. During the summer of 2002 this even seemed like a genuine possibility, as rumors that Jiang was attempting to hold onto power and to not give up his posts as president and party leader circulated. Whether it would have been due to a power struggle at the top or a grassroots revolt from below, such a move would have likely resulted in a regime crisis. At the 16th Party Congress in early November 2002, however, Hu Jintao was named Jiang's successor as party leader and the transition from Jiang to Hu has since gone smoothly and is now complete.[35]

To Chang, the imminent crisis will not be caused by a leadership succession, but rather by an economic collapse resulting from the unavoidable failure of China's state-owned enterprises and the banks that are forced to keep them afloat.[36] Once the economy fails, Chang argues, so will popular support. In making his argument about a coming collapse of China, Chang offers a virtual catalog of potential causes, including unrest among ethnic minorities and the unemployed, the ineffective nature of the state-controlled economy, the threat posed by the Internet to the party's monopoly on information, and the exhaustion of Marxist ideology. While interesting, Chang's analysis is overly critical of Chinese reform policy and exaggerates the potential for collapse arising from such factors, especially the Internet.

Some of the West's leading minds have also examined the issue of China's stability. In fact, a conference was held on this very theme at the Sigur Center for Asian Studies at George Washington University in 1998. The participants, which included Bruce Dickson, June Teufel Dreyer, and Dorothy Solinger, concluded that although nodes of instability certainly exist, there are no real ties binding the disparate threads together, leading to a state they label "stable unrest."[37] These scholars also identified in China many of the characteristics that played causal roles in the Soviet collapse, while also recognizing the presence in China of other factors that may contribute to stability, including sustained economic growth, leadership stability, interaction with the outside world, and a cohesive multiethnic population. Nevertheless, this group of distinguished China-watchers also concluded that CCP rule was unlikely to continue indefinitely.

More recently, more optimistic assessments of China's future have begun to appear. Gilboy and Heginbotham, for example, suggest that China has been able to reform successfully over the past decade and thus may be able to avoid a regime collapse.[38] Such a scenario sees China undergoing a transformation rather than an abrupt transition, with gradual evolution making a revolution unnecessary.

The Soviet Past and China's Future

China in the early days of the 21st century scarcely resembles the China of 1989, nor does it seem to be a country on the brink of collapse. Some China-watchers nevertheless continue to argue about the inevitability of a coming collapse. While the idea of a coming Chinese collapse is now more than a decade old, those that embrace such an idea are not discouraged by the passing of time nor China's continuing development. A recurrent theme in such writings is an analogy between the collapse of Communist rule in the Soviet Union and the situation in which the People's Republic of China finds itself.[39] The Soviet system was decrepit, ineffectual, and unable to satisfy the material wants of its denizens. Therefore, the argument goes, what transpired in the USSR is part of a natural progression, as authoritarian regimes eventually liberalize and blossom into pluralist political systems. From such a teleological assumption, the future of the world is liberal democracy, and China will eventually democratize as Russia and other former authoritarian states have begun to do.[40] We should remember, however, that the world was caught off-guard by the collapse of the Soviet Union, an event almost no one saw coming and whose causes we still debate.[41] Having missed the chance to predict what may have been the most important event of the Twentieth Century, perhaps some are now too eager to predict a similar collapse of Communism in China?

Arguments that suggest a Soviet-style collapse is on China's horizon are typically based upon rather shallow, simplistic, and even flawed understandings of precisely why the Soviet Union collapsed, thus leading to invalid inferences with respect to China. These accounts fail to recognize that the collapse of the Soviet Union was directly related to the initial conditions under which reform was implemented and the effects of specific policies chosen by Gorbachev as part of his policy program centered on perestroika and glasnost, particularly regarding the pace and scope of reform. The collapse of the Soviet system was thus the result of myriad factors and their interaction within a specific context in time and space. No matter how it was welcomed by many around the world, the collapse of the Soviet Union, therefore, was not preordained, nor is a Chinese collapse inevitable.

It was the collapse of Communism in the Soviet Union and Eastern Europe itself, rather, that initially led many scholars to predict a similar collapse of Asian Communism. Before the late 1980s, not only was no one predicting the collapse of China, no one was predicting the collapse of Communism in the Soviet Union and Eastern Europe. The fall of the Berlin Wall and the subsequent collapse of Communist regimes across the Soviet empire acted as a formative event for the understanding of the fundamental nature of Communist regimes across the globe, and thus for the future of China. With Eurocommunism rapidly relegated to the dustbin of history, we began to watch and wait for China and Asian Communism to follow a similar path.

The idea that it is the Soviet analogy that leads to predictions of China's collapse is supported not only by those who make such predictions, but by the fact that no one was making such predictions before the Soviet Union collapsed. In fact, in what is perhaps the most sober examination of Communist regimes in the 1980s, Brzezinski appears to have been the first serious observer to see the Soviet Union's demise on the horizon, while at the same time foreseeing an evolutionary transformation of China: "The reform of Chinese communism is probably fated to be successful. . . . [U]nlike its organic rejection by Eastern Europe, communism in China faces the prospects of organic absorption by the country's enduring traditions and values."[42] Brzezinski's predication was not naïve, it was an assessment based on the different trajectories of the two systems. Such a sober assessment of the Soviet and Chinese Communist systems could perhaps have only been made prior to the Soviet collapse, following which many people's thinking on regime transitions became clouded by the Soviet analogy and leading to the conclusion that Communist regimes cannot reform, only collapse. Brzezinski, however, while anticipating the collapse of the Soviet Union, was explicit in seeing a Chinese transformation, not a collapse.

Brzeziński's assessment that China would succeed where the Soviets would fail was made *before* the collapse of communism. The fact that this assessment predates the example of the Soviet collapse is significant, for I am arguing that it is this event that triggered the impulse of many to predict a similar collapse for China. Gilbert Rozman, writing in 1992, is an excellent example of a scholar whose thinking on the nature of Communist regimes was affected by the collapse of the Soviet Union. A specialist in both Soviet and Chinese reform efforts who had conducted path-breaking research in both countries, he was certainly among the best minds on the subject at the time. His keen eye saw Communist China's rapid demise:

> Despite the many twists and turns along the way, the eventual outcome appears to be the end of the old system of communism. In 1991 the Chinese leadership was still trying to halt this explosive process. To bolster its case it cited selective economic successes and the tumultuous effects of dismantling communism in the Soviet Union. Chinese communism, however, could do little more than buy time before the next wave of reform swept over it.[43]

While just how soon this next wave was expected to come along is not made clear, the process by which such a collapse would occur was explained by Rozman and Hakamada in the same volume:

> Official spokesmen even suggested that in 1949 communism had saved China and now it was China's turn to save communism. To most observers, however, this possibility seemed scarcely conceivable. Even the strategy of a gradual neo-authoritarian reform led by the Communist Party seemed far-fetched under leaders as unpopular as Li Peng. Instead, it could be expected that rising regional elites, closely tied to business interests, would play a major role in the next stage of transition. Once Chinese glasnost and democratization resumed, the survival of communism would be put to its last major test. Since much of the communist system was already being dismantled, the Communist Party it-

self could not be expected to retain its power for long even though uncertainty over its future leadership complicated efforts to predict the timing and process of transition.[44]

While Rozman was not the only scholar to predict an impending collapse of Communist rule in China, with his expertise in Soviet politics, he was certainly among the most qualified specialists to speak on the issue. Others were quick to join the cacophony of voices calling for China's impending collapse. Dickson has put forth perhaps the argument for a Chinese collapse that has been given with the strongest conviction, arguing that "the historical record suggests that communist governments do not evolve, but collapse. So while it would be foolish to predict *when* major political change will come to China, it is possible to say *how* it will come: suddenly and dramatically, not gradually and incrementally" (emphasis in original).[45] Dickson continued his assessment by arguing that a "peaceful, incremental, elite-sponsored transformation from Leninism to pluralist democracy is as remote a possibility in China as it was in the Soviet Union."[46] It is important, however, to avoid being so blinded by the Soviet analogy that we try to force-fit the Soviet model onto China. This is the trap that the doomsayers fall into, as they are so eager to predict a Soviet-style collapse for China that they incorrectly infer conclusions about China from the Soviet denouement.

While the predictions put forth in these and other works are based upon more than simple analogical deductions from the Soviet experience, it is clear that the Soviet denouement is still a major formative event that shaped the authors' thinking on the future of China, as it is explicitly mentioned by practically every author who writes on the topic of a coming Chinese collapse. Even Chang, who goes farthest in his work to identify unique causes of the impending Chinese collapse, makes specific mention of the similarity between the Soviet collapse and China's current situation:

> Although the parallels between the Soviet Union and China are not exact, of course, the essentials are the same. The Marxist-Leninist concepts that gave birth to both republics cannot be reformed; Gorbachev's effort to restructure Soviet society showed us that. The party of Jiang Zemin, which tries a different route to rejuvenation, will also be swept away as it too will not, or cannot, bring about the change that has to occur.[47]

More recent scholarship on the future of China seems to be less confined by the Soviet example. Increasingly, scholars are beginning to view China as *sui generis*, as a country with unique circumstances and unfettered by the Soviet past. Not surprisingly, such a view makes a transformation appear more likely than a collapse. Nevertheless, the Soviet analogy seems to linger in the minds of many, and the topic of a Chinese regime collapse is one that is likely to be around for the foreseeable future.

The New China

As the Soviet Union was beginning to emerge from the period of stagnation ushered in under Brezhnev's leadership, China was already developing special economic zones and installing the rudiments of a market economy, including private property and profit incentives. The result has been an economy that has grown at a rate of nearly 10 percent each year since 1978, with GDP quadrupling between 1980 and 1995 alone. In sharp contrast to the Soviet Union during perestroika, therefore, economic reform is not discrediting the Communist Party in China as it did in the USSR. In fact, it is strengthening it. By beginning earlier and allowing the benefits of the economic reforms to trickle down before embarking upon significant political reform, such as village elections, the CCP had already placed itself in a more advantageous position than the Communist Party of the Soviet Union, which went from reform to collapse in under five years.

While the Soviet Union's collapse was precipitated by a legitimacy crisis following economic stagnation and rapidly introduced market measures, China has been able to overcome its crisis moment and to re-embark upon the path of reform. Taking a more gradual approach, China has been able to produce sustained growth and, thanks to its ideological reconceptualization, retain legitimacy. Over the past decade, the CCP has proven itself able to carry through substantial reforms and to improve the material conditions of the country, which generates greater support among the masses. Simultaneously, the party is transforming, becoming less dogmatic and bringing members of the new elite into the party ranks. Additionally, progress continues to be made in democratization, as village elections become more democratic, the National People's Congress develops greater legislative power, and media liberalization spreads. Finally, today's party leadership is quite different from that of the 1980s in terms of personalities and views. At the beginning of the twenty-first century, China is quite different than it was in 1989 and, for that matter, its circumstances are radically different from that of the Soviet Union in its final days. Whether or not the PRC will ultimately prove successful at preventing revolutionary change and a regime transition, however, remains uncertain.

Russia after the Fall:
The Difficult Road of Post-Communism

The crisis of Soviet Communism resulted not only in the death of the USSR but also the birth of fifteen independent states, many of which had no prior history as modern states. All, however, have had to negotiate the difficult road of post-Communism and overcome the numerous obstacles that stand in the way of creating functioning market economies and establishing democratic forms of governance. Russia is in many ways the heart of the former Soviet Union, not only home to the former seat of the Soviet government but also heir to its international treaties and other obligations. While its prospects for market development and democratization are neither the best nor the worst among the successor states, Russia is a critical case and perhaps best illustrates the successes and failures of post-Communist reform in the former Soviet Union.

Since the Soviet collapse in December 1991, Russia has made considerable progress in carrying through economic, political, and social reforms. Four parliamentary elections, series of regional and local elections, and three presidential elections have all taken place. As a result, there has been significant turnover among Russia's political leaders, with Putin taking the presidential mantle from Yeltsin and United Russia replacing the Communist Party as the major parliamentary player. While the Russian economy continued into decline in the early years of the 1990s, substantial structural changes were carried out and at the dawn of the new millennium a recovery is underway that shows promise of increasing the country's standard of living and quality of life.

Of course, Russia has also faced serious dilemmas and challenges. As it began its journey along the path of post-Communism, Russia was immediately faced with several overwhelming tasks: to convert its decrepit command economy into a stable and productive free-market system; to maintain its territorial integrity; and to establish a democratic political system in a country with a long history of authoritarian rule. From the bloody stand-off between the Congress of People's Deputies and the Yeltsin government in the fall of 1993 to the decade-long war in Chechnya—which is also playing itself out in Moscow's movie theatres, subways, and stadiums—evidence of the country's many failures are readily apparent. Overall, however, Russia has made significant strides over the past decade toward the consolidation of democratic governance, development of a market economy, and the strengthening of its nascent civil society. These strides become clear by surveying the Russian political system as it evolved under the leadership of Boris Yeltsin and later under his hand-picked successor, Vladimir Putin.

Out From Under the Ruble

Following the collapse of the Soviet Union, Russia was not left in such an advantageous position as having to develop "democracy from scratch."[48] Rather, citizens and political actors were left to fend for themselves in the midst of a set of institutions that, having never been meant to function in a democratic fashion, had only been tweaked by Mikhail Gorbachev during his perestroika reforms to allow for democratic content amid the framework of what had been a totalitarian system. In this way, the newly-independent Russia was still largely governed by the Soviet-era constitution and legal code, not to mention mores and patterns of behavior. The development of the Russian political system in the early 1990s, therefore, should not be seen as developing democracy from scratch but rather as growing out from under the ruble of the Soviet collapse, as the country had to come to grips with its past before it could embark upon the path to its future.

One of the first legacies of the Soviet system that had to be addressed was the unclear division of powers between the executive and legislative branches, and indeed the actual power of these institutions in general. Not long after Boris Yeltsin became president and his deputy Ruslan Khasbulatov took over his old post as speaker of the legislature, a rift developed between the two that played itself out as a struggle between executive and legislative power. Khasbulatov opposed the rapid economic reforms being proffered by Yeltsin and Yegor Gaidar, his acting prime minister, and used his position in the legislature to block reform legislation, even refusing to confirm Gaidar as prime minister in 1992. During this period Yeltsin and Khasbulatov were countering each other's moves, although neither was yet in the position of being able to gain the upper hand.

This all changed in March 1993 when the Supreme Soviet initiated impeachment proceedings against Yeltsin. Russia's freely-elected leader struck back with a popular referendum on April 25, 1993, in which the people were asked if they supported the Yeltsin government, supported his economic policies, and whether they favored early presidential and/or parliamentary elections. While a slim majority of only 53 percent approved of Yeltsin's economic policies, 59 percent expressed confidence in him as president, with the electorate roughly evenly split on the issue of early presidential elections. Despite the lack of overwhelming support, Yeltsin considered the results a renewed popular mandate, and he began to make more authoritative gestures toward the legislature and policymaking in general. Then, on September 21, 1993, he issued a decree disbanding the parliament and calling for new parliamentary elections. Khasbulatov and Rutskoi, refusing to accept the fate left them by Yeltsin's unconstitutional move, barricaded themselves in the White House, while Rutskoi declared himself acting president and urged the crowd outside to march on the Kremlin. For nearly two weeks crowds stood outside the barricaded White House, some in support and others in defiance, until finally, on October 4, the military took armed action and began blasting the building. Rutskoi, Khasbulatov, and their supporters quickly conceded defeat and were arrested.

Yeltsin used these "October Events" to push ahead with reform and to craft a political system with more clearly-defined functions and powers, arranging for national and local elections and a referendum on the newly-drafted constitution. The constitutional arrangements called for a bicameral legislature and placed enormous powers in the presidency. While the Russian people were given the opportunity to voice their opinion on the new constitution in a constitutional plebiscite, they were not given any real choice, as they only had the power to approve or disapprove of the constitution offered to them. Disapproval meant continued gridlock under the old constitution, while approval meant consenting to a very strong presidential system. The constitutional referendum and elections of December 12, 1993, gave Russia a new constitution, but it also left the country with a sharply divided legislature, with no one party even receiving a quarter of the votes. The clearest winner was Vladimir Zhirinovksy's Liberal Democratic Party of Russia, which garnered over 22 percent of the vote, while Gaidar's

Russia's Choice tallied just more than 15 percent of the vote. The Communist Party followed closely with a very respectable 12 percent, considering it was greatly hindered from running a campaign.

Russia's fledgling democracy underwent the first test of its new institutions with the parliamentary elections of December 1995. This time without being hindered from campaigning, the Communist Party emerged as the clear winner, garnering 22 percent of the vote, leaving its competition far behind, with Zhirinovsky's LDP only garnering 12 percent and Our Home is Russia tallying 10 percent. Perhaps the most significant aspect of the 1995 parliamentary elections was the strong support for the Communists. As a Russian political scientist remarked following the elections, "The first thing to strike an observer is that, despite four years of unbridled anticommunist propaganda, what once again took first place in Russia were the popular ideas of socialism and the restoration of the Union and of Soviet power, for which at least one third of the electorate voted, casting their ballots for the Communists and for parties ideologically close to them."[49] Despite the old Communist regime's mistakes and failures, and the new regime's anti-Communist stance and propaganda, the people still held on to many of socialism's ideals and popular nostalgia for the past. This is actually not very difficult to understand, for in a period of such tumultuous change, it is very tempting to look to the past and remember the times when, even if there was not much freedom, the Soviet state provided a modest living for all.

A similar phenomenon was witnessed during the 1996 presidential elections held the next summer. In the first round of the elections, Yeltsin barely edged out Communist Party leader Gennady Zyuganov, who received 32 percent of the vote compared to Yeltsin's 35 percent. While the weak support for Zhirinovsky may have brought a sigh of relief (he received only 5 percent of the vote), the strong support for Zyuganov elicited fear in many, particularly Western leaders and Yeltsin himself. Yeltsin understood the true nature of the support shown for the Communists. Following the first round, he stated, "I think that you did not so much vote for our past life as you voted against the hardships of life today."[50] When given a clear choice between Yeltsin and Zyuganov in the run-off election, a majority of the Russian electorate voted for Yeltsin, giving him a renewed mandate and dashing the chances of returning a Communist Party member to the Kremlin.

The Path to the Putin Era

While the 1996 presidential elections secured Yeltsin his position for another four years, the constitution he placed before the people in December 1993 called for a two-term limit for the Russian president, meaning that his second term would be his last. Yeltsin's authoritarian tendencies had even led some to speculate that he was actually prepared to cancel the presidential elections that were originally scheduled for June 2000. Yet as the end of his second term approached, Yeltsin expressed publicly his wish to "go down into history as the president who ensured the first legitimate changing of power" in Russia.[51] The manner by which he handed over the reins of power, however, was cause for further speculation. His resignation in favor of then-prime minister Vladimir Putin just hours before the clock struck 2000 led many to believe that Yeltsin was trying to give his protégé an edge in the upcoming elections. While this was certainly true, more significant is the fact that this transfer of power was part of a negotiated settlement whereby Yeltsin would receive immunity from prosecution for crimes and "irregularities" committed during his tenure in office.

The results of the December 1999 Duma elections certainly indicated to Yeltsin that it was the most opportune moment for his chosen successor to stand for election. After all, this was the first post-Soviet election in which the support of a pro-Kremlin party almost equaled that of the Communist Party. While the CPRF still received the largest share of the vote with 24 percent, Unity was not far behind with 23 percent, and other centrist parties such as the Union of Right Forces (8.5 percent) and Fatherland/All Russia (13 percent) had also garnered significant support. And with the renewed war in Chechnya not yet too unpopular and Putin's popularity reaching record heights, victory was all but assured.

Putin, the former KGB officer and deputy governor of St. Petersburg, exploited these advantages to their fullest in his brief electoral campaign, which included such televised exercises of power and vitality as co-piloting a fighter jet into Chechnya and test driving a sports car on a closed course.[52] Putin easily won election on March 26 with just under 53 percent of the vote, with a distant second place going to Communist Party leader Gennady Zyuganov, who received slightly less than 30 percent of the vote. This figure, which is roughly equivalent to the level of support he received in the first round of the 1996 election, evidenced his relatively stable support among more than a quarter of the electorate. On the other hand, Zhirinovsky's 2.7 percent showed that his popular appeal had waned and signaled the end of his bid for the presidency, although not the end of his role in Russian politics.

With the inauguration of Putin as Russia's second president in May 2000, the country underwent its first turnover of presidential power and did do so in accordance with the constitution. In this regard, the Putin presidency is significant because as Russia continues to operate within democratic institutions and according to constitutionally-prescribed procedures, democracy in Russia continues to develop. This record was immediately and unnecessarily blemished, however, as electoral abuses quickly came to light, including the burning of ballot papers, bullying voters, and inventing entire electorates in Putin's favor.[53] Putin certainly enjoyed widespread popular support, making such actions entirely unnecessary, except for guaranteeing that a run-off election would not have to be held. These abuses, which were committed with or without his knowledge, perhaps by some overzealous regional authorities who wished to express their support for the country's new leader, unnecessarily tarnished the Putin presidency from the start.

Russian democracy seemed immediately under attack once Putin took office. Putin's first order of business was to reassert central control over the country's vast territory and myriad political and economic interest groups. While perhaps a necessary remedy to counteract Yeltsin's tendency to allow the Kremlin's power to become dispersed so long as no direct threats were posed against himself or his position, the means by which Putin sought to reassert Moscow's power and control immediately put his reputation as a democrat into question by Western observers, foreign governments, and Russian liberals. By arresting or forcing into exile several oligarchs and shutting down the independent media outlets they owned, Putin struck fear in the hearts of those who saw such actions simply as anti-democratic rather than an attempt to curb the power and influence of a group of individuals who had used crime and corruption to build economic empires whose power rivaled that of the Kremlin itself. Nevertheless, Putin's actions were largely successful in curbing crime and restoring a sense of order and even pride among Russia's citizens, who had come to associate post-Communist government with Yeltsin's drunken behavior and physical ailments. In sharp contrast, Putin—an avid Judo practitioner and expert and decorated KGB officer—symbolized strength and pride.

Just how far Russia evolved under Putin's leadership was most clearly apparent during the 2003-2004 legislative and presidential elections. In the December 2003 Duma elections, a pro-Kremlin party was the clear winner for the first time in post-Soviet Russia, as United Russia received 37 percent of the vote, compared to the Communist Party's 12 percent, which still won them second place. As if this were not a clear enough sign that centrism had come into fashion, Putin ran practically unopposed in the March 2004 presidential contest as several leading liberals called for a boycott of the election.[54] The Communist Party and the Liberal Democratic Party each offered up candidates to the electorate, but their leaders refused to stand for election against Putin, instead putting up the relatively unknown politicians Nikolai Kharitonov and Oleg Malyshkin, respectively. Alongside the former collective farm director and the ex-boxer also stood Duma members Sergei Glazyev and Sergei Mironov, who, while somewhat known as parliamentary politicians, certainly were not members of any organized alternative political movement. The lone opposition voice was that of Irina Khakamada, who was sharply criticized for defecting from her liberal colleagues and running as an independent after her party would not even endorse her. Against such a field it is no surprise that Putin won reelection with more than 71 percent of the vote. The real question is, what did the election mean for Russian democracy?

The fact that Putin ran practically unopposed should not be taken to mean that democracy has come to an end in Russia. After all, the silence of the opposition was intentional and unprovoked by the Kremlin. As was obvious to everyone in Russia, no one stood any kind of chance against Putin, who has remained the most popular leader in Russia since 1999. Public opinion polls from January of 2004, on the eve of the election, put Putin's support at 72 percent with no one else even in sight. In such circumstances, when (barring a constitutional amendment) Putin will be forced to step down after his second term ends in 2008, it makes more sense to sit out the elections rather than waste resources on a lost cause. The March 2004 election, therefore, should be seen as more about testing the waters for 2008 than a true electoral contest. In this regard, the one conclusion that can be drawn is that the Communist Party remains a political force, although not a very powerful one. As one commentator phrased it, a second-place finish by Kharitonov "might slow the Communists' slide toward oblivion, but no one thinks he or his party is Russia's wave of the future."[55] Nevertheless, the fact that this relatively unknown politician was able to ride the coattails of the Communist Party and garner more than 13 percent of the vote indicates that the party is still a political player.

The true test of Russia's democratic nature looms just over the horizon. In 2008, at which time Putin is scheduled to step down from the presidency, his authoritarian tendencies will become undeniable if he refuses to do so, or the country's progress in democratization will become irrefutable as a new leader occupies the Kremlin, no matter what his political leanings. The final possibility is that the recent wave of democratic revolutions that is sweeping the former Soviet Union—from Georgia and Ukraine to Kyrgyzstan—may soon make its way to Russia. Given that in each case these transitions have coincided with electoral contests, however, we may still have to wait until 2008.

Post-Communist Economic Reform

In contrast to the country's political reforms, Russia's post-Communist economic restructuring began immediately after the collapse and has continued unabated since that time. The economic reform program launched on January 2, 1992, called for the simultaneous and rapid implementation of all major aspects of economic reform. Under the "shock therapy" program, price controls were lifted, except for a short list of consumer goods and energy products, privatization was pushed ahead, and measures were made to make the ruble convertible. The government raised taxes considerably, cut back on spending, and attempted to bring expenditures and revenue into balance. Finally, centralized planning was abandoned and the regulation of supply and demand was left to the market.

It was thought that by laying the groundwork for a free-market economy, the invisible hand of the market would take over and lead to a productive and stable economy. This probably could not have been further from the truth. The program led to hyperinflation, rapid depletion of savings, decreased production, and overall caused widespread hardship. Some of the effects were so devastating, in fact, that Yeltsin's own vice-president, Alexander Rutskoi, denounced the program as "economic genocide."[56] The year 1992 saw the greatest decline in GDP in any single year since the Soviet Union's collapse, with a decline from 1991 of almost 15 percent, while 1993 saw a still further decline of 9 percent over that of 1992, representing a substantial cumulative decline that continued throughout much of the 1990s (see table 4.2 below).

A major aspect of the economic reform program was the privatization of state property, devised and directed by Anatoly Chubais, Minister of the State

Committee for the Management of State Property. The privatization of state property is one of the most necessary changes involved in Russia's transition to a market economy, and it is perhaps one of the most challenging obstacles. The transfer of ownership of the economy from state to private hands in Russia has been described as "the world's most ambitious and rapid program of denationalizing state enterprises."[57] It can also be described as a fire-sale, as the vast majority of these enterprises were sold well below market value. Between 1992 and 1999, more than 140,000 state-owned enterprises were privatized, including 25,000 large enterprises employing thousands of workers.[58] While the privatization process was very successful at liquidating state assets, with about 40 million Russians becoming stockholders in privatized enterprises (more than in any other country in the world),[59] the process was far from equitable, resulting in both "winners" and "losers" of the transition from Communism.[60]

In the initial stage of privatization, from 1992-1994, Russian citizens were each given vouchers with a nominal value of 10,000 rubles to invest in a company of their choice, a paltry sum for the divestiture of the Soviet state. The idea was that Russia's new shareholders would invest in privatizing companies, perhaps even in the enterprises where they themselves worked. This could be done according to three different methods, involving varying proportions of shares being purchased by employees, managers, and outside investors and with the use of varying combinations of cash and vouchers. Given the rapid inflation, economic dislocation, and overall economic hardship prevalent at this time, most Russians chose to sell their vouchers to speculators at greatly discounted rates rather than make a long-term investment in Russia's turbulent economy. These speculators were then able to purchase controlling shares in enterprises at bargain-basement prices. Moreover, on many occasions these speculators were actually the enterprise's previous managers, which meant that privatization was more a means for the elite to transform itself and legitimize its ownership of the private property it had held under the Soviet system. While this process was effective at rapidly transferring ownership from state to private hands, no real economic benefits ensued from this stage of privatization, as there was no real infusion of capital or investment, nor were there serious changes in worker motivation or in organizational and managerial structures.[61]

The second stage of privatization was announced in the summer of 1994 and began the next year. During this "money" stage, privatization was conducted only for actual money and at market prices, with enterprises privatized by auction and investment bidding. Of the income derived from the sale of an enterprise, fifty-one percent was retained by the enterprise itself, while the rest was divided between federal and regional authorities.[62] In contrast to the voucher privatization stage of 1992-94, which in essence entailed the liquidation of state assets, the money stage of privatization was the beginning of Russia's true market transformation. Investors selected companies in which to invest that had real promise, managerial structures were altered once companies were privatized, and often enterprises were completely restructured, using whatever capital assets were available. Unfortunately, since privatization preceded eco-

Chapter 4

nomic growth, very few people had personal wealth to invest in this way. This left the market to those who did, who often had acquired their wealth in questionable and unscrupulous ways.

The privatization of state-owned enterprises is only part of the picture of economic restructuring, as privatization alone does not guarantee improved economic performance. As research by Aukutsionek et al. shows, privatized firms in which managers and outside investors dominate perform better than worker-dominated firms. As they point out, this finding may be the result of a selection bias, since managers and outside investors most likely initially purchased "shares in companies with better performance and restructuring prospects," leaving workers with less-profitable enterprises.[63] This research shows, however, that the form of ownership taken by newly-privatized enterprises is significant.

While privatization is perhaps one of the most fundamental changes necessary in order to increase Russia's economic productivity and efficiency, other factors are perhaps just as important, including the creation of new businesses and the development of market-based trade. By July 1998, almost 875,000 small businesses existed in Russia. While the number of small businesses that had been created in the post-Communist period certainly exceeds 1,000,000, many such enterprises were created in the early years of market development and quickly failed. Likewise, the development of market-based trade proved more problematic than many had assumed. As a result of shock therapy, markets had to be developed overnight to replace central planning. When markets failed to emerge efficiently, people resorted to barter, growing food on their personal plots, or simply did without (not to mention theft and criminal activity).

TABLE 4.2.
Average Annual Growth Rates for the Russian Economy, 1992-2002.

	GDP	Industrial Production	Agricultural Production	Consumer Prices	Disposable Income
1992	-14.5	-18.8	-9.0	2,650	-41.0
1993	-8.7	-14.6	-4.0	940	14.0
1994	-12.7	-20.6	-12.0	320	-8.0
1995	-4.2	-3.0	-8.0	131	-13.0
1996	-3.6	-3.5	-5.1	22	5.0
1997	1.4	1.9	0.1	11	2.5
1998	-5.3	6.6	-12.3	85	-13.8
1999	6.4	11.0	2.4	37	-15.1
2000	10.0	11.9	3.0	21	9.0
2001	5.0	4.9	11.0	19	8.5
2002	4.3	3.7	2.0	15	8.8

Source: Compiled from data in Keith Bush, *Russian Economic Survey*, Russia and Eurasia Program, Center for Strategic and International Studies. Washington, DC: September 2003.

Despite the sheer enormity of the task and many setbacks, including the Yeltsin regime's policy failures and half-hearted attempts to introduce structural reforms, the Russian economy was improving by 1998 and showed signs of turning around (again, see table 4.2). The fallout from the crisis that beset Asian markets in 1997-98, however, brought the Russian economy to its knees in August 1998. The economy slowly recovered over the next few years, and then began a period of spectacular economic growth following the election of Vladimir Putin in 2000 and the implementation of structural reforms, deregulation, and a tightened budgetary constraint.[64] For the first time in the post-Communist period, the Russian economy seems to be moving in a positive direction, with GDP growing steadily and production expanding in both the industrial and agricultural sectors. Whether or not Russia's economic growth over the past few years is attributable to Putin's reforms or simply a jump in world oil prices and the windfall profits Russian companies are enjoying from their oil exports,[65] the fact remains that the Russian economy today has stabilized and is experiencing significant growth. In short, therefore, we can conclude that Russia has successfully completed the first phase of the world's most daunting economic transformation. As a Western investment agency noted already in 2002, "competitiveness in Russian domestic industries has improved, macroeconomic stability has been achieved, and a basic market environment has been created."[66]

Civil Society and Freedom

The fate of democracy and freedom in Russia rests upon more than the holding of free elections and the establishment of an effective market economy. Russia also needs a citizenry that is interested, active, and politically efficacious. Only engaged citizens joined together in a civil society can serve as an effective check on the power of the state, whose power has grown exponentially under Putin's leadership. Russian society, therefore, needs to develop democratic values and a body of citizens who not only follow events and participate in formal political and informal civic activities, but who also make informed choices about the country's future. In developing such a citizenry, Russia faces formidable obstacles, not the least of which is nostalgia for the country's Communist past and former great power status. Nevertheless, several scholars express optimism over the growth of civil society in Russia today. Hudson, for example, argues that civil society is developing in Russia and expresses "cautious optimism" that civic groups have become a permanent feature of the country's political life.[67] Based on analysis of survey data on social networks and civil society in Russia, Gibson has also argued that social networks and civic attitudes among Russians are such that they are facilitating the country's democratic transition.[68]

In addition to civic organizations, churches and religious life are also important institutions of civil society and facilitate civic involvement through such means as charitable events and church-sponsored fairs, or *yarmarki*.[69] White and McAllister have even shown that Russians who attend Orthodox churches frequently are more likely to participate in civic and political life through such activities as voting, while Gvosdev has argued persuasively that Orthodoxy easily reconciles itself with modern politics.[70] Given its particular history, with a Christian tradition stretching back more than one thousand years and seven decades of militant atheism in its more recent past, churches are an excellent indicator of civic and religious involvement in Russia. After all, as part of its policy of "forced secularization," the church was systematically attacked in the Soviet Union, and the vast majority of churches were destroyed or converted to state property during the Communist era.[71] Between 1989-1999, however, believers fought to reclaim and rebuild their old parishes, with the number of Orthodox churches in Russia rising from approximately 7,500 to 19,000 during this period.[72] Since the overwhelming majority of churches were either reclaimed from the state or built anew from scratch during this time, this serves as a good indicator of civic involvement in Russia today.

The lack of freedom was perhaps the most repugnant characteristic of the Soviet Union, and its attainment was a dream not only of dissidents, but of ordinary people and government reformers as well. More than a decade after the collapse of the USSR the citizens of Russia are still struggling to attain and maintain the freedoms that seemed to be within their grasp during the heady days of perestroika, glasnost and demokratizatsiya. While even a casual observer can plainly see that Russian citizens today enjoy greater freedom than they did twenty years ago, the creation of an autonomous civil sphere in which freedoms will be consistently guaranteed is still very much a work in progress.

The religious sphere has been one of the most contested areas of public life since the collapse of the Soviet Union. The church was one of the first social institutions to benefit from perestroika, with Gorbachev meeting with the Holy Synod of the Russian Orthodox Church in April 1988 and agreeing to recognize the church as a legitimate public institution. Thus ended the policy of militant atheism which had stood for almost 70 years, and from that point on religion in Russia underwent a renaissance. The new situation was soon codified with the 1990 law "Freedom of Conscience and Religious Belief," a very liberal law that introduced religious equality for the first time in Russian history. As with all new policies, however, its exact effects could not be known in advance. One consequence of the law which might have been predictable, but was probably unintended, was a dramatic increase in evangelism and proselytism.[73] As Western religious organizations began to operate in Russia and new religious movements began to emerge, they were met with resistance not only by many of their intended converts, but by government officials and the Russian Orthodox Church as well, who viewed such activities as presenting a threat to Orthodoxy and even to Russian national identity.[74]

As resistance swelled, an attempt was made in 1993 to amend the 1990 law. Although passed by the Supreme Soviet, President Yeltsin vetoed the amendment that would have altered religious freedom in Russia fundamentally by restricting sharply the rights of foreign religious associations and by rendering state support to Russia's "traditional confessions," i.e., Orthodoxy, Islam, Judaism, and Buddhism.[75] With the situation not being rectified at the federal level, many regions began to take it upon themselves to draft and enact regional laws on religion which were more restrictive than the 1990 federal law. The first region to do so was Tula, which passed a restrictive law in November 1994. This law was quickly used as a model by other regions, and in a brief period of time many regions had placed on the books laws which violated the federal law and constitutional guarantees.[76] The contradiction between the federal law and an increasing number of regional laws was resolved in 1997 with the passage of the new law "Freedom of Conscience and Religious Associations," which essentially set up a two-tier system, distinguishing between religious "organizations" (which have operated in Russia for at least 15 years) and religious "associations." While the former are granted a broad range of privileges, the latter are permitted to worship but face restrictions on their property rights, educational activities, publishing, and evangelism.

The religious freedom situation in Russia has evolved somewhat since the passage of the 1997 law, with the Constitutional Court and other courts interpreting the law somewhat less restrictively than was initially anticipated. In fact, there is great diversity in religious freedom across Russia, with some regions and agencies violating the law with their overzealous interpretations of its restrictive nature while others enforce it only lackadaisically.[77] Nevertheless, as is regularly documented by the *Keston News Service* and the *Forum 18 News Service*, the curtailing of religious freedom in Russia is not something that has been completely eliminated. The most egregious cases involve the Catholic Church, whose bishops and clergy regularly experience difficulty entering the country, and evangelical Protestant groups who regularly complain of suppression of their religious freedom. Meanwhile, the Russian state continues to develop a close relationship with the Orthodox Church, practically assuming the role of state church in all but name.

Besides religious freedom, other freedoms are also critical components of an open society and vital for the proper functioning of pluralism and democracy. One of the most important is perhaps freedom of the press. As Owens points out, commenting on the importance of a free press for civil society, "information is power—in this case, power that the public will use to inform itself while making choices about votes, purchases, investments, membership in organizations, participation in mass movements, support for legal challenges, and other expressions of power that can act to counterbalance the power of the state and strong economic entities."[78] In acting as a check upon the operations both of the state and of the major economic actors in society, the media function as the eyes and ears of the general public to ensure that the rules governing political and economic life are followed and to prevent any dangerous concentration of power that might threaten civil liberties.[79]

As Bovt and Zassoursky each point out, post-Soviet Russian society presents numerous challenges to the media to fulfill these functions.[80] During Soviet times, of course, the media could not perform its function of governmental watchdog, as they were directly controlled by the state and were simply used for disseminating information and political propaganda to the people. This changed under Gorbachev and his policy of glasnost, as the media were allowed to publicize events that previously had been kept secret and even permitted to speak out against the regime in later years. Eventually the floodgates opened and independent newspapers and television and radio stations emerged to mitigate the interests of an unleashed citizenry.

Under Yeltsin, the media flourished in terms of their ability to publish and criticize, although many media groups ran into financial difficulties and their criticism bordered on yellow journalism. It was also not as free as it could have been, since they were controlled by a small number of business tycoons, known as the oligarchs, who were able to amass tremendous financial resources during the transition from Communism. Despite their negative points, Yeltsin found common ground with the oligarchs since they both shared the same greatest fear—a return of the Communists to power. The oligarchs and their media empires thus heavily supported Yeltsin's electoral victories.

The media also played an important role in Putin's election campaign. As soon as he got into office, however, Putin launched an attack on the media and the oligarchs who controlled them, thus limiting the power of the press. Vladimir Gusinsky and his Media-Most empire wound up in open opposition to Putin's regime and was soon demolished, while in January 2002 the last independent national television channel in Russia, TV-6, was closed down, further diminishing the voice of an independent media in the country.

It is difficult to discern which was Putin's target: the independent media or simply the oligarchs who ran them. Despite outspoken opposition in the West to the attack on the free press in Russia, Russians themselves did not seem as worried. In March 2000, 55 percent of Russians polled said that they expected and hoped that Putin would strengthen state control over the media.[81] Regarding the closing of TV-6, only 7 percent of Russians thought that Putin played a major role in this affair, considering it instead a conflict among "economic actors."[82]

As Bovt summarizes the situation, it is "clear that the media in contemporary Russian civil society are not yet in any position to articulate the concerns of society as a whole or to act to defend democratic and market reforms in any decisive way."[83] The decline of media freedom in Russia will certainly impede the strength of civil society and inhibit the Russian people's ability to govern themselves and to oversee the state and restrain it from imposing itself upon society.[84]

The Soviet Past and Russia's Future

Russia's transition to democracy and the free market is inextricably linked to its Soviet past. While movement forward implies movement away from that past, the past is alive and well in Russia today and significantly affects the way people—both the governed and those who govern—view the world and their place in it. Throughout the 1990s, the country's Communist legacy was one of the most significant aspects of the country's past and path-dependence on the road to post-Communism. This became abundantly clear following the Communist Party's strong showing in the December 1995 Duma elections and Gennady Zyuganov's close race against Yeltsin in the summer of 1996. Its performance in the 1999 Duma elections, where it once again received more votes than any other single party and defeated the "party of power," further testified to the resilience of Communist support. It was only in the December 2003 Duma elections that a pro-Kremlin party was able to emerge as the clear winner in post-Soviet Russia, relegating the CPRF to second place for the first time in a decade.

The country's Soviet past manifests itself in more ways, of course, than simply support for the Communist Party. Perhaps more significantly, most Russians regret the end of Communist rule. Survey data from 1999 indicates that, while almost 22 percent of Russians would choose their present life if they had a choice, slightly more than 64 percent would choose their life prior to 1991. And when asked explicitly about their feelings about the collapse of the Soviet Union, 77 percent said that they regret it.[85] Similarly, a 2001 survey found that more than 13 percent of Russians considered the Soviet collapse a catastrophe of global proportions, with 43.5 percent considering it a misfortune for many of the people living in the successor states.[86]

While Communist nostalgia and the CPRF may be becoming increasingly irrelevant in the new millennium, it is not because their symbols and messages are no longer popular. Rather, others have more effectively taken up the mantle of the Soviet past and resurrected it in a slightly different form. From Putin himself on down, including a large number of members of the president's administration, Duma members, and even regional governors, personnel from the security services, military, and police have begun to appeal to Russia's citizens as representing the very best the Soviet Union had to offer while effectively distancing themselves from the regime's evils. Festooned in many of the symbols of the Russian empire, these new "centrists" speak proudly of the country's past and with optimism about its future, a message found quite appealing by a society wrestling with economic difficulties, violence in the streets, and ubiquitous corruption. The fact that this new class is actually a reconstituted Soviet elite also lends further support to the thesis of the persistence and transformation of the old elites in post-Communist Europe.[87]

More than a decade after the Soviet collapse, Russia has yet to achieve the democratic governance and economic prosperity for which the reformers had hoped. Indeed, post-Communist development in Eastern Europe and the former Soviet Union has proven to be a much more problematic and lengthy process than perhaps everyone had assumed. While Russia has seen its share of setbacks over the past decade, it has seen significant success as well. Despite the bumps along the way, Russia has come quite far along the path of post-Communism and has made significant strides toward the consolidation of democratic governance, the development of a market economy, and the strengthening of its nascent civil society. It is still too soon, of course, to reach any final conclusions regarding Russia's future, but its break with the more heinous aspects of its past seems complete.

Post-Post-Communism

The year 1989 certainly proved to be a critical juncture in the history of Communist regimes. Prior to this time, no consolidated Communist state had ever collapsed, and yet within a mere two years only four Communist states would remain. Two of these, North Korea and Cuba, were Communist only in name, having over the years evolved into personal dictatorships simply guised in the rhetoric of Marxism-Leninism. China and Vietnam, meanwhile, were "groping for reforms that, in effect, were tantamount to a repudiation of the Marxist-Leninist experience."[88] While China and Vietnam have reformed their systems to such an extent that the practice of applying the label Communist to them can be brought into question,[89] the fact that these states are still ruled by Communist parties and operate within the confines of a Marxist-Leninist ideology—however greatly revised it may be—does not change the fundamental nature of these systems. Much like the earlier periods of reform in both the Soviet Union and China, change *in* the system does not amount to a change *of* the system.

Of course, it was against the express wishes of the Soviet Union's reform architect, Mikhail Gorbachev himself, that an attempt to restructure the state led inadvertently to that very state's own demise. The post-Communist period in Russia has also shown that even a change of the system does not guarantee that development will be easy. Russia today still struggles with the trauma of its past and the difficulties of carrying through a dual-transition to democracy and the free market. While success is apparent in many areas, including laying the foundation of a functioning market economy and a political system that is becoming increasingly institutionalized, the attainment of democracy, freedom, and economic prosperity is still very much a work in progress.

Contrary to the expectation at the time, the events of 1989-1991 did not relegate all of the world's Communist regimes to the "dustbin of history." While the Soviet Union did shortly implode in the midst of its attempt to reform itself, more than a decade later the world's most populous country still stands as a testament to the resilience of Communist rule and the ability of a Communist system to carry through changes sufficient to prolong its life. Beginning with Deng's southern tour in 1992, China has proven itself able to carry through substantial reforms that have improved the material conditions of the country. These changes have also involved a virtual transformation of the CCP, which has become less dogmatic and has brought into its ranks members of the new elite. Meanwhile, progress continues to be made in democratization, as village elections become more democratic, the National People's Congress develops greater legislative power, and media liberalization spreads.

It remains to be seen, of course, whether or not the PRC will be able to navigate successfully a unique reform path and transform itself into a freer and more prosperous society without collapsing in the process. As we have seen, however, a Chinese collapse is not inevitable or historically predetermined due to the collapse of the USSR. The failure of the Soviet system was related directly to the initial conditions under which reform was implemented and the specific policies chosen by Gorbachev and other leaders. And if China can successfully draw lessons from the Soviet experience, the chances of a Chinese collapse may diminish even further.

Notes

1. Yuri Savenkov, "Russian Federation Parliamentarians in China," *Izvestiya*, December 26, 1991, 6.

2. Christopher Marsh and Paul Froese, "The State of Freedom in Russia: A Regional Analysis of Freedom of Religion, Media and Markets," *Religion, State & Society* 32, no. 2 (June 2004): 137-149.

3. Bruce Gilley, *Tiger on the Brink: Jiang Zemin and China's New Elite* (Berkeley and Los Angeles: University of California Press, 1998), 176-177.

4. Gilley, *Tiger on the Brink*, 184.

5. Sun, *The Chinese Reassessment of Socialism*, 82.

6. Sun, *The Chinese Reassessment of Socialism*, 82-83.

7. All figures are from: Liu Guoguang, Wang Luolin, Li Jingwen, Liu Shucheng, and Wang Tongsan, eds., *Economics Blue Book of the People's Republic of China, 1999: Analysis and Forecast* (Armonk, NY: M. E. Sharpe, 1999), 509.

8. Wu Naitao, "State-Owned Enterprises No Longer State Run," *Beijing Review* (November 16-22, 1992), 17-21.

9. "Leaders on Reform of State-Owned Firms," *Beijing Review*, March 24-30, 1997, 5.

10. X. L. Ding, "Who Gets What, How? When Chinese State-Owned Enterprises Become Shareholding Companies," *Problems of Communism* 46, no. 3 (May/June 1999): 32-33.

11. Ding, "Who Gets What, How?"

12. Hgok Ma, Ka-ho Mok, and Anthony B. L. Cheung, "Advance and Retreat: The New Two-Pronged Strategy of Enterprise Reform in China," *Problems of Post-Communism* 48, no. 5 (September/October 2001): 53.

13. Ma, Mok, and Cheung, "Advance and Retreat," 52.

14. Ma, Mok, and Cheung, "Advance and Retreat," 52-61.

15. Elizabeth Perry, "China in 1992: An Experiment in Neo-Authoritarianism," *Asian Survey* 33, no.1 (January 1993): 15.

16. *Statistical Yearbook of China, 2000* (Beijing, 2001), 105.

17. Liu, Wang, Li, Liu, and Wang, *Economics Blue Book*, 56.

18. Joseph Fewsmith, *China Since Tiananmen: The Politics of Transition* (Cambridge, UK: Cambridge University Press, 2001), 172.

19. Fewsmith, *China Since Tiananmen*, 173, and Robert Scalapino, "The People's Republic of China at Fifty," *NBR Analysis* (National Bureau of Asian Research) 10, no. 4 (October 1999): 11-15.

20. Jean C. Oi, *Rural China Takes Off: Institutional Foundations of Economic Reform* (Los Angeles and Berkeley, CA: University of California Press, 1999), 62-63, 80-88.

21. "Changes in China's Main Economic Indicators," *China & World Economy* 11, no. 4 (2003): 60.

22. Sasha Chang, *China Country Briefing* (Beijing: Bank One, NA, 2001).

23. Lianjiang Li and Kevin O'Brien, "The Struggle over Village Elections," in Goldman and MacFarquhar, *The Paradox of China's Post-Mao Reforms*, 129-144.

24. Li and O'Brien, "The Struggle over Village Elections," 131.

25. Zweig, *Democratic Values*, 21-26.

26. Tianjian Shi, "Mass Political Behavior in Beijing," in Goldman and MacFarquhar, *The Paradox of China's Post-Mao Reforms*, 145-169. See also Tianjian Shi, *Political Participation in Beijing* (Cambridge, MA: Harvard University Press, 1997).

27. Shi, "Mass Political Behavior in Beijing," 155.

28. Minxin Pei, "Domestic Changes in China and Implications for American Policy," in Christopher Marsh and June Tuefel Dreyer, eds. *U.S.-China Relations in the Twenty-first Century* (Lanham, MD: Lexington Books, 2003), 51-52.

29. Tanner, "The National People's Congress," 100-128. See also Murray Scot Tanner, *The Politics of Lawmaking in Post-Mao China: Institutions, Processes, and Democratic Prospects* (New York: Oxford University Press, 1998); Murray Scot Tanner and Chen Ke, "Breaking the Vicious Cycles: The Emergence of China's National People's Congress," *Problems of Post-Communism* 45, no. 3 (May-June 1998): 29-47; and Kevin J. O'Brien, *Reform Without Liberalization: China's National People's Congresses and the Politics of Institutional Change* (New York: Cambridge University Press, 1990).

30. Tanner, "The National People's Congress," 102.

31. Tanner, "The National People's Congress," 101-103.

32. Gang Guo, "Party Recruitment of College Students in China," *Journal of Contemporary China* 14, no. 43 (May 2005): 371-393.

33. Jie Cheng and Yang Zhong, "Defining the Political System of Post-Deng China: Emerging Support for a Democratic Political System," *Problems of Post-Communism* 45, no. 2 (January-February 1998): 30-42; Timothy Brook and B. Michael Frolic, *Civil Society in China* (Armonk, NY: M.E. Sharpe, 1997); and Suisheng Zhao, ed. *China and Democracy: Reconsidering the Prospects for a Democratic China* (New York: Routledge, 2000).

34. Dickson, "Unsettled Succession," 72.

35. Andrew Nathan, "Authoritarian Resilience: China's Changing of the Guard," *Journal of Democracy* 14, no. 1 (January 2003): 6-17.

36. Gordon Chang, *The Coming Collapse of China* (New York: Random House, 2001).

37. The papers from the conference were published in David Shambaugh, ed., *Is China Unstable? Assessing the Factors* (Armonk, NY: M. E. Sharpe, 2000).

38. George Gilboy and Eric Heginbotham, "China's Coming Transformation," *Foreign Affairs* 80, no. 4 (July-August 2001): 26-39.

39. Mel Gurtov, ed. *The Transformation of Socialism: Perestroika and Reform in the Soviet Union and China* (Boulder, CO: Westview, 1990); Rozman, *Dismantling Com-*

munism; Minxin Pei, *From Reform to Revolution*; Graeme Gill, "The Political Dynamics of Reform: Learning from the Soviet Experience," in *China After Socialism: In the Footsteps of Eastern Europe or East Asia?*, Barrett McCormick and Jonathan Unger, eds. (Armonk, NY: M.E. Sharpe, 1996), 54-72.

40. See, for example, Jie Cheng and Yang Zhong, "Defining the Political System of Post-Deng China: Emerging Support for a Democratic Political System," *Problems of Post-Communism* 45, no. 2 (January-February 1998): 30-42.

41. See "The Strange Death of Soviet Communism: An Autopsy," a special issue of *The National Interest* 31 (Spring 1993). One person actually did predict the collapse of the Soviet Union: Bernard Levin in a 1977 article in *The Times* (London). This article is reprinted on 64-65 in this issue of *The National Interest*.

42. Brzezinski, *The Grand Failure.*

43. Rozman, *Dismantling Communism*, 16.

44. Shigeki Hakamada and Gilbert Rozman, "China: The Process of Reform," in Rozman, *Dismantling Communism*, 179.

45. Dickson, "Unsettled Succession," 71.

46. Dickson, "Unsettled Succession."

47. Dickson, "Unsettled Succession," 253.

48. M. Stephen Fish, *Democracy From Scratch*: Opposition and Regime in the New Russian Revolution (Princeton, NJ: Princeton University Press, 1995).

49. Boris Slavin, "The Ideas that the People Went For," *Pravda*, December 23, 1995, 1.

50. "The New Life is More to be Cherished than Grievances," *Rossiskaya Gazeta*, June 28, 1996, 3.

51. *ITAR-TASS*, June 8, 1999.

52. *Kommersant*, March 21, 2000, 1; *Nezavisimaya Gazeta*, March 22, 2000, 1.

53. Yevgenia Borisova, "Baby Boom or Dead Souls," *Moscow Times*, September 9, 2000.

54. Christopher Marsh, Helen Albert, and James W. Warhola, "The Political Geography of Russia's 2004 Presidential Election," *Eurasian Geography & Economics* 45, no. 4 (July 2004): 188-205.

55. David Holley, "Russian Hopefuls' Quixotic Quest Plants Seeds for 2008," *Los Angeles Times*, March 14, 2004.

56. Celestine Bohlen, "Yeltsin Deputy calls Reforms 'Economic Genocide'," *New York Times*, February 9, 1992.

57. Darrell Slider, "Privatization in Russia's Regions" *Post-Soviet Affairs* 10, no. 4 (1994): 367-396.

58. Victor Supyan, "Privatization in Russia: Some Preliminary Results and Socio-economic Implications," *Demokratizatsiya* 9, no. 1 (2001): 146.

59. Supyan, "Privatization in Russia."

60. Joseph Blasi, Maya Kroumova, and Douglas Kruse, *Kremlin Capitalism: Privatizing the Russian Economy* (Ithaca, NY: Cornell University Press, 1997).

61. Sergei Aukutsionek, Igor Filatochev, Rostislav Kapelyushnikov, and Vladimir Zhukov, "Dominant Shareholders, Restructuring and Performance of Privatized Companies in Russia: An Analysis and Some Policy Implications," *Communist Economies & Economic Transformation* 10 (1998): 495-518; Supyan, "Privatization in Russia."

62. Supyan, "Privatization in Russia," 148.

63. Aukutsionek, Filatochev, Kapelyushnikov, and Zhukov, "Dominant Shareholders," 511-512.

64. Anders Åslund, "Russia's Economic Transformation under Putin," *Eurasian Geography & Economics* 45, no. 6 (2004): 397-420.

65. Marshall Goldman, "Anders in Wonderland: Comments on Russia's Economic Transformation under Putin," *Eurasian Geography & Economics* 45, no. 6 (2004): 429-434; and Philip Hanson, "Putin and Russia's Economic Transformation," *Eurasian Geography & Economics* 45, no. 6 (2004): 421-428; Anders Åslund, "Putin's Second Term is Likely to Differ from His First: A Rebuttal," *Eurasian Geography & Economics* 45, no. 6 (2004): 435-438.

66. Ernst & Young International, Ltd. *Doing Business in the Russian Federation* (Moscow: Ernst and Young, 2002), 5.

67. George Hudson, "Civil Society in Russia: Models and Prospects for Development," *Russian Review* 62, no. 2 (2003): 212-213.

68. James Gibson, "Social Networks, Civil Society, and the Prospects for Consolidating Russia's Democratic Transition," *American Journal of Political Science* 45, no. 1 (2001): 51-69.

69. Andrew Greeley, "Coleman Revisited: Religious Structures as a Source of Social Capital," *American Behavioral Scientist* 40, no. 4 (1997): 587-594; Robert Wuthnow, "Mobilizing Civic Engagement: The Changing Impact of Religious Involvement" in *Civic Engagement and American Democracy*, Theda Skocpol and Morris Fiorina, eds. (Washington, DC: Brookings Institution, 1999), 331-363; Corwin Smidt, ed. *Religion as Social Capital: Producing the Common Good* (Waco, TX: Baylor University Press, 2003); Inna Naletova, "Orthodox *Yarmarki* as a Form of Civic Engagement," in Christopher Marsh, ed., *Burden or Blessing? Russian Orthodoxy and the Construction of Civil Society and Democracy* (Boston: Institute on Culture, Religion and World Affairs, Boston University, 2004), 85-90.

70. Stephen White and Ian McAllister, "Orthodoxy and Political Behavior in Postcommunist Russia." *Review of Religious Research* 41, no. 3 (2000): 359-372; Nikolas K. Gvosdev, *Emperors and Elections: Reconciling the Orthodox Tradition with Modern Politics* (Huntington, NY: Troitsa Books, 2000).

71. Paul Froese, "Forced Secularization in Soviet Russia: Why an Atheistic Monopoly Failed," *Journal for the Scientific Study of Religion* 43, no. 1 (2004): 35-50.

72. Nathaniel Davis, *A Long Walk to Church: A Contemporary History of Russian Orthodoxy.* Second Edition. (Boulder, CO: Westview Press, 2003).

73. Sabrina Ramet, *Nihil Obstat: Religion, Politics, and Social Change in East-Central Europe and Russia* (Durham, NC: Duke University Press, 1998), 265-274.

74. Metropolitan Kirill of Smolensk, "Gospel and Culture," in John Witte and Michael Bourdeaux, eds. *Proselytism and Orthodoxy in Russia: The New War for Souls* (Maryknoll, NY: Orbis Books, 1999), 66-76.

75. Harold Berman, "Freedom of Religion in Russia: An Amicus Brief for the Defendant," in Witte and Bourdeaux, *Proselytism and Orthodoxy in Russia*, 275-76.

76. Lauren B. Homer and Lawrence A. Uzzell, "Federal and Provincial Religious Freedom Laws in Russia: A Struggle for and against Federalism and the Rule of Law," in Witte and Bourdeaux, *Proselytism and Orthodoxy in Russia*, 284-320.

77. Marsh and Froese, "The State of Freedom in Russia."

78. Brad Owens, "The Independent Press in Russia: Integrity and the Economics of Survival," in Christopher Marsh and Nikolas Gvosdev, eds., *Civil Society and the Search for Justice in Russia* (Lanham, MD: Lexington Books, 2002), 110.

79. Georgy Bovt, "The Russian Press and Civil Society: Freedom of Speech vs. Freedom of Market," in Marsh and Gvosdev, *Civil Society and the Search for Justice in Russia*, 93.

80. Bovt, "The Russian Press," and Ivan Zassoursky, *Media and Power in Post-Soviet Russia* (Armonk, NY: M. E. Sharpe, 2004).

81. "Russians Favour Putin Strengthening Control Over Media," VCIOM Survey, March 3-19, 2000. Available at: www.russiavotes.org.

82. "What do you think was the main Reason for the Closure of TV-6," and "Do you think Putin Played a part in deciding the fate of TV-6?" VCIOM Survey, January 25-28, 2002. Available at: www.russiavotes.org.

83. Bovt, "The Russian Press," 105.

84. Bovt, "The Russian Press."

85. *SSSR i SNG v Rossiiskom Obshchestvennom Mnenii* (Moscow: ROMIR, 2001), tables 2 and 3. Available online at: http://www.romir.ru.

86. *Novaya Rossiya: Desyat' Let Reform Glazami Rossiyan* (Moscow: Institut Kompleksnykh Sotsial'nykh Issledovanii, Rossiiskaya Akademiya Nauk, October 2001), question 46.

87. John Higley, Judith Kullberg, and Jan Pakulski, "The Persistence of Postcommunist Elites," *Journal of Democracy* 7, no. 2 (1996): 133-147.

88. Brzezinski, *The Grand Failure*, 12.

89. Pei, *From Reform to Revolution*, 2.

Chapter 5

Learning from Your Comrade's Mistakes

The Communist Party of the Soviet Union . . . is the most advanced, the most experienced, and the most theoretically cultivated party in the world. This party has been our model in the past, it is our model at present, and it will be our model in the future.

–Mao Zedong, 1953[1]

That model has failed which was brought about in our country. And I hope that this is a lesson not only for our people but for all peoples.

–Mikhail Gorbachev, 1991[2]

T HE People's Republic of China and the Union of Soviet Socialist Republics both faced lethal crises as they attempted to reform their communist systems. While the Soviet Union collapsed under the weight of reform, more than a decade later China stands as a testament to the resilience of the Communist regime in Beijing. Moreover, as the CCP leadership pursues policies that may bring about a Chinese transformation, such as increasing party legitimacy, pursuing controlled liberalization, and even appealing to Chinese nationalism, the chances of a regime collapse in China today are much less than they were a decade ago, and for that matter, less than they had been in the Soviet Union in its final days.

Juxtaposed one to the other, the Soviet and Chinese reform experiences look quite different. As the preceding analysis of their "unparalleled reforms" has illustrated, however, placing them side by side actually distorts the fact that events unfolded in both countries nearly simultaneously and with a significant degree of interaction. This begs the question, did events in one Communist giant have a significant impact on the course of events in the other? In particular, did leaders and political actors attempt to draw lessons from each other's experiences with reform?

Answers to this set of questions are crucial for understanding why specific policy strategies were chosen and what the implications of this may be for the future of both countries, as well as for the way scholars understand the dynamics of regime transition more generally. In regards to the Chinese case, while the CCP chose to pursue controlled, gradual reform, the issue of why this policy strategy was chosen remains unexplained. Is it simply due to cultural differences and the level of commitment to Marxist principles by Chinese leaders, as Brzezinski has argued?[3] Did Chinese leaders simply have a different vision than their Soviet counterparts? Or, are Chinese leaders seeking to learn lessons from the collapse of Communist rule in the Soviet Union and Eastern Europe as they attempt to implement policies that will lead the country along the path of gradual reform while simultaneously buttressing their own political power?

In this chapter, I argue that the course of reform in China has been inextricably linked to events throughout the Communist and post-Communist world, particularly after the tumultuous events of 1989. I present a substantial body of evidence in support of this thesis, including statements by party leaders, internal reports on the subject by government agencies, and samples of the extensive body of scholarly research on the causes of the collapse of Communism in the Soviet Union and Eastern Europe and the lessons to be drawn from that experience. I begin by tracing China's experience with learning from the Soviet Union back to the Bolshevik Revolution, and follow this trend through to the decision to abandon the Soviet model and the Chinese reaction to perestroika and the collapse of Communism in Eastern Europe and the USSR itself. Finally, I explore the possible lessons China may be drawing from the new Russia, where continuing struggles with economic transformation, political development, and declining military strength lead many Chinese to believe that their choice of controlled liberalization rather than democratization has been vindicated.

Lesson-Drawing and the Chinese Transformation

China's experience learning from the Soviet Union does not begin with the collapse of Communism in the USSR. As mentioned in the introduction, it actually begins with the success of the Bolshevik Revolution in Russia and the conscious attempt to emulate the Soviet experience. The first concrete steps were taken with the formation of the Chinese Communist Party back in 1922, which was followed shortly thereafter by a significant number of Chinese Communists going to Moscow for study, including Deng Xiaoping himself. As Deng's daughter points out in her biography of her father's early years, his file from that time "tells us something about him." It seems that while student Dozorov (as Deng was known in Russian), was a very bright student and exhibited leadership qualities even at this early time, he still had "not eliminated the characteristics of a Party member with the Kuomintang."[4] Perhaps Deng's embracing of the Soviet model was not quite as strong as some have thought, which would have made his decision to abandon the Soviet model upon his rise to power all the more easy. One thing is clear, however, China's experience interacting with and learning from the Soviet Union has a long history indeed.

Following the Communist victory in the Chinese Civil War, Mao Zedong was quite explicit in not only stating that China must learn from the experience of the Soviet Union, but also in explaining why and in what ways. As Mao explained,

> We are going to undertake this grand construction of our country. The task we are facing is arduous, and we have little experience. So, we need to learn seriously from the Soviet Union, from their advanced experiences. All of us, Communist Party members or not, cadres (old or young), technicians, working class and farmers, all must sincerely learn from the Soviet Union. Not only should we learn from them the theories of Marx, Engles, Lenin, and Stalin, but also we should learn from their advanced technology. We will push this learning to a nationwide climax in order to construct our country.[5]

As early as 1956, however, with the 20th Party Congress of the CPSU, China began to reconsider its choice of role model. After the Cultural Revolution came to a close and the decision was made to reassess Chinese socialism, the decision was also made to abandon the Soviet model outright. In fact, in exploring their options, Chinese leaders even sought the advice of Western economists, some of whom were specialists on the Soviet economy. Their task was to predict how the Soviet economy might evolve in the future, and "to gain insight about what might happen to China if substantial reforms" were not made and it retained the Soviet economic model.[6] The advice they got was sobering, and left them aware of the difficult task that lay ahead and of the necessity to pursue reform.

Once the decision was made to abandon the Soviet model, the only question that remained was how to restructure the economy. Chinese leaders set up an Economic Reform Investigation Group, which at first gave consideration to the East European models offered by Romania, Hungary, and Yugoslavia, countries that had each developed their own unique systems of socialism and whose standards of living seemed to the leaders in Beijing to be higher than neighboring countries. While Romania was a close ally of the PRC, its economic model was dismissed due to its reliance on a high level of compulsory investment.[7] Hungary's New Economic Mechanism (NEM) and Yugoslavia's "market socialism" both seemed to offer attractive strategies for restructuring and running a socialist economy, and certain aspects of these systems turned up in the Chinese economy within a few years, including enterprise autonomy and the retention of profits from production that exceeded the plan.

Once the Soviet Union initiated its own economic reforms under Gorbachev's leadership, another model became available. Chinese leaders were dubious of perestroika from the very beginning, however.[8] Having wrestled with economic reform for almost ten years, leaders in Beijing knew how difficult it was to reform a Soviet-type economy. Gorbachev, moreover, was attempting to

carry out sweeping reforms of the economy simultaneously with political reforms. It was at this point that Chinese leaders rejected the Soviet reform model
and decided to stick to their own path. During his report to the Seventh National
People's Congress in March 1989, Premier Li Peng clearly indicated that China
would not follow the Soviet path of glasnost and perestroika.[9] The next month,
as demonstrations got underway in Tiananmen Square, Li said that "democracy
should not be implemented too rapidly and that China would not 'mechanically
copy' the policies adopted in the Soviet Union."[10]

    While party leaders had rejected the Soviet model, many Chinese felt dif-
ferently. In fact, the strides being made in the Soviet Union toward democracy
in 1987-1988 impacted students and the new elite that was forming as a result of
the already decade-old reforms in China.[11] This fact became abundantly clear
when Mikhail Gorbachev arrived in Beijing in mid-May 1989 to negotiate improved Sino-Soviet relations. Gorbachev's presence in the Chinese capital actually spurred on student protests, with the number of protestors swelling to over a
quarter million in the days leading up to his visit. As Keller observed, "Some
Chinese, including restive students, hope that Mr. Gorbachev's visit will inspire
broader democratization of their society,"[12] while others saw in him "a vigorous
symbol of political liberalization" and regarded his visit as "an implicit rebuke
to the aging leadership of China."[13] In the words of one poster held up by the
students, "In the Soviet Union, they have Gorbachev, in China, we have
whom?"[14] The students were not only motivated by Gorbachev and his reforms,
they actually hoped that he would intervene on their behalf with the CCP leadership to bring about further reform in their own country. As Wang Dan, a student
leader from Peking University, said at a news conference, "As a great political
reformer, we urge Mikhail Gorbachev to talk to the government on our behalf,
for humanitarian reasons."[15]

    While it is clear that Gorbachev symbolized political reform and liberaliza-
tion to the demonstrating students, and that his presence in Beijing impacted to a
significant degree the way events unfolded, his effect on events should not be
overemphasized. The demonstrating students were not only invigorated by Gorbachev's visit, they also saw the press corps as an opportunity to publicize their
cause. Many of the people that flooded Tiananmen Square in mid-May, moreover, were also moved by the students who were on hunger strike and putting
their lives on the line for their beliefs. As Kristof reported, "intellectuals said
that they admired what Mr. Gorbachev had done in the Soviet Union," but "they
emphasized that it was sympathy for the hunger strikers rather than Mr. Gorbachev's presence that brought them into the streets."[16] Once Gorbachev and the
press left Beijing, however, CCP leaders in Zhongnanhai forcefully cleansed the
streets and Tiananmen Square of the demonstrators.

Lessons of the Collapse of Communism in Eastern Europe

As the CCP was recovering from the turbulent events of May-June 1989, events were stirring half a world away that would resonate back to China. The collapse of Communism in Eastern Europe worried Chinese leaders greatly, and forced them to come to grips with the fact that, rather than representing the future of the world, socialism was in crisis. This hadn't been the case prior to the Tiananmen events, however. Throughout the 1980s, China had watched developments in Eastern Europe with great interest, and while the events of 1980-1981 in Poland were disturbing to leaders in Beijing, the progress of economic reforms was initially viewed with enthusiasm.[17] As Tubilewicz persuasively argues, throughout the first half of 1989, the Chinese media had been reporting events in Eastern Europe in a largely positive light, presenting the reforms in Poland and Hungary as consistent with socialism and as mainly aimed at building "national understanding" and restoring "domestic stability."[18] Some more liberal voices even used their coverage of reforms in Eastern Europe as a means to promote similar reforms in China, dismissing the opinion of some that there was a danger of antisocialist forces seizing power or undermining economic reforms.[19]

This situation changed drastically as the events of 1989 unfolded. The Chinese press began to take on a more critical tone, and began to criticize East European governments for "trying to abandon socialism."[20] As one Communist regime in Eastern Europe after another fell in the fall of 1989, leaders in Beijing watched with amazement and fear. They did more than sit idly by, however. They criticized Gorbachev's policies as "not in conformity with true Marxism-Leninism," launched a public relations campaign in support of one-party rule and communist ideology, and reached out to Communist leaders in Romania, Bulgaria, Cuba, and North Korea, offering them moral support and advice on how to avoid unrest. In fact, in November and December 1989, high level exchanges took place between Beijing, Bucharest, and Pyongyang as Communist leaders searched for strategies for dealing with sources of instability—both real and potential.

Once the Ceausescu regime was toppled in late December, however, fear turned to panic. According to former National Security Advisor Brent Scowcroft, who was in Beijing at the time, Chinese leaders "had taken great comfort" in Romania's "apparent impregnability." But when Ceausescu and his wife were executed in the final days of December, Scowcroft recalls, "I believe the Chinese leaders panicked."[21] They did indeed.

The dramatic events in Bucharest were presented in the Chinese press as the result of "wrong policies," with fault being directed at Ceausescu for creating a cult of personality, monopolizing the highest positions of the state and party, and violating the basic principles of Marxism.[22] Qian Qichen, a veteran diplomat and Soviet expert, had insisted in an article published after Ceausescu's arrest on December 22 that "socialism has not failed and capitalism has not triumphed."[23] In actuality, however, party leaders "were haunted by parallels between the revolt that overthrew Rumania's dictator and Beijing's student-led protests" at

Tiananmen.[24] The very day following Ceausescu's execution, the CCP called mid- and high-level officials in to their offices to receive an internal memorandum on the collapse of Communism in Eastern Europe and to be "instructed" on how to "correctly understand" the event.[25] In the memorandum, Jiang Zemin himself admitted that "We cannot say that China will remain intact from the recent changes."[26]

The party memorandum blamed Gorbachev for "subversion of socialism," while pointing out that the Romanian Communist system was actually "imposed" by Moscow and was therefore different from China's genuine Communism, which sprang from its own revolution. When speaking about the events in Romania with foreigners, these officials were instructed to neither take a stand for nor against Ceausescu or the Romanian people. When speaking "to Chinese, of course, we should say the demise of Communism was a blunder."[27]

The party's inner circle got an even more vivid educational experience. As Yang reports, shortly after the fall of the Communist regime in Romania, Deng Xiaoping and several politburo members and veteran cadres gathered to watch videotapes of the whole affair, which had been compiled by the Ministry of Foreign Affairs.[28] The standoff between the Ceausescu regime and crowds of people in Bucharest seemed to those assembled to be "a microcosm of the Tiananmen incident." But as Yang describes, most of those watching the footage were not familiar with the subsequent part of the story—the arrest and execution of the Ceausescu couple:

> This old comrade and his wife looked pale and depressed. They were questioned and obviously had been physically tortured. The couple heroically refused to sign the judgment paper of the military court. They were dragged to the execution ground, forced against the wall, and finally shot. The bodies fell like heavy rocks, jerked on the ground, and eventually lay still in puddles of blood.[29]

Those gathered to view the film let out a few soft sighs, followed by a few minutes of silence, before someone blurted out, "We'll be like this if we don't strengthen our proletarian dictatorship and repress the reactionaries." To which Deng replied, "Yes, we'll be like this, if we don't carry out reforms and bring about benefits to the people."[30]

While the collapse of Communism in Eastern Europe certainly shook the Middle Kingdom, there were numerous differences between Eastern Europe and China that prevented an analogy from being drawn too rigidly, such as the imported vs. genuine nature of their Communist revolutions and their degree of autonomy from Moscow. The CCP leadership recognized these differences and emphasized them in its interpretation of what had occurred, including in the internal memorandum mentioned above. China's true counterpart, of course, was not Eastern Europe but the Soviet Union itself. But before long, this analogy would prove no less unsettling.

Looking into the Mirror

Rozman has pointed out that shortly after the collapse of the Soviet Union the CCP began to cite the tumultuous effects of dismantling communism in the Soviet Union in order to shore up support for the Communist regime in Beijing. Was this just a political tactic, or is it a belief genuinely held by the CCP leadership? It is not unreasonable to suspect that the Soviet collapse would have impacted the thinking of the party leadership and other Chinese in this way. Indeed, it gave a drastically different meaning to the Chinese saying, popular in the 1950s, that "the Soviet Union's today will be our tomorrow" (*Sulian de jintian jiu shi women de mingtian*). How could a party-state modeled after the Soviet Union, based on a parallel ideology, and facing similar dilemmas consider the events of 1989-1991 in Eastern Europe and the Soviet Union to be of no consequence to itself?

Evidence that the Chinese have sought to learn lessons from the collapse of the Soviet Union is not difficult to find. Deng Xiaoping himself, the intellectual leader of the CCP during the fall of the Berlin Wall and the collapse of the Soviet Union, personally believed that there were lessons to be learned from the Soviet collapse, and that these lessons could be used to strengthen the People's Republic of China. Not long after the collapse, Deng remarked publicly that "some [socialist] countries have gotten into serious trouble. It seems that socialism has been weakened, but people . . . can learn from these lessons. This can help us improve socialism and lead it on the path to healthier development. . . . Do not think that Marxism has disappeared, has fallen out of use, or has failed."[31]

Jiang Zemin, who rose to power in the wake of the Tiananmen crackdown, held a similar view on the significance of the Soviet collapse: "After more than seventy years of socialist construction in the Soviet Union" the great tragedy of the Soviet collapse occurred. "Why? The reasons and the lessons inherent in this need to be concluded profoundly and comprehensively," if this is done properly, "there will be new development of Marxism-Leninism."[32]

In 1996, after the wave of collapse was over and China found itself still standing, Jiang Zemin began to call explicitly for serious examination of the reasons for the Soviet Union's collapse in order to understand the implications for China's future. The country's leading Russia scholars heeded the call and sought to draw lessons from the Soviet collapse: "The study of the reasons for the Soviet Union's collapse is very important for China at this time . . . [it] will help us improve the process of our reform. . . . [It] will help us build the foundation of socialism with Chinese characteristics and help us govern the country far into the future, and to keep China safe, stable, and standing."[33]

Perhaps even more outspoken on the topic has been current president Hu Jintao. In a speech to the fourth plenary conference of the sixteenth session of the CCP in September 2004, Hu stated that he would do more to learn from the mistakes of the Soviet collapse than had Jiang. In his speech, Hu placed great blame on Gorbachev for the collapse:

> Gorbachev is the ringleader of the Soviet great change, a socialist rebel, not the so-called "person who has rendered meritorious service." Talk which claims him to be a "person who has rendered meritorious service" is not standing in the interests of the Soviet people or the enterprise of human progress. It is just that he advocated glasnost and pluralism. This caused the entire CPSU and the people to fall into chaos. The Soviet Union and the CPSU collapsed under the impact of his "Westernization" and "bourgeois liberalization." [34]

Not only have policymakers and leaders such as Jiang and Hu been impacted by the Soviet collapse, Chinese of all persuasions have also been profoundly affected by the failure of Soviet Communism. As Zhao points out, many Chinese intellectuals decided,

> that the post-Cold War transformation in Eastern Europe and the former Soviet Union was not as positive as expected. The West, its values and systems, did not make much difference to postcommunist countries. . . . Even those who supported the 1989 student movement concluded that if China were to initiate the dramatic democratic reform promoted by the West, the nation could well have suffered a similar disorder to what Russia had. [35]

Research by Peng on democracy and political discourse in China suggests that the collapse of the Soviet Union affected not only elites, but ordinary Chinese as well. In his research Peng found evidence of a political orientation that "favors a strong 'corporatist' state to guide the transition from state socialism to a market economy," an approach that "values a free market but also emphasizes the government's role in guiding the economy and an active state sector." [36] Those who hold such views point to "the disruptive experience of the Soviet bloc" and argue "that a strong state may be necessary to maintain political stability in the transition period." [37] What is perhaps most significant is that such ideas are not only held by those in favor of a corporatist state. "Those leaning toward a social democratic paradigm," who are generally supportive of private property rights, the free market, and a decreased role of the state in economic management, are also worried about the wholesale adoption of values associated with Western liberalism, arguing "that today the Russian people are suffering because Russia has adopted this path." [38]

Following Jiang's call for analysis of the Soviet collapse, research institutions that had previously studied the USSR as a means of generating insights about its adversary, such as the Institute for Soviet and East European Studies at the Chinese Academy of Social Sciences (now renamed the Institute for East European, Russian, and Central Asian Studies), switched their focus to examining the implications of the Soviet past for China's future. Other research centers were created, such as the China Reform Forum at the Central Party School, whose purpose is to analyze regime evolution and collapse, especially with reference to the former USSR. In Shanghai, a national Center for Russian Studies was created at the East China Normal University. Similar changes took place in academic publishing, with new journals, including *Eluosi Yanjiu* (Russian Studies), published out of the Center for Russian Studies at East China Normal University, springing up alongside existing academic journals devoted to the study of the Soviet Union, such as *Sulian Dongou Yanjiu* (Soviet and East European Studies), which was renamed *Dongou Zhongya Yanjiu* (East European and Central Asian Studies). While research institutes are not primary actors in the policymaking process, as Li points out in reference to foreign policy think tanks, they are important sources of analysis and innovative ideas, and their research impacts policy.[39]

Research into the Soviet collapse is not something the Party just left up to academics. The Communist Party formed working groups comprised of the country's leading specialists with the specific charge of studying the causes of the collapse and the lessons to be learned. These working groups have been the source of much of the research in this area, which has included government-sponsored conferences and has resulted in numerous books on the Soviet collapse, many with special sections devoted to the lessons to be drawn from the Soviet experience.[40]

Chinese scholars specializing in Russia have been busy amassing a large body of scholarship on the failure of Soviet Communism and the causes of the collapse of the USSR. While the focus of every study of Russia coming out of China is not explicitly on the lessons to be learned from the Soviet collapse, hardly any article or book on Russia being done in China does not contain some discussion of the parallels between the Soviet and Chinese Communist systems and the implications for China's future. In fact, Chinese scholarship on the former Soviet Union and Eastern Europe has remained fixated over the past decade on the collapse of Communism, which is more often referred to in Chinese as the "great change" (*jubian*). As they wrestle with Communist reform in their own country, Chinese scholars are particularly interested in determining the reasons for the failure of Soviet Communism in order to draw lessons that will facilitate the Chinese Communist system's preservation and further development. More than a decade after the Soviet collapse, this area of inquiry is still a major preoccupation of academic research, with every issue of the major Russian studies journals including one or two analyses of the causes of the Soviet *denouement*. In the West, of course, the business of studying the Soviet collapse was popular for a brief moment between 1992-93, and since then most scholars have moved on to the seemingly more topical questions of democratic development and state-building. Accordingly, such topics receive little attention in the Chinese academy. It is important to recognize this difference, however, for the fact that this topic has received much more attention in China than it has either in the West or in the former Soviet countries themselves is not insignificant.

It is, of course, impossible—and unnecessary—to review here all of the Chinese scholarship done on the Soviet collapse over the past decade and a half. I will thus survey some of the representative works and common themes of this body of literature.[41] The works considered here are not only examples of this rather large and extensive body of scholarship, they are also some of the finest products of this effort. A close reading of this body of work makes one thing clear—the image of the Soviet collapse has fundamentally affected the way China views itself and its future.

Chinese Views on the Failures of Soviet Socialism

Within weeks of the August 1991 attempted coup in the Soviet Union, Chinese intellectuals began thinking about what the collapse of Communism in the USSR would mean for China. In an internal document attributed to the Ideology and Theory Department of the *China Youth Daily*, entitled "Realistic Responses and Strategic Choices for China after the Soviet Coup," a group of party and government officials active in consulting for the post-Tiananmen leadership explored the changing situation and what it meant for China.[42] Four of the article's seven points focus explicitly on the implications of the collapse of Communism in the Soviet Union for the future of Communist rule in China. It acknowledges similarities between the two countries in terms of their ideology, institutions, and multinational character, simultaneously pointing out the critical differences. For one, they argue that China began to reform much earlier than the Soviet Union, before the situation became critical, and its reforms have been much more successful. In regards to nationalities issues, they point to the fact that the Soviet Union was much more ethnically diverse than China, emphasizing that over ninety percent of Chinese are ethnically Han, whereas in the Soviet Union only slightly more than half were ethnic Russians. Some responsibility is also placed on Russian Orthodoxy, which they maintain is a conservative religion that hinders reform, whereas China is not burdened in such a way. Finally, the fact that the Soviet Union on the eve of collapse was quite distant in time from the Bolshevik Revolution is seen as significant, since there were no leaders around from the revolutionary period in whom people could believe.

More significant than what they think led to the Soviet collapse are their recommendations for China. They argue that it would be wrong to remake the Chinese system along capitalist lines as the USSR attempted to do, moving from the extreme left to the extreme right. Their recommendation is for the Party to transform itself from a revolutionary party into a ruling party and to stop wasting time focusing on class struggle. They suggest that the Party should combat corruption and seek the people's support by giving them more democracy and liberty, but within certain limits. The answer is not to Westernize, but rather to turn to China's traditional beliefs such as Confucianism. But of all these similarities and differences, the most profound impact of the collapse of the Soviet Union for China is the issue of ideology. Accordingly, they recommend that party ideology be relaxed so that the people can support a common set of values and the Party can gain wide popular support.

With Marxism-Leninism no longer seen as effective in mobilizing loyalty and legitimating the state, it was necessary to develop a new ideological basis upon which to legitimate CCP rule. It is here that the call was first made to turn to Chinese nationalism to promote the Party's legitimacy. While Zhao has pointed out that the CCP is attempting to use nationalism as a new base of legitimacy for the party,[43] it has remained overlooked that the strategy of attempting to use nationalism in this way was arrived at after careful examination of the disintegrative role played by the CPSU's loss of legitimacy and the rise of ethnic nationalism in the collapse of the Soviet Union.

Almost all of the same themes first enunciated in the *China Youth Daily* piece in September 1991 have been expanded, elaborated upon, and documented in the burgeoning literature on the collapse of the Soviet Union in contemporary China. Most such studies point to the CPSU and the Soviet system itself as the primary underlying causes, arguing that the CPSU never made the transition from a revolutionary party to a ruling party, remaining too dogmatic and inflexible, as did the system it controlled. Of course, individual leaders had control over the Party to varying degrees at various points in Soviet history, so these studies also acknowledge that some fault rests with Soviet leaders for not initiating reforms. Gorbachev, the author of the Soviet Union's most comprehensive reform agenda, is even the subject of criticism, since his perestroika made too many mistakes and is seen as naïve. Mention is also made of how the systemic crisis that the Soviet Union ran into meant that high levels of productivity were never achieved, resulting in a loss of popular support.[44] This situation was confounded by the ethnic factor, which is referred to as "the powder keg of the Union's collapse."[45] This same study even makes a strong case that the protracted Soviet conflict in Afghanistan played a key role, arguing that the myth of Soviet invincibility was destroyed on the battlefields of Afghanistan, especially among the Soviet Union's non-Russian population.[46]

Lu and Jiang's major effort to reconsider the Soviet experience and the underlying causes of the Soviet collapse begins with an historical reconsideration of the Soviet experience from the Bolshevik Revolution to the collapse of the Communist regime. Lenin, although viewed as naïve, is seen consistently as a good leader overall, and he is especially praised for his New Economic Policy (NEP), a set of market measures that permitted private enterprise in agriculture and trade. While Chinese scholarship previously considered this set of policies as a partial restoration of the capitalist mode of production and thus a betrayal of communism, the NEP is held in very high regard in contemporary China.

The conclusion of Lu and Jiang that it is Stalin who bears the greatest responsibility for the Soviet Union's failure comes as no surprise. But unlike what some might expect, Stalin is not considered the "betrayer of the revolution" or blamed for the purges, rather he is criticized for abandoning the NEP, attempting to export communist revolution, and pursuing territorial expansion. One of the most interesting aspects of this work is how the contributors point out that there were numerous times throughout the Soviet era when reform could have been launched, thus averting the country's eventual demise. Again, Stalin is seen by all the contributors to this work as the one leader who led the USSR down the wrong path, but every other leader, from Khrushchev to Gorbachev, is also held responsible for not embarking upon a program of comprehensive reforms, reforms that would have abandoned the dogmatic approach to socialist construction and would have instituted market mechanisms. The only real debate on this point is whether or not Gorbachev could have led a reform program that would have revitalized the Soviet Union without leading to its eventual collapse. Most Chinese scholars argue that this was highly unlikely, since the system's problems were too numerous by that point to correct them. One voice speaks out in dissent, however. Gao Fang, a very senior and eminent scholar in China, argues that if Gorbachev "had been a creative Marxist," he would have been able to effectively reform the Soviet Union and avoid a collapse.[47]

In looking at the immediate causes of the collapse of the Soviet Union, Lu, Jiang, and the other contributors to this volume also pay attention to the nationalities question, although they place great confidence in the ability of economic benefits to quell calls for autonomy and independence. What is more congruent with Western scholarship on the topic is the argument, made by Ge Linsheng and Hu Yanfen,[48] that Gorbachev unleashed nationalist aspirations with glasnost, which raised the ambitions of those who wanted to seek independence. This point is later elaborated upon, with Gorbachev's naïveté regarding the nationalities question as the subject of investigation. Lu, Jiang, and their colleagues argue that Gorbachev failed to pay sufficient attention to nationalities problems, perhaps hoping that if the country's other problems were fixed then this issue would be resolved in the process. In carrying through his reform agenda, however, they argue that Gorbachev made three critical mistakes. The first is that he promoted open discussion of history through glasnost, without realizing that there were many ghosts in the Soviet closest. Second, glasnost led to open debate in society, which they argue led to a challenge of the CPSU's position and its loss of legitimacy. Finally, Gorbachev's inability to hold the union together is seen as the final link in the chain of causation that pulled the Soviet Union down.

As Huang points out in a recent work published in commemoration of the ten year anniversary of the collapse of the Soviet Union, the fall of the USSR is not only a great tragedy, it is also a mirror for China, one that illuminates the suffering that accompanies such a collapse while simultaneously indicating to China a better way to govern itself.[49] Such a theme is not unique, but rather it resonates throughout the entire body of work on the topic in China. Huang lists what he argues are the six factors that led to the collapse of European Communism. The first is ideological dogmatism and trying to adhere too rigidly to theory, which is blamed for leading to economic stagnation and eventually decline. Closely related to this factor is that of over-centralization of the economy. The third factor is an excessive degree of bureaucracy, with the bureaucracy holding a monopoly of power. The excessive costs of the arms race and the general competition with the United States are not overlooked either, and Huang suggests that such resources would have been better spent on economic construction and the improvement of living standards.

The fifth factor, that of the rapid ideological shift that was required as the Soviet Union underwent perestroika, is one that has received relatively little attention in the West. It is often overlooked in the West that, in fact, the Soviet regime went from declaring profit to be theft to promoting capitalism practically overnight. Huang considers the speed with which this was attempted to be a critical mistake, however, and sees the ideological shift from "left-wing" dogmatism (rigid adherence to the tenets of Marxism-Leninism) to capitalism and freedom of thought to be too much, too soon. Here, a careful reading makes it obvious that Huang sees this as a major factor leading to the loss of legitimacy of the CPSU.

The sixth and final factor, that of Soviet minorities, also relates to the issue of legitimacy. Unlike most scholars in the West, however, Huang thinks the Soviet regime could have effectively dealt with the nationalities question, seemingly through financial means (thus putting him in agreement with Lu and Jiang). While he repeatedly states that the nationalities question was never dealt with "properly," he neglects the issues of autonomy, sovereignty, and culture, and instead seems to argue that, had the Soviet economy functioned better and the minority regions of the Soviet Union been equal recipients of the benefits of that economy, they would have been content to remain a part of the Soviet empire. Of course, such an interpretation is made with the author being very conscious of the facts surrounding China's own nationalities problems and the CCP's current policy of placating the minorities through financial means.

While Huang maintains that these six factors were instrumental in the collapse of the Soviet Union, he argues that there are two main reasons that brought about the collapse: the failure to reform during earlier periods and the ubiquitous corruption in the Soviet system, especially among party leaders. The link connecting these factors with the collapse of the Soviet regime is again legitimacy. Huang seems to argue here that economic prosperity and honest leadership could have saved the Soviet Union. Such an opinion is widely shared in China, and is at least partly based upon the hope that such a strategy will help save China.

Thou Shalt Have No Other Gods

A factor that is conspicuously absent from the Chinese academic literature on the Soviet collapse is the role played by religion and religious institutions. While this factor, along with the role of civil society more generally, has received much attention in the West, Chinese scholars seem to have overlooked its significance.[50] Chinese government officials, however, have not. In fact, the CCP's religious policy is perhaps the policy area where the impact of events in Eastern Europe and the Soviet Union is most clear, with many internal policies and official reports stating explicitly that China must "manage" correctly religious affairs if it is to avoid the sort of collapse that occurred in Eastern Europe and the Soviet Union.

As early as the fall of 1989, the role of "peaceful evolution" was seen as being closely tied to the events occurring in Eastern Europe. A code word in China for a purposeful strategy Western nations use to pressure socialist states to "evolve" (read: collapse), including the use of economic incentives and the promotion of human rights,[51] peaceful evolution was seen by many to be at the center of the collapse of Communism in Eastern Europe and the Soviet Union.[52] In regards to Czechoslovakia and East Germany in particular, the social turmoil in these satellite states was seen as having its roots in the West's peaceful evolution strategy and the "antisocialist activities" of opposition forces and the Roman Catholic Church (which is seen as a key player in peaceful evolution).[53] As Ramet summarizes this line of thought, "the CCP concluded that religious organizations, particularly the Catholic Church, had played a role in destabilizing the communist systems of Eastern Europe, and it was determined to take the necessary steps to prevent the same thing from happening in China."[54]

In an internal document from the Bureau of Religious Affairs of the State Council, entitled "China's Current Religious Question: Once Again an Inquiry into the Five Characteristics of Religion,"[55] Ye Xiaowen examines the disintegrative role religion played in the Communist states of Eastern Europe:

> The disintegration of the Soviet Union and the dramatic change in Eastern Europe resulted from their domestic political and economic failures and the sharpening of social contradictions there, including the failure of their policy toward religion over the long term that resulted in the alienation of religious believers. Religion became a weapon in the hands of the dissidents for inciting the masses and creating political disturbances, thus hastening the collapse of the Soviet and East European communist parties.[56]

Quite in line with the chain of events laid out by Chinese scholars in the literature reviewed above, Ye, head of the Bureau of Religious Affairs, only adds religion to the laundry list of factors that pulled down Communism in Eastern Europe. The role played by religion, according to Ye, was two-pronged. On the one hand, he argues that religious revival is often coupled with conflict and war: "When there is national oppression . . . religion plays the role of a sacred banner under which the nation fights national oppression and serves as an important tie for national unity."[57] Additionally, foreign religious organizations are seen as attempting to infiltrate the Chinese system and bring about a peaceful evolution. As Ye explains, "Today, with the support of the Vatican, the Catholic underground has few followers in China but considerable capabilities. . . . The various departments must coordinate their efforts and fight a prolonged general defensive war against infiltration by hostile foreign religious forces."[58]

It is quite clear that Chinese leaders have learned from the East European example that the church and other civil society actors can play important roles in tearing down Communism. They have done more than identify this as a factor, however—they have also sought to implement policies that they hope will prevent a similar occurrence in China. The impact of the collapse of Communism in Eastern Europe and the Soviet Union has remained overlooked by Western scholars seeking to explain the causes of China's religious policy,[59] which is so often critiqued for its repressive nature. But a review of some internal documents relating to religious policy in China reveals that this is the single most important factor pointed to as justification for the country's over-restrictive religious policy.

According to Luo Shuze in an internal document published under the auspices of the theoretical journal of the CCP (*Qiushi*), China must remain "vigilant against hostile international forces using religion to try to Westernize and divide" the country.[60] As Luo argues, since the 1980s, "one of their strategies for subverting socialist countries has been the cultivation of religious forces in those countries and the use of religion as their tie with the underground political forces." In employing such a strategy, Western forces hope "to divide" China and "to achieve pluralistic political beliefs through pluralistic religious beliefs."[61] In "the name of religion," Western forces "engage in activities designed to divide the nationalities" as they attempt "to achieve the objectives of undermining national unity, subverting the socialist system, and splitting the great motherland."[62]

By their own admission, China's policymakers are pursuing its restrictive religious policy due to their understanding of the role religion played in the collapse of Communism in Eastern Europe and the Soviet Union. The most explicit statement to that effect is by Luo, who argues in the same document:

> We need to learn from the lessons of the disintegration of the Soviet Union and the precipitous changes in Eastern Europe. One of these lessons is the lowering of vigilance against Western infiltration by the use of religion. As a result of the errors of the former socialist countries in the Soviet Union and Eastern Europe in their handling of the religious question, religion became an instrument in the hands of the political dissidents for stirring up trouble when the domestic politics and economy became mired in trouble and all kinds of social contradictions sharpened. That hastened the downfall of the Soviet and East European communist parties.[63]

Such ideas are not limited to general theoretical works; similar ideas can be found in all corners of China in offices responsible for implementing religious policy. An excellent example is a secret memorandum from the Tongxiang Municipal Public Security Bureau which instructs religious affairs bureau offices at the village and township levels about strategies for curbing illegal religious activities.[64] The justification for issuing this memorandum was that "infiltration and subversive activities on the part of outside hostile forces that use religion as a means to Westernize and divide our country have increased." These "outside forces" are "energetically fostering anti-government forces in an attempt to 'gospelize' China, trying vainly to bring about in China the kind of evolution [i.e., peaceful evolution] that is taking place in Eastern Europe and the former

Soviet Union."[65] Such a view on the role of religion in the collapse of Communism helps explain China's policy of excessively controlling and regulating religious activities, especially those of Western churches and missionaries, and provides an excellent example of how the image of the Soviet collapse has affected policy development in a specific area.

Lessons of the Soviet Collapse

Are the ideas of Chinese scholars and policymakers about the Soviet collapse really any different from those that we in the West have identified, and that we reviewed in chapter 3? While many are the same, such as economic stagnation, ethnic nationalism, and the rise of civil society, there is a great difference in the fundamental understanding of how these factors operate. While most Western scholars believe that Communist rule cannot work and that all Communist systems are doomed to failure in the end, Chinese scholars see things differently. Thus, they see the Soviet collapse as the result of leadership failure and bad policy choices, and point to naïve leaders and masses who were too quick to just toss the whole experiment into the dustbin of history. In this sense, they are joined not only by Soviets of an earlier period, but by many contemporary members of post-Soviet societies who have become disillusioned with post-Communism and the transition to democracy and the free market.

The themes that resonate throughout the Chinese literature on the collapse of the USSR focus on the role of the Party and popular support. The CCP needs to transform itself into a ruling party and to take on more autonomy from the central leadership and more legislative initiative.[66] It is also suggested that the Party permit other voices to exist in society, whether in the form of other parties or through a strengthened role for interest groups. They are not suggesting that the Party give up its privileged position as the CPSU did, however, as this is seen quite consistently as perhaps the most direct cause of the Soviet collapse. Perhaps most significantly, there is a consensus that the Party should work to earn the people's support and trust by clamping down on government corruption, abandoning ideological dogmatism, and concentrating on improving living standards of ordinary people. This is seen as especially important regarding the country's ethnic minorities, which must have rights and privileges and be kept satisfied with their existence within the Middle Kingdom.

Lest the picture seem entirely bright, it is clear by reading between the lines that force is not ruled out as a means of quelling dissent, whether in the form of ethnic separatists, student protesters, or the Falun Gong. In addition to the actions of the regime in Beijing, this conclusion can be arrived at by the sharp criticism of Gorbachev's failure to use force consistently in Eastern Europe and in the secessionist republics, which is seen as a critical mistake that led to the Soviet collapse. Gorbachev is the subject of much criticism in China for his "failure" in this regard, as he is in Russia among a sizable segment of the population that regrets the collapse of the Soviet Union. The ethnic dimension to the Soviet collapse thus greatly informs Chinese thinking on reform, and for a culture that places tremendous emphasis on order, to many political leaders and ordinary citizens the violent means of suppressing dissent often employed are justified (or rationalized) by the ends of regime stability.

Lessons from the New Russia

Apart from the lessons of the Soviet collapse, Chinese leaders must have learned other important lessons from the post-Communist period as well. One of the most obvious such lessons they could have learned is that the collapse of the Soviet Union did not bring the kind of peace, prosperity, and stability to Eastern Europe and the former Soviet Union that had been expected. Indeed, while several East European states are making strides toward democracy and economic development, such as the Czech Republic and Hungary, the examples of war-torn Yugoslavia and the festering problem of the trans-Dniestr region provide a more troubling analogy. Of course, China's true counterpart is not Eastern Europe but Russia. Here the war in Chechnya, a decade of economic hardship, and greatly diminished international stature offer no better prospect.

It should come as no surprise that, in light of such facts, Chinese leaders and many common Chinese feel that their choice has been vindicated. While Chinese intellectuals certainly lamented the violent means used to quell the student protestors in June 1989, the events in Eastern Europe and the Soviet Union over the next several years indicated that, had the Chinese Communist regime fallen at that time, things might actually have turned out worse, resulting in economic decline, an increase in corruption, and even civil war. Such ideas permeate the scholarly research in China on post-Soviet Russia.[67]

While most Western scholars would consider the difficulties Russia has faced in its transition to democracy and the free market to be short-term costs that are unavoidably associated with a regime transition, and just part of the price that has to be paid to enjoy the benefits of living in a democracy—even a transitioning one—many Chinese are skeptical. Chinese intellectuals are quick to point out that democracy is often held up as a good above all other values. This point is most clearly articulated by Zhang, who maintains that the West places too much emphasis on democracy and not enough on stability and prosperity, which are equally important.[68]

The themes that are most often expressed in Chinese scholarship of post-Communist Russia deal with the difficulties of the country's economic restructuring, including shock therapy, privatization, and the general economic downturn. An excellent example is an article by Wang Jingcun, in which the author critiques the means used to transform Russia's economy, particularly privatization and shock therapy.[69] Wang argues that privatization was nothing more than the state giving away its property without any real compensation in return, since the prices state property was sold for did not in any way represent their real value.[70] Moreover, Wang suggests that since there were very few domestic funds available for Russians to purchase these assets, the state in essence simply transferred ownership to Western countries. As Wang concludes, the price of these policy choices was not just an economic downturn, but a liquidation of state assets as well.[71]

Shock therapy also comes under attack by Wang, who points specifically to Western advisors such as Jeffrey Sachs who convinced Russian leaders to pursue such a doomed approach.[72] Such an opinion is shared by Su Kaiyi, who also argues that the West "actively pushed" shock therapy, and that it was "this theory which led the Russian leadership to make serious mistakes."[73] Perhaps the most interesting thing about Su's article, however, is his view of the role of peaceful evolution and the intentions of Russian policymakers. As Su argues, "the majority of those who rose to power" in the wake of the Soviet collapse "were prisoners of the Western strategy of peaceful evolution who chose the course of complete Westernization as their development strategy, actively leaning toward the West and clinging to the hope of receiving their recognition and quickly making the transition to the Western world."[74] In the view of Chinese scholars (and many Western scholars as well), this policy failed miserably, and resulted in Russia's economic downturn, the rise of the oligarchs, and the country's weak position in the international system.

The Yeltsin era as a whole is described as an economic downward spiral from which Russia could not escape. As Tan Zhoujian sums up the period, despite eight years of reform, Yeltsin was not "able to get the Russian economy out of crisis. This crisis was no ordinary crisis associated with fluctuations in economic cycles—it is an emergency and a deep and total crisis" encompassing the agricultural, social, economic, and political spheres.[75] Tan compares Russia's economic situation during the Yeltsin period with that of the Soviet Union during the civil war and World War II, and even with the United States during the Great Depression, and finds it worse in terms of the decline in GNP, not to mention Russia's experience with debt and inflation.[76]

For these reasons, the election of Vladmir Putin as president in March 2000 was welcomed by Chinese scholars, who saw Putin as the type of leader who could bring about stability and restore order to Russia.[77] As Wang Chenzai expressed it, Putin was likely to take advantage of "the experiences and lessons of the USSR and the experience of the past 8 years of reform" in order to carry through "domestic and foreign policies that utilize the support of the majority of the population and the fundamental political forces of the country to lead Russia along the path to its rebirth."[78] More concrete analyses of Putin and his policies were offered by Fu Linyun and Zhang Lian in their examination of Putin's electoral victory. The authors expressed satisfaction with the fact that the election took place within the confines of the law, in a peaceful atmosphere, and in one round, and they attributed Putin's victory to his success in appealing to the hearts of the people, who want "to live honestly" and "with pride" once again.[79] Other factors that were said to have contributed to his victory were the support of the Western powers and the advantages he had by being Yeltin's protégé and the acting president. Finally, Putin benefited from the fact that the Russian economic situation had begun to turn around in 2000, registering economic growth for the first time in 10 years.[80] Nevertheless, the authors point out that Putin had nothing to do with the economy's performance and that much remains to be done before the economy truly recovers from the economic crisis caused by shock therapy and privatization.

Given such views on Russia's economic restructuring, it is no surprise that when Chinese scholars compare Russia's transition with that of China, Russia comes up short. As Bao Xifen phrases it, "Chinese reforms have been crowned with colossal successes," while "reforms in Russia have run into difficulties and its wheels are spinning in place."[81] One reason such comparisons find China in the lead is their almost exclusive focus on economic reforms rather than offering a balanced account of both economic and political reforms. While throughout the 1990s Western scholars largely acknowledged Russia's economic difficulties but gave the country credit for the strides it was making in democratic development, Chinese scholars either focused on the economic situation in Russia when they were ostensibly examining political reforms (for instance, they focused on standards of living and the role of the oligarchs rather than freedom of religion or the right to participate in elections), or they viewed political developments in Russia through a Marxist lens. For example, Su argued that the political system that had been put into place after 1991, while being a multiparty system and having separation of powers, was actually that of bourgeois democracy.[82] Bao argued that political reform in Russia has been on the wrong path ever since Gorbachev came to power, and also points out that "in Russia even until today there are people who are trying to restore the USSR and the Soviet political system," a fact seemingly long since forgotten in the West.[83]

Such ideas point to another lesson that Chinese leaders have learned from post-Soviet Russia—that Communist parties and politicians have long-term viability, and that relinquishing power to opposition forces is perhaps not really necessary. It is probably no mere coincidence that Jiang Zemin's 1996 call for research on the failure of Soviet socialism followed the return to power of many Communist parties in Eastern Europe and the Russian Communist Party's strong showing in the December 1995 Duma elections, not to mention party leader Gennady Zyuganov's close race against Yeltsin in the summer of 1996. Several years later, the CPRF continued to show itself to be surprisingly resilient. Its performance in the 1999 Duma elections, where it once again received more votes than any other single party and defeated the "party of power," further supported the idea that Communist parties need not be so quickly relegated to the "dustbin of history."

In fact, some Chinese scholars see the CPRF as a major political player in Russia, pointing to its strong showings at the polls and even the fact that parliamentary leaders such as Seleznev and Kasyanov have been members of the Communist Party. In his analysis of the CPRF and the presidential elections of 1996, Wang Shouze points out that, despite the fact that the CPSU and its general secretary were removed from power, the CPRF steadily moved back into the forefront of politics as the "fashionable" liberal-democratic parties lost appeal and Russian politics appeared to begin to lean left again. As he concluded, "the rebirth of the CPRF is an indisputable fact."[84] Huang even argued that there is movement toward the development of a two-party system in Russia, with the prized positions going to the "party of power" and the CPRF, which is "the biggest and best organized of all political parties" in the country.[85]

Are such ideas far from the mark? While Russia is still a ways away from developing into a two-party system, and it is not a foregone conclusion that the CPRF will ever be able to capture more than a quarter of the Russian electorate, support for the Communist Party in Russia is rather strong and consistent compared to most other parties. As discussed in chapter 4, moreover, support for the CPRF is actually low compared to the segment of the population that regrets the end of Communist rule, with more than 60 percent of Russians saying that, if given the choice, they would prefer to live their life prior to 1991, and 77 percent of Russians saying that they regret the collapse of the Soviet Union. Even regimes like Poland, Lithuania, and Romania, whose Communist revolutions were exported from Moscow, witnessed a resurgence of Communist support in the years following Communism's collapse. All of this suggests to the Chinese that the collapse of Communist Party rule is not inevitable. If Communist parties can retain support in countries where socialism failed and so many mistakes were made, what are the prospects for a Communist China that consistently attains some of the world's highest rates of economic growth?

Finally, it is perhaps Russia's position in the international system that most frightens China's leaders and policymakers. While the Soviet Union stood shoulder to shoulder with the United States throughout the Cold War, today Russia is a mere shadow of its former self, and its international stature has greatly diminished. For example, an author writing under a pseudonym in the pages of *Nanfang Zhoumo* has argued that Russia needs to find its rightful place in international affairs. As a declined superpower, it cannot play the role of a pole in a multipolar world and it should find a proper role to play, with the author suggesting that Russia might find a place in the world as a mediator between other powers.[86]

Chinese perceptions of Russian foreign policy in general range from bad to worse, but perhaps all are in agreement that Russia is a declined superpower that maintains illusions of great power status, a theme similar to that voiced in *Nanfang Zhoumo*. The more optimistic assessments consider that Russia was duped by the West's strategy of peaceful evolution and attempted complete Westernization, including abandoning its ties with its formerly Communist allies and attempting to align itself with the West. Chinese scholars consider this to have been a "fond illusion," for although Russia was promised quite a bit, less has actually arrived, and in the process the country became bogged down in foreign debt. Other Chinese analysts point to the collapse of the Warsaw Pact, NATO expansion, and even the presence of U.S. troops on CIS soil as evidence of the fact that Russia has basically been relegated to the position of a peripheral state in the international system.[87] No matter what the specific interpretation of Russia's current position in international affairs, as a rising regional power that already feels "encroached upon,"[88] the foreign policy implications of a Soviet-style collapse provide Chinese leaders with yet another troubling analogy.

The Impact of the Soviet Past on China's Future

The year 1989 was a critical juncture in the history of Communist regimes, as both China and the Soviet Union were confronted with lethal crises that resulted from their attempts to reform Communism and revitalize their societies. While the Soviet Union shortly imploded in the midst of its attempt to reform itself, the Middle Kingdom seems to have overcome its reform crisis and to have found new sources of stability. As the evidence reviewed in this chapter makes clear, not only have the reform efforts in these Communist giants resulted in different outcomes, the reform processes themselves did not take place in isolation of events in other parts of the world, with there being a high degree of interaction between actors in Eastern Europe, the Soviet Union, and China. This level of interaction provided the opportunity for Chinese leaders (and citizens) to draw lessons from experiences in Eastern Europe and the Soviet Union, and later Russia. A recent report by the U.S.-China Security Review Commission even makes reference to this fact, pointing out that

> Chinese leaders have repeatedly stressed to their Communist Party supporters and the Chinese people that they have no desire to repeat in China the political and economic collapse that took place in the former Soviet Union. They seek to maintain and strengthen the Communist Party's political and social control while permitting freer economic activity. They consistently limit the freedom of the Chinese people to obtain and exchange information, practice their religious faith, to publicly express their convictions, and to join freely organized labor unions.[89]

This factor, however, has been overlooked (or at least under-examined) by Western scholars, among whom the theme of a coming collapse of China has been very popular. While such analyses have been based on the analogy of the Soviet collapse, they are misleading and only half right. The collapse of the Soviet Union is a critically informative event for understanding the future of China, but there is another important fact that remains overlooked—the Chinese can draw analogies, too. In fact, the very same conditions that lead some to unwisely forecast an imminent Soviet-style collapse in China may actually make it *less* likely: for while the flawed understandings of the Soviet collapse may have clouded some Western thinking on Communist transitions, Chinese policymakers are attempting to draw lessons from that experience that may serve to buttress their political power. With such a scenario offering very little to comfort those in positions of power in China, and with the harsh realities of post-

Communist Russia having destroyed the illusion of a prosperous transition to democracy and the free market, it is no wonder that the image of the Soviet collapse became a catalyst that triggered a fundamentally different reform strategy than that pursued by the CPSU, with Chinese policymakers seeking to draw lessons from the Soviet collapse that would help them better navigate the waters of Communist reform.

Why do most China-watchers miss this as a factor when assessing China's future? As suggested in chapter 2, scholars of comparative politics are guided by theories that do not adequately take such variables into consideration. In fact, most comparativists would not even think of asking how events in one country affect events in another, rather being solely interested in comparing the processes and outcomes as if the two events were completely isolated from one another. In the modern world system, in which advanced communication technologies keep all those who wish to be informed up to the minute with developments on significant events across the globe, this is simply not the case. It is also important to recognize that the scholarly practice of viewing events of one order as the same or similar is not limited to outside analysts, but inside actors often employ the same analytical tool. So even though we know that our thinking about the future of China is deeply affected by the collapse of the Soviet Union, we fail to acknowledge that the Chinese themselves may have been affected by the same event—only in this case seeking to prevent a similar outcome.

No more than a few analyses of China's reforms make any mention of the ways in which the collapse of the Soviet Union affected Chinese politics, but if we want to understand the reform strategy of the CCP leadership, we must understand the impact of the Soviet collapse and how policymakers are attempting to draw lessons from that experience that will help them keep their regime in power as they play a balancing act with the forces of modernization and democratization. While there is no guarantee that they will be successful, an understanding of this factor leads to a different view on the future of China, one that includes the very real possibility that policy lessons learned from the Soviet experience may help stave off a regime collapse indefinitely.

China in the early days of the twenty-first century scarcely resembles that of more than a decade ago, nor does it seem to be a country on the brink of collapse. The best explanations for why the Communist regime has been able to stave off collapse, moreover, relate directly to specific policies pursued by the CCP leadership, policies made with a conscious eye on the failure of the Soviet socialist experiment and Russia's problematic transition. While China embarked upon its reform path in the late 1970s and has continually adjusted its policies along the way, one critical juncture that had a profound impact on the course of Chinese reform and fundamentally altered its trajectory was the collapse of the Soviet Union. And while the Soviet collapse continues to shape Western thinking regarding the future of China, it weighs even more heavily upon Chinese reform strategists.

Gao Fang, a senior Chinese scholar of the Soviet Union, argues that "the greatest difference between the reform of the Soviet Union and Eastern Europe is that they failed, which led to the death of the party, the country, and socialism. We have succeeded, which has led to the thriving of the party, the country, and socialism."[90] Unlike in the West, therefore, the failure of Soviet socialism is not seen as predestining the failure of Communist rule in other countries. In fact, it is seen in quite opposite terms. Those in the West waiting for China's coming collapse would therefore be well advised to consider other options, for China is doing its best not to make the sort of mistakes that led to the collapse of the Soviet Union.

Notes

1. "Oppose the Bourgeois Ideology in the Party" (August 12, 1953), as translated in Michael Y. M. Kau and John K. Leung, eds., *The Writings of Mao Zedong, 1949-1976,* vol. 1, *September 1949-December 1955* (Armonk: NY: M. E. Sharpe, 1987), 331.

2. Quoted in John Lichfield, "U.S. Insomniacs Phone the Gorbachev-Yeltsin TV Show," *The Independent* (London), September 7, 1991.

3. Brzezinski, *The Grand Failure.*

4. From "Party Member Criticism Plan," CPC Branch of the Sun Yat-sen University, June 16, 1926. As contained in Deng Maomao, *Deng Xiaoping, My Father* (New York: Basic Books, 1995), 107-108.

5. Quoted in Zhou Shangwen, "Zhong'e jingjin zhuangui chushi tiaojian de bijiao," *Elousi Yanjiu* 2 (2003): 40.

6. Marshall Goldman, "China Rethinks the Soviet Model," *International Security* 5, no. 2 (Fall 1980): 50.

7. Goldman, "China Rethinks the Soviet Model," 59.

8. Such a point is made by Zhou Shangwen in several of his writings from the 1990s. Xu Kui, however, former director of the Institute for Russian, Central Asian, and East European Studies at the Chinese Academy of Social Sciences, argues that in fact Chinese leaders welcomed perestroika and glasnost initially, only changing their opinion of Gorbachev's reforms between 1989-92, at which point they felt they had gone too far. Xu Kui, interview by author, Beijing, PRC, July 14, 2002.

9. As cited in Soled, *China,* 108.

10. Kristof, "China's Hero of Democracy," A10.

11. Author interviews with participants of the May-June 1989 demonstrations; details of interviews withheld to protect identity of participants.

12. Bill Keller, "The Soviets and Chinese Get Down to Business," *New York Times,* May 14, 1989, 1 (Section 4).

13. Keller, "Gorbachev Visits Beijing for Start of Summit Talks," A1.

14. Sheryl Wu Dunn, "150,000 Lift their Voices for Change," *New York Times,* May 16, 1989, A12.

15. Keller, "Soviets and China Resuming Normal Ties After 30 Years," A1.

16. Nicholas Kristof, "Crowds in Street Ask Deng's Ouster," *New York Times,* May 18, 1989, A1.

17. Halpern, "Learning from Abroad," and Jeanne Wilson, "'The Polish Lesson': China and Poland 1980-1990," *Studies in Comparative Communism* 23, nos. 3-4 (Autumn/Winter 1990): 259-268.

18. Tubilewicz, "Chinese Press Coverage of Political and Economic Restructuring of East Central Europe."

19. Tubilewicz, "Chinese Press Coverage of Political and Economic Restructuring of East Central Europe," 932.

20. Tubilewicz, "Chinese Press Coverage of Political and Economic Restructuring of East Central Europe," 933-934.

21. George Bush and Brent Scowcroft, *A World Transformed* (New York: Alfred A. Knopf, 1998), 566.

22. Tubilewicz, "Chinese Press Coverage of Political and Economic Restructuring of East Central Europe," 935.

23. David R. Schweisberg, "China Minister Condemns East Bloc Reform," *United Press International*, December 23, 1989.

24. "Upheaval in the East: China," *New York Times,* December 28, 1989, A1.

25. "Upheaval in the East: China," A1.

26. "The Fall of Ceausescu: Remaining Communist Countries on Defensive," *The Guardian*, December 23, 1989.

27. "Upheaval in the East: China," A1.

28. Benjamin Yang, *Deng: A Political Biography* (Armonk, NY: M. E. Sharpe, 1998), 256-257.

29. Yang, *Deng*, 257.

30. Cited in Yang, *Deng*.

31. Quoted in Lu and Jiang, *Sulian jubian shencengci yuanyin yanjiu*, 3.

32. *Lun dang de jianshe* (Beijing: Zhongyang wenxian chubanshe, 2001), 410.

33. Quoted in *Lun dang de jianshe*, 2.

34. "Hu Jintao sizhong quanhui neibu jianghua."

35. Suisheng Zhao, "Chinese Nationalism and Authoritarianism in the 1990s," in Zhao, *China and Democracy*, 261.

36. Yali Peng, "Democracy and Chinese Political Discourses," *Modern China* 24, no. 4 (October 1998): 437.

37. Peng, "Democracy and Chinese Political Discourses," 437.

38. Peng, "Democracy and Chinese Political Discourses," 438.

39. He Li, "The Role of Think Tanks in Chinese Foreign Policy," *Problems of Post-Communism* 49, no. 2 (March-April 2002): 33-43.

40. In addition to Lu and Jiang, 1999, see Lu Nanquan, Jiang Changbing, Xu Kui, Li Jingjie, *Sulian xingwangshi lun* (Beijing: Renmin chubanshe, 2001); Zuo Fengrong, *Zhiming de cuowu—sulian duiwai zhanlue de yanbian yu yingxiang* (Beijing: Shijie zhishi chubanshe, 2001); Gong Dafei, Xu Kui, Yang Zheng, eds., *Sulian jubian xin tan* (Beijing: Shijie zhishi chubanshe, 1998); Chen Xinming, *Sulian yanbian yu shehuizhuyi gaige* (Beijing: Zhonggong zhongyang dangxiao chubanshe, 2002); and Pu Guoliang, "Lun suweiai tizhi de lishi diwei jiqi shijian jiaoxun," *Dongou Zhongya Yanjiu* 1 (2001): 70-75.

41. A brief sampling of some of the most interesting and rigorous analyses includes: Gao Fang, *Sulian dongou jubian yuanyin yanjiu* (Beijing: Zhongguo renmin daxue chubanshe, 1992); Lu Nanquan, "Sulian jubian de genben yuanin," *Shijie jingji* 9 (1996); Lu and Jiang, *Sulian jubian shencengci yuanyin yanjiu*; Wang Zhengquan, "Sulian kuatai de genben yuanyin," *Eluosi Yanjiu* (December 2001): 5-9; Zhou Shangwen, "Sugong

changqi buneng zuodao sangedaibiao yingchu de jiaoxun," *Eluosi Yanjiu* (December 2001): 10-13; Zuo Fengrong, "Daozhi sugong baiwang de ji ge guanjianxing yinsu," *Eluosi Yanjiu* (December 2001): 28-34; Pan Deli, "Lun sulian jubian de sixiang zhengzhi genyuan," *Dongou Zhongya Yanjiu* 5 (2001): 2-7; Pan Deli, "Sugong xianjingxing de sangshi yu sulian jubian—xuexi 'sangedaibiao' sixiang, dui sulian jubian yuanyin zai renshi," *Dongou Zhongya Yanjiu* 6 (2001): 1-8; Huang Weiting, *Sugong wangdang shinian ji* (Jiangxi: Jiangxi Gaoxiao Chubanshe, 2002).

42. Sixiang lilun bu, *Zhongguo qingnian bao*, "Sulian zhengbian hou zhongguo de xianshi yingdui yu zhanlue xuanze," (September 1991). Reprinted in *Zhongguo zhichun* (January 1992): 35-39.

43. Zhao, "Chinese Nationalism and Authoritarianism in the 1990s."

44. Xu Zhixin, "Lun sulian shibai de jingji genyuan," *Dongou Zhongya Yanjiu* 3 (2001): 1-10.

45. Zhang Shengfa, "Sulian jieti yuanyin zai tan," *Eluosi Yanjiu* (December 2001): 16-27.

46. Zhang, "Sulian jieti yuanyin zai tan."

47. Gao Fang, "Youguan sulian jubian ji ge zhongyao wenti de fenxi," in Lu and Jiang, *Sulian jubian shencengci yuanyin yanjiu*, 151.

48. Ge Linsheng and Hu Yanfen, "Sulian jieti de minzu yinsu," in Lu and Jiang, *Sulian jubian shencengci yuanyin yanjiu,* 195-208.

49. Huang, *Sugong wangdang shinian ji.*

50. Another explanation may be, as raised in discussions with some Chinese scholars, that the nature of this topic is just too sensitive to write about in such an open forum as a journal. Indeed, the lack of written sources in this area may in fact indicate that the topic is taken very seriously by academics and government officials.

51. For Deng Xiaoping's refutation of Western nations using human rights as an excuse to exert pressure on China, see "First Priority Should Always be Given to National Sovereignty and Security," December 1, 1989. Available online at: http://www.humanrights-china.org

52. See, for example, Rui Bian, "Xifan tuixing 'heping yanbian' de zhanlue mubiao," *Banyue Tan* 19 (October 10, 1989): 56-59; and "Xifan tuixing 'heping yanbian' de shoufa," *Banyue Tan* 20 & 21 (October 25 and November 10, 1989): 57-59 and 56-57.

53. Tian Juanbao, "Jiekesiluofake," *Jingri Sulian Dongou* 3 (1990): 17-21.

54. Ramet, *Nihil Obstat*, 40.

55. Ye Xiaowen, "China's Current Religious Question: Once Again an Inquiry into the Five Characteristics of Religion," March 22, 1996. This document is reprinted in *China: State Control of Religion* (New York: Human Rights Watch/Asia, 1997), 116-144.

56. Ye, "China's Current Religious Question," 133.

57. Ye, "China's Current Religious Question," 130.

58. Ye, "China's Current Religious Question," 133.

59. See, for example, Carolyn Evans, "Chinese Law and the International Protection of Religious Freedom," *Journal of Church and State* 44 (Autumn, 2002): 749-774. The partial exception is Lambert, who at least acknowledges that the Soviet collapse affected Chinese thinking on religious policy. Tony Lambert, "The Present Religious Policy of the Chinese Communist Party," *Religion, State & Society* 29 (2001): 121-129.

60. Luo Shuze, "Some Hot Issues in our Work on Religion," *Qiushi* 5 (1996). This document is reprinted in *China: State Control of Religion,* 65-70.

61. Luo, "Some Hot Issues in our Work on Religion," 65.

62. Luo, "Some Hot Issues in our Work on Religion."

63. Luo, "Some Hot Issues in our Work on Religion."

64. United Front Work Department of the Tongxiang Municipal Committee of the Chinese Communist Party, "Opinion Concerning Carrying Out the Special Struggle to Curb Illegal Activities of the Catholic and Protestant Christians According to Law," 1997. This document is reprinted in *China: State Control of Religion*, 71-79.

65. "Opinion Concerning Carrying Out the Special Struggle to Curb Illegal Activities," 73.

66. Huang, *Sugong wangdang shinian ji*, and Pan Guang, "Zhizhengdang de zhidao sixiang guanxi dao guojia de xingwang—cong sulian jieti kan 'sangedaibiao' sixiang de zhongyao yiyi," *Dongou Zhongya Yanjiu* 6 (2001): 9-14.

67. See, among others: Hu Jian, "Eluosi jingji zhuangui moshi de sikao—jianlun zhonge jingji zhaungui de bijiao," *Dongou Zhongya Yanjiu* 2 (2001): 79-84; Lou Fang, "Eluosi: cong jihua dao shichang de jiannan guodu—toushi 21 shiji jingji gaige mubiao," *Dongou Zhongya Yanjiu* 6 (2001): 32-36; Xu Poling, "Zhongdongou yu eluosi jingji zhuanxing shinian: duibi yu jiejian," *Dongou Zhongya Yanjiu* 1 (2001): 22-29; *Analiticheskii Tsentr Gossoveta KNR o Vnutripoliticheskoi Situatsii v Rossii* (Moscow: Institut Dal'nego Vostoka, Rossiiskaya Akademiya Nauk, 2000); *Kitaiskie Politologi o Kharaktere i Rezul'tatakh Perestroiki v Rossii v "Epokhy El'tsina"* (Moscow: Institut Dal'nego Vostoka, Rossiiskaya Akademiya Nauk, 2000); *Otsenki Kitaiskimi Politologami Vnutrennei Situatsii v Rossii v Kanun Parlamentskikh i Prezidentskikh Vyborov* (Moscow: Institut Dal'nego Vostoka, Rossiiskaya Akademiya Nauk, 1999); *Politologi KNR o Sovremennoi Politicheskoi Zhizni Rossii* (Moscow: Institut Dal'nego Vostoka, Rossiiskaya Akademiya Nauk, 1998); Liu Zuxi, ed. *Dongou jubian de genyuan yu jiaoxun* (Beijing: Dongfang chubanshe, 1995). See also *Ekonomicheskie Reformy v Rossii i Kitae Glazami Rossiiskikh i Kitaiskikh Ekonomistov: Sbornik Statei* (St. Petersburg: Sankt-Peterburgskii Gosudarstvennii Universitet, 2000).

68. Zhang Shuhua, "Minzhu de jianxin yu shenhua de pomie," —dui eluosi shinian zhengzhi zhuangui de fenxi yu fansi" *Dongou Zhongya Yanjiu* 4 (2001): 12-19.

69. Wang Jincun, "Osobennosti Rossiiskoi modeli perestroiki ekonomiki i prichiny ee porazheniya," in *Analiticheskii Tsentr Gossoveta KNR o Vnutripoliticheskoi Situatsii v Rossii*, 19-28.

70. Wang, "Osobennosti Rossiiskoi modeli perestroiki ekonomiki i prichiny ee porazheniya," 24.

71. Wang, "Osobennosti Rossiiskoi modeli perestroiki ekonomiki i prichiny ee porazheniya," 25.

72. Wang, "Osobennosti Rossiiskoi modeli perestroiki ekonomiki i prichiny ee porazheniya," 27.

73. Su Kaiyi, *Eluosi Yanjiu* (1999): 44.

74. Su, 45.

75. Tan Zhoujian, "Itogi El'tsinskoi Epokhi i Perspektiby Ekonomicheskogo Ravitiya Rossii," in *Kitaiskie Politologi o Kharaktere i Rezul'tatakh Perestroiki v Rossii v "Epokhu El'tsina,"* 59.

76. Tan, "Itogi El'tsinskoi Epokhi i Perspektiby Ekonomicheskogo Ravitiya Rossii,"

77. See the various articles on Putin's election in *Rossiya: Ot "Epokhi El'tsina" k "Epokhe Putina"* (Moscow: Institut Dal'nego Vostoka, Rossiiskaya Akademiya Nauk, 2000).

78. Wang Chenzai, "Chto Sobiraetsya Delat' Putin," in *Rossiya: Ot "Epokhi El'tsina" k "Epokhe Putina,"* 62.

79. Fu Linyun and Zhang Lian, "Vesennii Grom na Severe: Prezidentskie Vybory v Rossii i Tendentsii ee Politiki. Prezident Putin: Nachalo Novoi Ephoki ili Prodolzhenie Staroi?" in *Rossiya: Ot "Epokhi El'tsina" k "Epokhe Putina,"* 31-37.

80. Fu and Zhang, "Vesennii Grom na Severe," 34.

81. Bao Xifen, "Sravnenie Reform v Kitae i Rossii," in *Kitaiskie Politologi o Kharaktere i Rezul'tatakh Perestroiki v Rossii v "Epokhu El'tsina,"* 29.

82. Su, 44.

83. Bao, "Sravnenie Reform v Kitae i Rossii," 32-33.

84. Wang Shouze, "Guanyu egong de chengsheng he yeliqin de xuanju," *Jingri Dongou Zhongya* 5 (1996): 7-11.

85. Huang Yunshan, "Eluosi zhengzhi shenghuo fazhan wu nian," *Jingri Dongou Zhongya* 1 (1997): 13.

86. Rong Liang, "Elousi de 'Xinzhuang'," *Nanfang Zhoumo*, September 30, 2002.

87. See, for example, Xu Zhixin, "Eluosi duiwai zhengce de jiaoxun," *Dongou Zhongya Yanjiu* 2 (2002): 54-58, and Pei Yuanying, "A Multi-Dimensional View of Russian Diplomatic Strategy," *Foreign Affairs Journal* (Beijing) 65 (September 2002): 55-59.

88. June Teufel Dreyer, "Encroaching on the Middle Kingdom? China's View of its Place in the World," in Marsh and Dreyer, *U.S.-China Relations in the Twentieth-Century*, 85-103.

89. "U.S.-China Security Review Commission Report," reprinted in Ibid., 125.

90. Fang, "You guan sulian jubian ji ge zhongyao wenti de fenxi," 137.

Chapter 6

What Moscow Refuses to Learn from Beijing

We have learned from the Soviet Union in the past, we are still learning today, and we shall learn in the future. Nevertheless our study must be combined with our own concrete conditions. We must say to them: We learn from you, from whom then did you learn? Why cannot we create something of our own?
–Mao Zedong[1]

The Chinese leadership really started reforms, while we were only theorizing, not knowing how to begin. My attitude toward the People's Republic of China changed respectively. One may say, I was converted to a new faith.
–Oleg Troyanovskii, Soviet ambassador to China[2]

MIKHAIL Gorbachev's visit to Beijing in mid-May 1989 was meant to improve Russia's foreign relations with the PRC, but it had profound consequences both for the future of Communist rule in the Soviet Union and for political stability in China. Not only did Gorbachev's presence in the Chinese capital spur on student protests and lead to calls for a "Chinese Gorbachev," the events also left an imprint on Gorbachev himself and forced him to contemplate what the future might hold in store for his perestroika. Gorbachev was not the only one to take the opportunity to reflect on the course of reform in the two Communist giants; journalists and commentators had similar thoughts. As a *New York Times* journalist commented at the time, "experts have long recognized that economic change . . . has progressed a good deal farther in China, while political liberalization . . . is far more advanced in the Soviet Union. Gorbachev's visit here has helped advertise this to the ordinary citizens of each country, and has also raised hopes that each can learn something from the other."[3] While the Chinese did take advantage of this and other opportunities to learn from their Soviet comrades, Gorbachev was very reluctant to consider any aspect of the Chinese experience as applicable to the Soviet situation. Nevertheless, there were some very important lessons to be learned from this experience regarding political stability, economic reform, and the use of force. Some of

China during this time was quite different than that portrayed by Soviet scholarship of it, of course, as China had begun to move away from Maoism already by 1978. China was certainly not experiencing "neo-Maoism" in the 1980s, therefore, as Soviet specialists claimed. Economic reforms were also more successful than they were given credit for, since the Soviets were critiquing the reforms for deviating from Marxist principles as they had come to understand them in the Soviet Union. Of course, the criticism for China's deviation from Marxist principles was correct, but this was understood by Soviet China specialists as a bad thing at that time. In the end, Soviet scholarship on China gave no credit to China and the CCP for the reassessment of Chinese socialism and for relaxing Marxist dogma, significant first steps in the Chinese reform process that could have been effectively adopted by Soviet reformers.

Rozman has argued that, "struggling to find a reform strategy of its own as its economy stagnated and its international position became more isolated, the Soviet Union could have turned to China for lessons on how to proceed. It could have met the challenge of China's revitalization by energetically debating what was happening and how it might prove relevant for initiatives at home."[10] Due to the nature of Soviet scholarship on China during this time, however, this simply was not an option. In the end, "the Soviet Union and then Russia failed to examine China more closely, to understand in a timely fashion the significance of its transformation, and to learn appreciably from its example."[11]

Rozman has also argued that during Gorbachev's "desperate search for perestroika and then a path to marketization, neglect of the Chinese experience seems scarcely comprehensible."[12] In fact, given the content of Soviet scholarship on China, which was anything but positive or optimistic about the potential for successful reform in China, it is quite understandable that Gorbachev did not give serious consideration to pursuing a Chinese model of reform. With his thinking about China as a possible model shaped largely by the slanted scholarship of the government's think tanks and his own preconceptions of the Middle Kingdom, no good lessons on Communist reform seemed available. Indeed, Gorbachev's position on this topic has not changed over the years, as he continues to argue that the Chinese model was not applicable. As his friend and colleague Zdenek Mlynar put it when discussing the issue with Gorbachev recently, "I don't think that China has found a solution that could have served as a model for you back then."[13] Gorbachev's own comments on the issue are perhaps more telling: "The reforms in China, incidentally, have been going on since 1974, and their most difficult problems still remain unsolved."[14] In another exchange between the two friends, the two agreed that it is still not clear whether or not "China will end up the same way as the USSR."[15]

Despite the misinformation on China coming out of the country's think tanks, Gorbachev had other sources of information. Most significantly was from Oleg Troyanovskii, his ambassador to China. Troyanovskii, who spent considerable effort researching China's reforms, experienced a "conversion of faith" to the Chinese model after a few years. As he wrote in his memoirs, "the Chinese leadership really started reforms, while we were only theorizing, not knowing how to begin. My attitude toward the People's Republic of China changed respectively. One may say, I was converted to a new faith."[16] This conversion, however, had no effect on Gorbachev himself.

Others in the Soviet Union had raised the Chinese model as an example. For example, Fedor Burlatskii, an adviser to Gorbachev, gave a praiseful commentary on China in *Literaturnaya Gazeta* in June 1986.[17] To intellectuals such as Burlatskii, China seemed like a more applicable model. Rather than attempting to emulate certain aspects of the Soviet Union's chief rival, i.e., the United States, why not turn to its Communist comrade, China? After all, in the decade since Mao's death China had experienced renewed dynamism and had seen substantial economic growth, while the Communist Party elite had retained control of the organs of the state. Gorbachev wanted more sweeping change, however, and he was critical of the Chinese model for only providing economic liberalization while retaining political repression. Gorbachev was convinced that the USSR needed to go further and to carry through a complete restructuring of society.

Gorbachev still showed respect for Chinese reforms. During his visit to Vladivostok in the Russian Far East in July 1986, Gorbachev praised:

[The] Soviet people regard with understanding and respect the aim put forward by the CCP of modernising the country and building in the long term a socialist society worthy of a great people. As far as one can judge, our priorities and those of China are similar: the acceleration of socioeconomic development. Why not support one another and cooperate in realising our plans, where this is evidently to the benefit of both? The better our relations are, the more we can exchange experience with one another.[18]

Gorbachev was not interested in exchanging experience with China, however, at least not by copying Chinese-style reforms. It does seem that he did draw a negative example from China's reform efforts during this time, as he saw the CCP's failure to embark upon political liberalization as a serious mistake. Beginning in 1987, he began to argue that economic reform required simultaneous political reform to be successful. Indeed, Gorbachev still remains convinced of this, recently stating: "Now, with a certain distance from those events, I of course see many things differently, but in my fundamental positions nothing has changed: I would do it all over, and I would begin again with the struggle for 'more democracy, more socialism'."[19]

One might respond to Gorbachev by pointing out that the same path would invariably lead to the same destination—regime collapse. Gorbachev does not see democratic reform as the problem, however:

The reason for the failure of the reforms is not that we took the path of democratic change. The reasons lay elsewhere, in the vindictiveness of the reactionary forces and the excessive revolutionism of the radicals. It is true that there was not always sufficient logic in our actions, but as far as the basic choice is concerned, in my opinion, there simply was no other way.[20]

Was it not possible to pursue democratic reforms more gradually, or perhaps in a different fashion? Might there have been a route to democracy that did not entail the traumas of a regime and systemic collapse? Perhaps Gorbachev now sees that all Communist regimes are doomed to collapse, and that there is no other way to reform such a system. This is what his comment regarding the Chinese path seems to suggest: "You can object that in China they are taking a different path. But I do not think that the reforms in China are being carried out taking the specific conditions of the country into account. Only the future will show to what extent they prove effective."[21]

The fact that Gorbachev flouted the Chinese experience in developing his reform agenda does not mean that he was not the kind of leader who would learn from abroad. In fact, he was very interested in emulation—but from the West or Hungary,[22] not from China. As Gorbachev himself said during a visit to Hungary in June 1986, the Soviet leadership was following developments there with "attention and respect," and it felt free "to borrow whatever is useful, whatever is suitable for our country" from the Hungarians and other allies.[23] In this case, Colton correctly points out that Hungary certainly was not a useful model, since decentralization "would be much harder to achieve and control in a country of 280 million people (to Hungary's 10 million), sprawled over eleven time zones and with economic priorities that include provisioning and arming a huge military establishment."[24] More than a decade of democratic reform in Russia illustrates that emulating Western democracy and capitalism is perhaps even more difficult.

The first opportunity Gorbachev had as leader to draw lessons from China was thus upon his initial pursuit of reform. As he began formulating his perestroika agenda, China had already been reforming for 8-10 years. While Gorbachev only drew negative lessons from the Chinese experience, this does not mean, in the final analysis, that Chinese reforms were not applicable to the Soviet situation, only that, given the information available to him and his value premises, he concluded that they were.

The Impact of Tiananmen

The second opportunity Gorbachev had to draw lessons from China's reform experience was during his visit to China in May 1989, at the height of the Tiananmen Square demonstrations. Gorbachev had a front-row view on the events in China, as he arrived in Beijing to sign an accord of friendship with the PRC just as the Tiananmen student protests were underway. Witnessing the student demonstrations at their height left Gorbachev keenly aware of the problems that can arise when the speed of reform does not keep pace with the expectations of the people. As he remarked to his Chinese hosts, "we also have hotheads who, in most cases, favor the renewal of socialism, but who are more intent on that renewal than on the leadership of the party which began the policy. They want it all done in one night. This is not the way it happens in life. This happens only in fairytales."[25] Other political leaders had similar impressions: "This shows what can happen if a government does not keep up with its people," remarked a member of Gorbachev's entourage (which included such leading figures as Eduard Shevarnadze and Aleksandr Yakovlev). Referring to conservatives in the Soviet leadership who favored slowing down reforms at that point, he added, "I wish they could see it."[26]

Despite the Chinese leadership's best efforts at shielding Gorbachev from the student protests, the events were just too large to avoid. While they were able to have him land at a different airport than originally planned, the driver that brought Gorbachev to downtown Beijing made a mistake and actually brought him right in front of Tiananmen Gate, where Gorbachev gained a full view of the protests. Gorbachev also had great interest in the events in China, and he kept himself well informed of what was going on. He even called a special meeting, which lasted two hours, with senior Soviet journalists and diplomats at the Soviet embassy who briefed him and answered his questions about what was going on. As *New York Times* reporter Bill Keller described it, "drinking tea with the journalists until midnight, Mr. Gorbachev heard a detailed account of the student demonstrations, including the assessment of some Soviet journalists that the protests were a major force that would ultimately push the Chinese government to liberalize its policies."[27]

Gorbachev's meeting with Chinese journalists on May 17 sheds light on what he was thinking at the time. One hard-hitting and persistent Chinese journalist asked Gorbachev, "You mentioned during the meeting with Chinese leaders that China and the Soviet Union can learn a great deal from each other. When you look at Beijing today and see hundreds of thousands of people carrying banners, including some against Deng Xiaoping, what experience for the Soviet Union can you derive from this?" The Soviet leader was very diplomatic in his response, answering "I would not assume the role of judge and would not try to give marks to everything that is happening in China today. . . . I wish only that solutions will be found that will continue the successful movement of China and the Chinese people along the path on which they have embarked."[28] Gorbachev's persistent interlocutor did not back down, however, retorting "I wasn't completely satisfied with your answer. . . . What do you think: Will we see the same painful events here in the Soviet Union?" After attempting to skirt the issue yet again, Gorbachev finally replied,

> these are profound processes, they cannot take place easily . . . they sometimes become painful, but in the end they will bring us to a new stage of development, will give socialism a second wind. In any case, we have embarked on a path of profound revolutionary transformations and will proceed along this path confidently and firmly. If anyone thinks that this road will lead us to the dustbin of history, I think he will be deeply disappointed.[29]

Such statements make it clear that, at the time, Gorbachev did not foresee something like this happening in the USSR, and he certainly did not see the complete regime collapse that would come in under three years. His audience did not let Gorbachev off the hook, however, and continued by asking him how he would react if similar events were to take place in Moscow. Gorbachev's response was prophetic: "In the Soviet Union, when problems of this or a similar nature arise, we will examine them concretely and find political methods of solving them, so that problems that arise within the framework of the political process will be solved on the basis of democracy and glasnost, preserving the basic values to which we have sworn allegiance."[30] Little did he know that similar events were about to unfold before his eyes back in the Soviet Union, and that he would find it difficult to proceed in a manner consistent with the values of democracy and openness he had so firmly expressed.

Gorbachev returned to Moscow before the actual crackdown occurred on June 3-4, but once news of the tragedy broke and received worldwide attention, he was forced to face the issue once again. At the outset, Gorbachev tried to retain his nonjudgmental position, and refrained from condemning the events outright. In fact, in the first official Soviet reaction to the events, a declaration by the Congress of People's Deputies on June 7, it was unclear who had used weapons and who had fired first. As Lukin points out, the declaration stressed that it was not the time for "hasty conclusions," that the event was an "internal affair," and expressed the hope that the "friendly Chinese people" could "turn this tragic page of their history as quickly as possible."[31] Gorbachev hastily pushed this document through the parliament, and deputies were so upset when they began to learn what had really happened in China and how they had been duped into passing such a declaration that they began to take matters into their own hands.

While Gorbachev was clearly attempting to go against his earlier position of respect for democracy and glasnost in order to promote his foreign policy agenda of closer relations with China,[32] in this case democracy and glasnost backfired. Other political figures and the new democratically-elected parliament were less willing to go along with Gorbachev's plans, and they even rallied against the Soviet government for its failure to condemn the events in China. The fact that the Soviet media was also more free and that people were less afraid to go against the regime also worked against Gorbachev. As part of glasnost and demokratizatsiya, the debates on the floor of the parliament were broadcast live on television, allowing the Soviet public to watch reformist legislators and opposition leaders speak out vehemently against the events in China and demand that the Soviet government take decisive action against Beijing.[33] The media then began to broadcast information on what had really happened in China and to cover the rallies that were being staged in Moscow in support of the protestors in China. In such a way, the events in China took center stage in the Soviet Union, affecting not only political leaders who had recently visited China, but all segments of Soviet society, from parliamentary deputies to ordinary Soviet citizens.

As Lukin points out, reforms "in China are invariably compared in the USSR to the reforms of perestroika," which led directly to the Tiananmen events being taken very seriously in the Soviet Union, because this event became "directly linked in the mind of the public to the brutal clamp-down in Tbilisi which happened only weeks before . . . and was seen as an indicator of the possibility that perestroika in the USSR could be discontinued."[34] A good example of such an analogy is offered by the editor of *Moskovskie Novosti*, A. Vlasov, who argued in an editorial on June 11 that the path to change,

> must not be a bloody one. The tragic events in Tbilisi have convinced us of that. They happened at the time when the conflict in China that culminated in the massacre on the morning of June 4 was only just beginning. We found enough courage to give an honest account of the events in Georgia in order that no such thing should happen again. So why should we pretend to be indifferent watching how the disaster, which is similar to ours, only on a much greater scale, is moving to our good neighbor's house?[35]

Deputies in the parliament also drew their own lessons from the events in China. One outspoken deputy was the dissident scientist Andrei Sakharov, who made a speech on the floor of the parliament in which he said "The hand of frightened reactionary forces is the same everywhere: be it Minsk, Vilnius, Yerevan, Tbilisi, or in Chinese cities."[36] When the initial discussion turned to the issue of the events in China, however, Gorbachev had Sakharov's microphone switched off, so the above statement and others like it never made it into the official record, nor were they broadcast over the airwaves. Sakharov's statement was quickly made public, however, and was read at a public rally. The following passage summarized the feelings of many Russians at the time: "Peaceful popular actions in Beijing, Shanghai, Harbin, Nanjing, Chengdu and other cities in the country took place under slogans calling for deepening reforms, combating corruption, greater democratization, freedom of speech and assembly. We, citizens of the country which has launched perestroika, fully appreciate these slogans."[37]

While Gorbachev had told his Chinese hosts that if "problems of this or a similar nature arise" they "will be solved on the basis of democracy and glasnost," in his first trial he immediately resorted to old Soviet methods in an attempt to contain the situation. It was too late, however, for democracy had progressed too far and it would not be possible to keep things under wrap without resorting to repression and possibly even coercive force. In the end, Gorbachev acquiesced and changed his position on the events in China. On August 1, at the opening session of the Supreme Soviet, Gorbachev gave his last official speech on the Tiananmen tragedy, remarking, "we deplore the turn of events" in China. "We are in favor of the most acute problems being solved through political dialogue between the authorities and the people. That is our belief. Such is the method we have chosen for ourselves. But a people solves its own problems on its own. This is our principled and, I believe, irreversible position."[38]

Learning to Use Force

Although the fallout from the Tiananmen tragedy was over by late summer, Gorbachev's real challenge was only just beginning. While things were settling down in Moscow, unrest was stirring in the satellite states of Eastern Europe. Very quickly Gorbachev would have to apply the lessons he had learned from Tiananmen, first in dealing with independence movements in Eastern Europe, and shortly thereafter in dealing with secessionist-minded republics, a process that only ended with the collapse of the Union itself in December 1991.

On the very same day that the crackdown occurred in China, parliamentary elections were held in Poland, with the opposition party Solidarity garnering 99 percent of the seats they contested. In fact, De Nevers argues that the coincidence of the timing "may have given the Polish leadership additional incentive to make its support for the election results clear."[39] As Timothy Garton Ash reported the events, "In Warsaw, we watched the first pictures from Tiananmen Square while waiting for the election results. 'Tiananmen' was a word that I would hear muttered many times in Central and East European capitals over the next few months."[40] The events in China thus had a wide-ranging impact on Eastern Europe, providing lessons to struggling regimes, opposition forces, and even common citizens.

In places like East Germany, Czechoslovakia, and Romania, Communist leaders viewed the Tiananmen crackdown as a legitimate use of force, and variously called the event an "internal affair" or a legitimate move to curtail "counterrevolutionary" forces. Some even later referred to the use of force to put down similar protests in Eastern Europe as the "Chinese solution."[41] Egon Krenz, East German politburo member and head of internal affairs, even sent a message of support to Chinese Communist leaders on June 4,[42] while Romanian Communist leader Nicolae Ceausescu sent a similar letter, expressing his wish that China, "under the leadership of the CCP," should "overcome the current difficulties caused by the actions of the counter-revolutionary elements."[43] Finally, Communist party newspapers in Czechoslovakia and East Germany both published articles defending the CCP's actions regarding the events in Tiananmen Square.[44] Meanwhile, however, protests in support of the student demonstrators sprung up as well, such as the one held in Prague immediately following the crackdown.[45]

While political actors in Eastern Europe were affected by the events in China, the question we have to address here is whether or not Gorbachev's own thinking about the revolutions in Eastern Europe was affected by his experience with the events in China and his perception of their value and utility. Based on the available evidence, it is not possible to answer such a question conclusively, so one can only speculate as to the lessons he could have drawn from that experience while addressing similar issues in the satellite states. It is very possible, however, that Gorbachev's refusal to use force to stem the tide of reform in Eastern Europe has its roots in China. After all, Gorbachev could have calculated that, if Soviet citizens were so enraged by his refusal to condemn the events in Tiananmen, how would they react if he were to resort to a "Chinese solution" himself?

While only Gorbachev knows the answer to this question, the fact is that Soviet forces were used to put down protests in the Soviet Union after the Tiananmen events had happened. The first occasion was on January 19-20, 1990, when Soviet forces were used to "uphold Soviet power" in Baku, Azerbaijan, where ethnic conflict had been erupting between Armenians and Azerbaijanis. In what was labeled by the Kremlin a "humanitarian effort to save Armenians," Soviet forces ran through the streets of Baku firing indiscriminately, leaving around two hundred dead and several hundred wounded.[46]

One year later, on January 13, 1991, Soviet forces were used once again to quell revolution in the republics, this time with tanks rolling the streets and Soviet paratroopers dropping into downtown Vilnius, Lithuania, resulting in the death of fourteen people. This "bloody Sunday" was precipitated by increasingly vociferous calls for Lithuanian independence.[47] While the Lithuanian Supreme Council had declared independence on March 11, 1990, this had only resulted in an economic embargo against Lithuania, which Moscow later lifted once Lithuanian leaders agreed to suspend its declaration of independence. In the final days of 1990, however, and into the beginning of the new year, the situation in Lithuania became increasingly unstable, and by January 11, the first blood was spilled as Soviet troops took control of individual buildings in Vilnius, including a press building and a police academy.[48] Then on January 13, taking advantage of the West's engagement in the Persian Gulf, Soviet forces attempted to reestablish control of the rebel republic.

While Gorbachev has denied giving the order to use force, assigning blame to the commanding officer of Soviet forces in Lithuania, it is highly unlikely that he was not involved in the decision to use force. Was he willing to resort to a "Chinese solution" to hold the country together? By this point, Gorbachev realized that if Lithuania were to leave the Union, other Soviet republics would follow suit, as indeed they did, with the other Baltic republics almost simultaneously driving toward independence, followed in quick succession by the Caucasian republics and Ukraine.

Despite the abhorrent nature of the crackdown in Vilnius, the fact is that it remained limited in scope and did not involve the level of force necessary to keep Lithuania in the Union. But why was force used on such a small scale? Was a renegade Soviet commander really responsible for the tragedy, and it was brought to an end by Gorbachev before it had time to escalate (again, that Gorbachev was not involved in the decision to use force is unlikely)? Or, did Gorbachev call it off once the crackdown received international attention and became the subject of global outrage? Or, was Gorbachev himself not able to endure the whole affair, and found himself in the same position as his Chinese comrades only two years earlier? Of course, no single factor determines a specific course of action. A combination of these and other factors thus must have been at work in Gorbachev's decision calculus, but the tragic events in Tiananmen must certainly have weighed heavily on his mind.

The last attempt to hold the Union together by force was during the August 1991 coup, the failure of which signaled the end of the Soviet Union. While the coup was carried through by Communist leaders appointed by Gorbachev, Gorbachev himself did not go along with their plans. The coup plotters had hoped that they could convince Gorbachev to sit by quietly while they carried out the "dirty business" themselves and reestablished control of the spiraling Soviet Union.[49] While he refused to go along with their plans, he was powerless to do anything to stop them. Gorbachev was facing the event that he had told his Chinese interlocutors that he would never face.

Once again, democracy had spread too far for anyone to hold back the tide, for Muscovites and other citizens had learned lessons from these events, too. As James Billington, U.S. Librarian of Congress and an eyewitness to the coup attempt, reports, "the defenders rallied to the White House in response not to anyone's articulated appeal or program, but to remembered televised images of the recent past: of Lithuanians forming a human wall to defend their government building, and of that lone figure in Tiananmen Square who turned away a tank."[50] In facing off against the coup plotters, therefore, the citizens of Moscow were fighting to prevent a replay of the events in Vilnius, Baku, and Tiananmen. They were also joined in their efforts by political and military leaders who did not wish to see a repeat of such events in the Soviet capital. In particular, Eduard Shevardnadze and Aleksandr Yakovlev, who had accompanied Gorbachev on his visit to Beijing in May 1989, had risked their own lives by joining Boris Yeltsin in the Russian White House, which the coup plotters were preparing to take by force.[51]

Once the coup was put down and Gorbachev had regained control, the Soviet regime would not use force again in an attempt to hold the Union together, a fact which contributed greatly to the actual collapse of the USSR within a few months. As Gorbachev and others faced the events that unfolded in the Soviet Union and Eastern Europe from the time of the Tiananmen protests to the collapse of the USSR in December 1991, China's experience must have figured in their calculations about available options and the potential outcomes of certain courses of action. No matter whether positive or negative lessons were drawn, the image of the Tiananmen tragedy loomed large in the minds of all in the Soviet world. Tiananmen, therefore, was an important factor in the collapse of the Soviet Union, for as Tucker points out, "the Chinese democracy movement helped to create an environment in which citizens of other communist countries dared to aspire to a new political order." [52] The fact that "the Chinese themselves succumbed to a brutally repressive regime did not stem the tide elsewhere,"[53] and in fact indirectly contributed to the collapse of Communist rule in other parts of the world.

Just what lessons Gorbachev drew from China's experience with crisis we cannot be sure, but the fact is that when confronted with similar circumstances, first in Eastern Europe and then in the Soviet Union itself, he reacted differently. Although force was used in Baku and Vilnius, it was under different circumstances and on a much smaller scale. And in the final analysis, Gorbachev packed up his office and went home rather than resorting to the level of force that would have been required to hold the Union together.

The Domino that Didn't Fall

As the Soviet Union was coming down, Russian leaders took notice of the fact that China was still standing and seemed to be moving past the crisis that had only recently shook the Middle Kingdom. In fact, in December 1991, in the USSR's final days, a group of Russian parliamentarians paid an official visit to China. Vladimir Lukin, who served as chairman of the parliament's Committee on International Affairs and Foreign-Economic Ties and who headed the delegation, praised China for the success of its economic reforms, observing that they "accomplished one of the greatest achievements in the history of mankind: doubling the wealth of a people of more than 1 billion in 10 years' time!" He also opined that, "We may be progressive in understanding the need for modern-day political structures, but are we really progressive when it comes to creating a normal life for people?"[54]

After the collapse of the Soviet Union, it seemed that Gorbachev's policy of simultaneous reform which had resulted in the disintegration of the country was perhaps not the best model of reform, as China was still standing while the USSR had found its way into the "dustbin of history." Indeed, this fact was not missed by the leader of post-Soviet Russia, Boris Yeltsin. Just one year after the collapse of the Soviet Union, speaking in Beijing, Yeltsin said that "Russia is interested in the Chinese experience of reform," noting that "we can take something to enrich our reforms. In principle, the general thrust of the Chinese model could be accepted."[55] In speculating about what just such a model might entail, Yeltsin said that the Chinese tactic of reform is "not to hurry, not to force, and without revolutions," adding that this is "very important . . . and for us, it has significance." He also said that, "to a large extent I have changed my opinion of this country."[56] It took the collapse of the Soviet Union itself, however, for Moscow to pay attention to the drastic transformation underway in the Middle Kingdom.

Unfortunately, perhaps the opportunity to learn from China's reforms had already passed by that time. The situation was accurately summed up by Mikhail Bely, head of the Department of Asia and the Pacific of the Ministry of Foreign Affairs, who on the eve of Yeltsin's December 1992 visit to Beijing commented that,

> Certain democratic circles cannot accept China because of its communist regime, on the other hand there are circles which consider that we should learn from the Chinese example and develop reforms along the model suggested by China. I think that the experience of reforms in China really has certain points which we can make good use of. But the road chosen by China . . . attempts to find ways to reform the command and administrative system through evolution,

which is a unique experience. We have entered another road, and it would be absurd to go back and follow the Chinese way.[57]

Bely is correct in his assessment, for once the Soviet Union had collapsed, China's model of gradual economic reform and slow political liberalization was no longer an option, not even if they were to resort to force. Once the reform program was launched, there was just no way to turn back the clock. Indeed, as Yegor Gaidar, an economist by training and Yeltsin's first prime minister, argued, Poland and other East European transition states became the only applicable examples. As he later recalled, "We watched everything that was taking place in Eastern Europe very attentively and in detail and with a great interest. It was understood that it had a most direct relation to what could happen in the Soviet Union, an alternative to the [options] we might have. Especially in Poland . . . we thought that Poland was the most important for us as a source of lessons, experience, and assessments of possible alternatives."[58]

Gaidar's attempt to follow the Polish model of rapid transformation led the Yeltsin administration to pursue "shock therapy," a program that sounds about as appealing as the medical treatment, but which is perhaps less effective. In fact, Poland had, in turn, modeled its shock therapy program after that of Bolivia, and had even enlisted the assistance of economist Jeffrey Sachs, the program's mastermind. While Bolivia might have been a useful model for Poland, shock therapy was disastrous in a country as large and with such a diversified economy as Russia.[59] Within a few years, popular support for such radical measures began to wane. Indeed, this is one of the primary purposes of shock therapy, to implement sweeping reforms rapidly before popular support dies off, since people are willing to put up with hardship over the short term, but not for an extended period of time. Likewise, once support for shock therapy diminished in Russia, the Yeltsin administration began to pursue more gradual reforms.

Perhaps Yeltsin still felt certain aspects of the Chinese experience were useful. Information on the October Events of 1993 that has been recently brought to light indicates that Yeltsin's battle against "communist hardliners and rightwingers" was in fact nothing more than a crackdown against his political opponents.[60] It turns out that the armed protestors who made their way to the Ostankino television tower were actually accompanied by a column of armored vehicles loyal to Yeltsin, and that the "attackers" had less than two dozen weapons among them, while the tower was protected by 450 heavily armed policemen. The fact that the attack against Ostankino was used by Yeltsin to justify the use of force to "restore order" (read: suppress his opposition), and then to introduce a new constitution and political system, leads one to wonder whether or not he was resorting to a Chinese solution of his own.

With Yeltsin's resignation on New Year's Eve 1999, power passed to Vladimir Putin. Upon his assumption of the presidency, Putin has not shown any interest in pursuing Western-style reforms, instead focusing primarily on restoring order and stability, objectives dear to the hearts of Chinese leaders. While

Putin does think that China is an "interesting model," he is not a very outspoken advocate of Chinese-type reforms.[61] According to Irina Khakamada, a leader in the center-right Union of Right Forces and a 2004 Russian presidential candidate, Putin and his advisers have been studying the "Chinese variant," and while they note that China is not a democracy, they are impressed by its stable government and its success in attracting international capital from major institutional investors.[62] Putin also seems to believe that openness is a prerequisite of successful reform, however. Speaking at Peking University in December 2002, Putin told his audience that reforms to accelerate the economy are good, but that they must be carried "out with maximum openness," so that "even insignificant miscalculations and mistakes can be understood."[63]

Putin's economic advisor, Andrei Illarionov, is more outspoken about his views on the success of China's economic reforms. A longtime critic of Gaidar's reforms, Illarionov has argued that China's reforms have not been gradualist, but liberal, with the "government burden on the economy" decreasing more quickly and to a greater degree in China than in Russia.[64] An admirer of China's reforms who is also a liberal, Illarionov concludes that the "Chinese reform experience shows that only the utmost liberal economic policy can stop Russia's increasing lag behind its neighbors and other countries of the world."[65]

Illarionov's opinion is not widely shared by Russian liberals. For example, Yabloko party leader Gregory Yavlinskii has argued that the Chinese experience is not applicable to Russia, and that the country remains in trouble.[66] Boris Nemtsov, who is currently leader of Union of Right Forces but who at the time was deputy prime minister, remarked on an official visit to China in 1997, "To me, Chinese Communists look more like Gaidar than Zyuganov."[67]

While liberal in name only, the LDPR is not surprisingly positively predisposed to the Chinese reform experience. Aleksei Mitrofanov, a leading figure in the party and its chief foreign affairs expert, believes that China's economic success proves the limits of a purely market-based economy. While market economies are quite successful at providing consumer goods and meeting popular demand for products, he argues, they are less effective at establishing a "harmonious" balance between domestic consumption and a state's strategic resources. Mitrofanov is thus a proponent of a mixed system, one that integrates centralized planning with aspects of a free market, similar to the Chinese model.[68]

The success of China's transformation has perhaps no greater admirers in Russia than the Communist Party and other splinter Communist groups. The CPRF has been one of the biggest critics of Russia's attempt to transform itself overnight, seemingly with little or no attention paid to the methods used or how just the outcome might be. Not surprisingly, many in the CPRF view China in a positive light. They point to the fact that China, which is still Communist, receives more American and Western investment than Russia, which attempted to emulate the West. Contrary to the opinion of the CPSU in the 1980s, today's CPRF believes that Deng's reforms are in line with Leninist thinking, particularly the NEP. They also consider Deng a great leader and attribute most of

China's success to him and his policies.[69] Finally, in the words of Oleg Rakhmanin, a former Communist who maintains close ties with party organs, Russian Communists can take great pride in the fact that "in the East, a great socialist state led by a 57-million-strong army of Chinese Communists is rising in all its magnitude."[70] To the CPRF and its supporters, therefore, socialism as a system is not ready for the dustbin of history, but can adapt and evolve with the changing times.

On the eve of the 2003 Russian parliamentary elections, 10 years after the first post-Soviet elections, CPRF leader Gennady Zyuganov debated the applicability of China's reforms to Russia with Yabloko leader Gregory Yavlinskii, with Zyuganov posing the question, "Why does China get $77 billion in investment and why is there none for 'democratic' Russia?"[71] The Communist Party leader continued by arguing that Russia should attempt to "emulate the Chinese example" and to restore a strong state that would be capable of fostering economic growth and rehabilitating the country's crumbling infrastructure. Yavlinskii vigorously contested Zyuganov's assessment and declared that "China is not an example for us," since China's economic success "cannot be emulated by Russia, since it relies both on exploitation of the domestic labor force and the existence of an overseas Chinese community that provides a great deal of the investments for the mainland."[72] Instead, Yavlinskii argued, Russia must focus its efforts on rejoining Europe and "complete its own internal transformation [and] to adopt European values and principles."

Learning from Your Comrade's Success

As Lukin points out, for "most Russian observers, the positive outcome of economic reforms in China is set against the background of the deepening Russian crisis. As a result, one can hardly find an outright rejection of the Chinese experience."[73] This is particularly true for Russia's China scholars, whose work on social, political, and economic change in China highlights the many parallels between the reform of the Soviet/Russian and Chinese systems while emphasizing the drastically different outcomes.[74] Opinions do vary, however, and while most scholars are in agreement over the success of China's transformation, they disagree over the issue of whether or not this experience was applicable to the Soviet Union and/or is applicable to Russia today. Many scholars have concluded that aspects of the Chinese reform model are applicable to Russia's transition, although their voices have largely gone unnoticed by the policymaking community and the general public.

In the late 1980s, as mentioned above, several scholars and intellectuals called for the Soviet Union to learn from China's experience with reform, but to no avail. Following the Soviet collapse, however, such calls became even loader and began to emanate from many of the country's universities and think tanks. The institute that has played the leading role in this regard has been the Institute of the Far East, the very same institution which during the Soviet era was the most outspoken critic of China, chiding its Communist comrade for its "capitalist and imperialist ways."

Since the early 1990s, the IDV has organized a broad range of activities, which Lukin points out, have been "aimed at the popularization of the Chinese economic reforms in Russia and at showing the advantages of the Chinese way compared to that chosen by the Russian authorities."[75] The institute's strategy focuses on holding seminars and conferences and publishing activities. In addition to holding an annual conference on China, the IDV also sponsors seminars and symposia with Russian and Chinese politicians, officials, and scholars, with the themes often focusing explicitly on the success of China's economic reforms. For example, the theme of the 2003 annual conference was the "Chances and Challenges of Globalization," and the introductory remarks of Mikhail Titarenko, the director of the institute, paid homage to China's success in integrating itself into the world economy without becoming a pawn of the West. Titarenko also observed that Russia can learn three things from China's experience with globalization: that the process must be humane, that it is irresistible, and that, if done properly, the results can be very positive.[76]

It is the institute's publishing efforts, however, that are probably the most active and influential. The orientation of IDV's journal, *Problemy Dal'nego Vostoka*, is now positive in regards to China and even South Korea, and is the primary outlet for research on Chinese reforms. The institute's series *Express-Information* is also an important publishing initiative which seeks to disseminate in Russian the work of primarily Chinese scholars. The institute also translates and publishes book-length works, such as *The China Miracle: Development Strategy and Economic Reform*, a work which makes several explicit references to the superiority of the Chinese model of reform over that attempted in Eastern Europe and the former Soviet Union.[77] Of course, the institute also publishes original monographs, and these also tend to view China's reforms in a largely positive light. Finally, in addition to their regular publishing activities, IDV also sends policy briefings and reports to various government agencies in an attempt to effect policy.

Mikhail Titarenko is not only the director of IDV, he is also an active researcher and one of the most outspoken proponents of a Chinese model. Most of the documents and reports issued by the institute are published under his name, in following with the general Soviet practice, but many are largely the result of collaborative work and research teams. One report of this type, published in 1997 under the title *Kitaiskie Reformy: Primer, Vyzov, ili Ugroza Rossii?* (Chinese Reforms: An Example, a Challenge, or a Threat to Russia?), expresses very clearly the institute's position on the relevance of China's reforms for Russia. The report begins by stating that "the striking contrast of the implementation and results of reforms in Russia and China . . . prompts [us] seriously to analyze the 'secrets' of the success of the reforms in China against the background of the alarming demise of our country's economy."[78]

The primary question that underlies the report is the reasons for the drastically different outcomes of the Soviet and Chinese attempts to reform. As they phrased it,

> Why did the economic reforms in China lead to a considerable boom in the economy, a significant although not equal rise in the living standards of the people, and a strengthening of the defense of the PRC, its internal stability and international stance, while in Russia reforms led to the reverse: a catastrophic decline in production, resulting in total economic chaos, making beggars of the majority of the population, creating a serious threat to Russia's security, bringing the country to the edge of a social explosion, and in the international arena in fact pushing it to the side of world politics?[79]

Titarenko and his colleagues concluded that the "secrets" to China's success rested in several areas. Perhaps most importantly, the objectives of the reforms were different. While China's goal was to transform itself into a modern and prosperous country, Soviet leaders attempted a complete transformation of the socio-economic system. China's success in carrying through its reforms was also due in large measure to the priority given to economic tasks over political ones and the consistent balance of reforms with stability. Additionally, the type of economy introduced in both countries was quite different, with China introducing a regulated market economy with the state remaining a dominant force in industry through state-owned enterprises. By contrast, Russia sought to introduce a purely market economy based upon private property seemingly overnight through the liquidation of state assets and privatization.

Titarenko is not alone in his belief that China's path to reform was superior to that followed in the Soviet Union and Russia. Such ideas are shared by the majority of the IDV's scholars, most notably by Boris Kulik, Igor Baliuk, Alexander Larin, Elena Bazheneva, and Andrei Ostrovskii. These scholars largely share a common opinion on the success of China's economic transformation and its future stability, the Middle Kingdom's relatively benign foreign policy, and the relevance of China's reforms to the Russian experience. It is also a common position among these scholars that the model that was pursued by the Yeltsin administration was that of an American or Western one, and that China is a more appropriate model. As Baliuk phrases it, the Chinese model is "much more consistent with the historical and cultural tradition of the Russian people than the idea of U.S. individualism, which had been, until recently, actively introduced by some politicians."[80]

Another leading scholar at the IDV who has written extensively on the relevance of China's reforms for Russia is Andrei Ostrovskii. An economist by training and a specialist in Chinese and Taiwanese economics, Ostrovskii is the same scholar who back in the late 1980s suggested the Russia should catch "the China train," a metaphor for following the path to reform modeled after that of China. While Ostrovskii has recently concluded that Russia "missed the China train, and caught a quite different train altogether,"[81] his earlier work is quite explicit in arguing that Russia can and should learn from the success of China's economic reforms. His article "Ekonomicheskie Reformy v KNR: Uroki dlya Rossii" (Economic Reform in the PRC: Lessons for Russia), is his most articulate expression of his ideas on the topic, and is perhaps the single best example of Russian scholarship that seeks to extract lessons from the Chinese reform experience for Russia.[82]

Ostrovskii begins by comparing the outcomes of the Russian and Chinese economic transitions, pointing out that in looking at "the results of the reforms of the Chinese economic system over the past 20 plus years, one must say that, in terms of economic accomplishments and from the point of view of the viability" of the country's economic productive capacity, "China had greatly outstripped Russia."[83] He also chides Russia for not paying attention to China's experience:

> In the 1970s, when China began its reforms, in the USSR this was looked upon as revisionism, and it was figured that China was moving too quickly along the path to the market. In 1991, on the contrary, in Russia it was figured that China was moving too slowly and needed to carryout more radical measures for the transition to the market and integration into the world economy. In such a way Russia practically ignored the Chinese experience entirely.[84]

The main points Ostrovskii makes in this article center around the speed of reform, political control over the reform process, and the nature of the market mechanisms introduced. Ostrovskii praises China for pursuing gradual reform, pointing out that in China the "transformation of the command-administrative system to a market economy" took place "while retaining and utilizing the country's industrial capacity developed during the 1950-1970s," particularly in the areas of the military-industrial complex and the fuel and energy sectors.[85] He also suggests that if China had attempted simultaneous and rapid reform, such as Russia attempted with shock therapy, the result would have been the same in China as it was in Russia—a collapse of economic productivity and a drastic decline in real income.[86]

Ostrovskii also argues that "the most important factor for carrying through reforms successfully has been the CCP's retention of control over economic and political processes," since this has allowed the party to lead reforms, not for the economy to be restructured haphazardly by different interest groups.[87] Here he is in agreement with his colleague Boris Kulik, who has argued that by retaining political control, the CCP has been able to organize and implement reforms, whereas the CPSU, "as a result of Gorbachev's apostasy, did not go further than a verbal announcement of reforms."[88] Ostrovskii also praises China for not copying the Western model of a market economy, and for retaining strong socialist aspects as part of its "socialist market economy" model, which has focused on raising the living standards of the whole country and retaining the positive aspects of economic planning.[89] Finally, Ostrovskii argues that Russia can still learn from the Chinese experience, and that it would be well served to adopt something along the lines of China's special economic zones. He has even suggested that Russia could employ "great leap forward" to help it recover from shock therapy.[90]

While the IDV may be the main scholarly voice in Russia calling for Russia to learn from the success of China's reforms, it is not the only voice. Scholars from other institutions have reached similar conclusions based on their own analyses. An excellent case in point is Anatolii Butenko of Moscow State University, who published an influential article on the "four lessons" of socialism with Chinese characteristics in an article in Pravda in the summer of 1995.[91] Butenko, who is also a member of the Institute for International Economic and Political Research at the Russian Academy of Science, sharply criticized Gorbachev and Yeltsin for their policies which failed to extricate Russia from its economic difficulties. The reasons they were ultimately unable to do so, Butenko argues, relate to several points, perhaps the most important being that the reforms were not based on any theory of reform, as they were in China. Butenko also argues that to pursue simultaneous economic and political reform, as was attempted in the Soviet Union, was ludicrous; it made infinitely better sense to resolve economic problems first, and then to address political ones. Additionally, the underlying causes of stagnation in the Soviet Union were never uncovered and no realistic plan was developed for reacquiring economic dynamism. Finally, Butenko points out that reform alone does not generate economic growth, arguing that this should have been the reformers' objective, not just restructuring the economy.[92]

While Butenko's assessment is not as sophisticated as Ostrovskii's, and overlooks some of the very real problems China continues to face in its transformation (such as corruption and the problems of China's state-owned enterprises), it is just one more example of a significant body of scholarly work in Russia on the relevance of China's reform experience for Russia. And by publishing this and similar articles in the national press, Butenko and other scholars are able to express their views about the success of China's reforms to everyone from policymakers to common citizens.

Russians' Assessments of the Chinese Miracle

In general, both elites and ordinary citizens pay less attention to what is going on in China than do government officials and scholars, except perhaps for those living in the Russian Far East, where Chinese traders coming across the border by the thousands raise fears of a Chinese takeover of the region.[93] Some Russian intellectuals do recognize China's success, however, and even common Russians have a general idea of China's relative success in transforming its economy into one of the most vibrant in the world.

Through the publication of popular books, Russian intellectuals not only express their own views of China's transformation, they also influence the understanding and attitudes of common citizens. A good example of a work that does this is Igor Malevich's *Vnimanie, Kitai* (Attention, China), which aims primarily to inform readers of the former Soviet Union about China's dramatic rise to a position of influence in the world.[94] Malevich, a former Soviet astronaut, structures his work around the question of whether China represents Russia's future or its past, only to conclude that it is in some ways both. Most significantly, however, Malevich wants to warn his readers of the potential dangers of a successful and powerful China. *Vnimanie, Kitai* is also noteworthy for the author's acknowledgement of the impact the Soviet collapse had on CCP leaders and their thoughts on reform.[95]

Another example is Andrei Devyatov's *Krasnyi Drakon: Kitai i Rossiya v Dvadtsat' Pervom Veke* (The Red Dragon: China and Russia in the 20th Century), which also focuses on the geopolitical implications of China's economic success.[96] Devyatov, a former Soviet defense intelligence officer, sees China's rise to global dominance as more of an opportunity than a threat, however, and calls upon Russia to join with China in establishing a multipolar world and balancing American influence. Unique among Russian popular writing on China, a full 100 pages of *Krasnyi Drakon* is devoted to lessons for Russia. This section, which begins by asking "why does socialism live and thrive in China, never caught on in the West, and collapsed in Russia," is sure to get readers to ask similar questions.[97]

Indeed, such questions are being asked by Russians. Positive assessments of China's transformation are particularly prevalent among Russia's new business elite. One Russian businessman from Ekaterinburg, who had supported Gaidar's Russia's Choice bloc and even participated in democratic demonstrations, has begun to question seriously the value of Russia's rapid democratic reforms before substantial economic reforms had been realized:

> Now I doubt whether it was right to reform the Soviet political system in such a dramatic way that the country collapsed. Transition to a market economy is the right thing to do. However, I doubt whether democratization of the political system was necessary at that stage of reform. Look at China. The economy is booming, the standard of living of the Chinese people is improving a great deal, and the international prestige of China has far surpassed that of poor, violent, and chaotic Russia.[98]

While scholars and intellectuals feel that the Chinese model of reform is superior to that of Russia, what do average Russian citizens think? According to a public opinion survey conducted in 2002, 42 percent of Russians have a positive view of China, an opinion that prevailed mostly among Communist sympathizers, senior citizens, and those with a higher education.[99] More interesting perhaps is the finding that, in comparing Russia with its eastern neighbor, 66 percent of respondents felt that China is developing more successfully, with almost half the respondents (49 percent) agreeing that China is in the lead in economics and industry. Nevertheless, 73 percent felt that Russia exerts more influence in

the world today, while only 2 percent felt that the Chinese people were better off
or that their political system was better than Russia's.

These data reveal some interesting popular attitudes, and we can infer from
them that a Chinese model of reform might be welcomed by many Russians.
While fully 2/3 of respondents feel that the Chinese path to reform is superior to
that of Russia, this does not necessarily translate into a positive general view of
China. In fact, the vast majority of respondents believe that Russia is still superior in many ways to China, for example, in terms of international stature or the
daily life of an average citizen. Perhaps most importantly, however, while we
cannot conclude that average citizens have actually learned anything from the
Chinese experience, they do appear to recognize the differences between the
Soviet and Chinese models of reform and to acknowledge the success of China's
economic transformation.

The Secret of China's Success

Many factors helped determine the path of reform in the Soviet Union and the
development model being pursued in post-Communist Russia. The impact of
lesson-drawing and interaction, however, has remained understudied and its
significance relatively overlooked. In particular, the impact of the negative lessons drawn from China during the Tiananmen demonstrations and their aftermath affected deeply those living in other Communist countries, both those in
positions of power and ordinary citizens hoping for a better life. This is particularly true for Gorbachev, for although he failed to draw any positive lessons
from China's experience with reform from 1978-85, he paid particularly close
attention to China between 1989-1991. In this regard, Gorbachev perhaps felt
vindicated in blazing a new trail of his own, since the demonstrators at Tiananmen were calling for political freedoms, which Gorbachev had given to the Soviet people with glasnost and perestroika. Unfortunately, he could not rest on his
laurels long, since as soon as he returned to Moscow from Beijing Gorbachev
began to witness the underlying discontent with reform among the Soviet population, which began to use their new-found freedoms to liberate themselves further and to pull down the Soviet Union in the process.

While lesson-drawing and interaction played a significant role in the unfolding of events in the 1989-1992 period, albeit as a source of negative lessons
for the Soviet Union, since that time China has had much less of an impact on
Russia and its reforms. Why has Russia not taken such an interest in China's
successes? As I have shown, it is not due to ignorance of the success of China's
reforms. Also, it is not due to a lack of initiative on the part of scholars in Russia, who have been trying to influence policy to no avail. It is also not due to a
lack of access to the halls of power, for many like-minded scholars have had
direct audiences with policymakers. For example, in 2001, Ostrovskii participated in a roundtable discussion sponsored by the *Otechestvo* (Fatherland) po-

litical movement, headed by Moscow mayor Yuri Luzhkov.[100] Here Ostrovskii summarized many of the same themes articulated in his earlier work to an audience that included influential Duma members and government officials. He and others have also spoken before the Federation Council on similar matters. And as Lukin has stated, there have even been occasions when documents have been handed directly to Soviet and Russian leaders, bypassing normal channels.[101] Even the Russian ambassador to China, Igor Rogachev, who has been ambassador since 1990 and who was even born in China, thinks that Russia can learn important lessons from China.[102] Why do Russia's policymakers consistently reject China's experience as applicable to Russia's situation?

Russia might not be trying to learn for a few reasons. One is perhaps ethnocentrism. Many Russian policymakers argue that China is a Third World country and has nothing to teach Russia, despite the fact that Russian scholars who specialize in China think in quite different terms. After all, why should Russia, the heir to the great Soviet empire, look to a developing nation such as China as a model? There are some valid points to this argument, since the transition from an undeveloped to a developing country has few concrete lessons for a developed and industrialized country such as Russia that is undergoing a transition from plan to market.

In the minds of Russian policymakers, and many ordinary citizens, the United States and the West in general provide a much more attractive model than China, and indeed this is precisely the type of system leaders such as Gorbachev and Yeltsin sought to emulate. If the goal is to emulate Western democracy and capitalism, then it is natural to reject the idea of China as a model to emulate. Moreover, the fact that China did not collapse means that the impetus to learn from China's experience is less than it was for China to learn from the collapse of Communism in Eastern Europe and the Soviet Union. These facts indicate that the perceived relevance of an experience and the seriousness of its implications are important factors in lesson-drawing.

Finally, it may be that policymakers are not simply ignoring the lessons of China's transformation at all, but that they fear what might happen if Russians today were to begin to question the course of reform followed up to this point with an eye to China and its relative success. Perhaps by rejecting the notion of the relevance of China's success for Russia and even by suppressing information about China the government is attempting to prevent Russian citizens from questioning the new system and the policies followed to put it into place. After all, the Russian people, given knowledge of the successes of Chinese reform, might learn from that experience and choose to support parties that would bring Russia back to a path that would more closely approximate the situation in China today under the CCP. While Gennady Zyuganov and the CPRF stand ready to lead Russia in such a direction, even such an idea is considered extremely threatening by Putin, his beloved United Russia party, and other leaders at the helm of the post-Soviet Russian state.

While such an idea may sound conspiratorial and extreme, it is an opinion held by several leading China scholars in Russia.[103] For evidence in support of such an idea, these scholars point to more than policymakers' simple rejection of the Chinese experience. They point out that there are virtually no sources of information on China in Russia. The mass media also apparently continually refuses to cover such issues in the news,[104] and the only TV coverage is of tragic events like SARS. And while the occasional visit of a Russian official to China may receive some coverage, it is not accompanied by any general discussion of the state of the country, as is the practice in the Western media. There is also the problem of financial resources. The Russian government purportedly barely provides any funds for China studies, leaving institutes such as the IDV and scholars at other institutions who wish to study hamstrung. Meanwhile, the IDV, which enjoys a monopoly in Russia on the study of China only because the government will not fund China studies anywhere else, is forced to use its limited funds to keep research on China alive in Russia. Relying upon scholarly publication as its sole means of disseminating information, e.g. scholarly monographs and their journal *Problemy Dal'nego Vostoka*, assures that the general public will not learn what is happening in China, only a select few academics in a very small community. Whether it is the result of a deliberate policy or not, the very low percentages of people who think that Russia should follow a Chinese model of reform can be explained in this way—how could it be otherwise in a society where information about China's success is not widely known? Given that the situation is unlikely to change drastically, the secret of China's success will remain safe in Russia.

Notes

1. Mao, "Speech at the Group Leaders' Forum of the Enlarged Meeting of the Military Affairs Commission," as translated in Stuart Schram, ed., *Chairman Mao Talks to the People: Talks and Letters, 1956-1971* (New York: Random House, 1976), 129. As cited in Dittmer, *Sino-Soviet Normalization, 29*.

2. Oleg Troyanovskii, *Cherez Gody i Rasstoyaniya* (Moscow: Vagrius, 1997), 346. Quoted in Lukin, *The Bear Watches the Dragon*, 150.

3. Keller, "Soviets and China Resuming Normal Ties After 30 Years," A1.

4. Throughout the Soviet period, the issue of whether or not Moscow's China-watchers could actually influence policy remained a contentious one, with estimates ranging from such scholarship finding its "way straight into the wastepaper basket" to more optimistic assessments that argued that it was "an important source of analysis for the Central Committee planning staff and the Foreign Ministry." See Chi Su, "Soviet China-Watchers' Influence on Soviet China Policy," *Journal of Northeast Asian Studies* 2 (December 1983): 25-49.

5. Rozman, *A Mirror for Socialism*.

6. For an excellent analysis of the changing nature of Sino-Soviet relations, see Lukin, *The Bear Watches the Dragon*.

7. V.A. Dolmatov, "Maoizm—ideinii i politicheskii protivnik mirovogo revoliutsionnogo dvizhenya," *Problemy Dal'nego Vostoka* 35 (1980): 196-199; P.B. Kapralov,

A.M. Krygalov, and A.V. Ostrovskii, "Nekotorye tendentsii v sotsial'no-ekonomicheskoi politike kitaiskogo rukavodstva," *Problemy Dal'nego Vostoka* 36 (1980): 105-116; L.M. Gudoshnikov, "Samorazoblachenie maoizma," *Problemy Dal'nego Vostoka* 37 (1981): 201-205; and N.E. Borevskaya, "Model' lichnosti po-maoistski," *Problemy Dal'nego Vostoka* 42 (1982): 151- 158.

8. D. A. Smirnov, "Maoistskaya kontseptsiya 'novoi demokratii'— pravorevizionistskaya versiya 'natsional'nogo' sotsializma," *Problemy Dal'nego Vostoka* 32 (1979): 92-105.

9. V.I. Akimov and S.S. Emel'yanova, "Dynamika razvitiya ekonomiki Kitaya," *Problemy Dal'nego Vostoka* 50 (1984): 43-52; S.R. Ratnikov and D.A. Radikovskii, "Diskussiya v KNR o puti razvitiya strany," *Problemy Dal'nego Vostoka* 52 (1984): 115-127; Z.A. Muromtseva, "Modernizatsiya sel'skogo khozyaistva KNR: Voprosy kapital'nikh vlozhenii," *Problemy Dal'nego Vostoka* 53 (1985): 96-106; and V.Y. Portyakov and S.V. Stepanov, "Spetsial'nie ekonomicheskie zony kitaya," *Problemy Dal'nego Vostoka* 57 (1986): 37-46.

10. Rozman, "Chinese Studies in Russia and their Impact, 1985-1992," 143-144.

11. Ibid. See also Gilbert Rozman, "China's Soviet Watchers in the 1980s: A New Era in Scholarship," *World Politics* 37, no. 4 (July 1985): 435-74, and Gilbert Rozman, "Moscow's China Watchers in the Post-Mao Era: The Response to a Changing China," *China Quarterly* 94 (June 1983): 215-42.

12. Rozman, "Chinese Studies in Russia and their Impact, 1985-1992," 144.

13. Gorbachev and Mlynar, *Conversations with Gorbachev*, 70.

14. Gorbachev, *Gorbachev*, 57.

15. Gorbachev and Mlynar, *Conversations with Gorbachev*, 194.

16. Troyanovskii, *Cherez Gody i Rasstoyaniya*, 346.

17. Fedor Burlatskii, *Literaturnaya Gazeta*, June 11, 1986, 10. Cited in Timothy Colton, *The Dilemma of Reform in the Soviet Union* (New York: Council on Foreign Relations, 1986), 154.

18. Mikhail Gorbachev, text of speech delivered in Vladivostok, July 28, 1986. Reprinted in Ramesh Thakur and Carlyle A. Thayer, *The Soviet Union as an Asian Pacific Power: Implications of Gorbachev's 1986 Vladivostok Initiative* (Boulder, CO: Westview, 1987), 219-220.

19. Gorbachev and Mlynar, *Conversations with Gorbachev*, 199.

20. Gorbachev and Mlynar, *Conversations with Gorbachev*, 70.

21. Gorbachev and Mlynar, *Conversations with Gorbachev*.

22. The fact that Gorbachev was interested in emulating Hungary's reforms is discussed in Colton, *The Dilemma of Reform in the Soviet Union*, 154. See also *Ekonomicheskie Reformy v Rossii i Vengrii: Opyt Sravnitel'nogo Issledovaniya* (Novosibirsk: IEiOPP SO RAN, 1996).

23. *Pravda*, June 10, 1986, 1. Cited in Colton, *The Dilemma of Reform in the Soviet Union*, 154.

24. Colton, *The Dilemma of Reform in the Soviet Union*, 155.

25. Keller, "Soviets and China Resuming Normal Ties After 30 Years," A1.

26. Bill Keller, "Gorbachev Praises the Students and Declares Reform is Necessary," *New York Times*, May 18, 1989, A1.

27. Keller, "Soviets and China Resuming Normal Ties After 30 Years," A1.

28. "A New Stage in Soviet-Chinese Relations," *Pravda*, May 20, 1989, 1-2.

29. "A New Stage in Soviet-Chinese Relations."

30. "A New Stage in Soviet-Chinese Relations."

31. Lukin, "The Initial Soviet Reaction to the Events in China in 1989," 121.

32. Lukin, "The Initial Soviet Reaction to the Events in China in 1989," 119-121, and Lukin, *The Bear Watches the Dragon,* 152-156.

33. Lukin, "The Initial Soviet Reaction to the Events in China in 1989," 121.

34. Lukin, "The Initial Soviet Reaction to the Events in China in 1989," 129.

35 A. Vlasov, "Posle 'Osvobozhdeniya Tian'an'men'," *Moskovskie Novosti,* June 11, 1989, 3. Quoted in Lukin, *The Bear Watches the Dragon,* 159.

36. Quoted from Lukin, "The Initial Soviet Reaction to the Events in China in 1989," 130. See also Sakharov's similar comments at a Pugwash meeting in Cambridge, Massachusetts, mentioned in Walter Clemens, *Baltic Independence and Russian Empire* (New York: St. Martin's Press, 1990), 255.

37. Lukin, "The Initial Soviet Reaction to the Events in China in 1989," 129.

38. Lukin, "The Initial Soviet Reaction to the Events in China in 1989," 124.

39. Renée De Nevers, *Comrades no More: The Seeds of Change in Eastern Europe* (Cambridge, MA: MIT University Press, 2003), 93, f66.

40. Timothy Garton Ash, "Ten Years After," *New York Review of Books*, November 18, 1999.

41. Norman Naimark, "Ich will hier raus?: Emigration and the Collapse of the German Democratic Republic," in Ivo Banac, ed., *Eastern Europe in Revolution* (Ithaca, NY: Cornell University Press, 1992), 72-95.

42. Luke Allnutt, "The Unfolding of 1989," *Transitions*, January 1999.

43. *Agerpres* (Romanian Press Agency), June 26, 1989.

44. "Reaction to Continuing Violence in China Reported," FBIS:EEU, June 8, 1989; "Continuing PRC Unrest Termed 'Internal Matter'," *Prague Domestic Service*, June 11, 1989, in FBIS:EEU, June 12, 1989; and "Events in China Termed 'Internal Affair'," *Rude Pravo*, June 14, 1989, in FBIS:EEU, June 16, 1989, all cited in De Nevers, *Comrades no More,* 196, f129, and *Neues Deutschland,* June 5, 1989, 1, cited in Naimark, "Ich will hier raus," 82, f35. See also "China: Aftermath of the Crisis," U.S. Department of State, Bureau of Intelligence and Research, Intelligence Research Report No. 210, July 27, 1989, 3.

45. De Nevers, *Comrades no More,* 170.

46. Tamara Dragadze, "Azerbaijan and the Azerbaijanis," in Graham Smith, ed., *The Nationalities Question in the Post-Soviet States* (New York: Longman, 1996), 280.

47. Marsh, "Power Capabilities, External Recognition, and Sovereignty."

48. Vardys and Sedaitis, *Lithuania,* 176.

49. Robert Service, *A History of Twentieth-Century Russia* (Cambridge, MA: Harvard University Press, 1997), 498.

50. James Billington, "Orthodox Christianity and the Russian Transformation," in Witte and Bourdeaux, *Proselytism and Orthodoxy in Russia,* 53.

51. Service, *A History of Twentieth-Century Russia,* 501.

52. Tucker, "China as a Factor in the Collapse of the Soviet Empire," 518.

53. Tucker, "China as a Factor in the Collapse of the Soviet Empire," 518.

54. Savenkov, "Russian Federation Parliamentarians in China," 6.

55. "Yeltsin Gives Press Conference in Beijing," *Xinhua News Agency*, December 18, 1992.

56. "Yeltsin Gives Press Conference in Beijing."

57. "Press Briefing on the future visit of Boris Yeltsin to China by the RF Foreign Ministry," *Interfax*, December 15, 1992.

58. Interview with Yegor Gaidar, from *Commanding Heights: The Battle for the World Economy,* May 15-June 19, 2003, on PBS, WGBH. Transcript available at: http://www.pbs.org/wgbh/commandingheights/shared/pdf/int_yegorgaidar.pdf.

59. For some interesting insights into the differences between the economic reforms of Russia, China, and Poland, see Wing Thye Woo, "The Art of Reforming Centrally Planned Economies: Comparing China, Poland, and Russia," *Journal of Comparative Economics* 18 (1994): 276-308.

60. Nick Paton Walsh, "How Yeltsin Crushed Democracy: Secrets are Spilled of 1993 Deception that Allowed President to Suppress Parliament," *The Guardian,* October 3, 2003.

61. Press Trust of India, September 28, 2003.

62. Nikolas Gvosdev, "Outside View: Putin and the Chinese model," United Press International, February 9, 2004.

63. "Putin Emphasizes Importance of Making Reforms Clear, Transparent," *ITAR-TASS,* December 3, 2002.

64. Andrei Illarionov, "Taina Kitaiskogo Ekonomicheskaya Chuda," in *Bulleten' po Problemam Ekonomicheskoi i Sotsial'noi Politiki* (Moscow: March 25, 1998). Cited in Lukin, *The Bear Watches the Dragon,* 211.

65. Illarionov, "Taina Kitaiskogo Ekonomicheskaya Chuda."

66. Remarks made at the Open Russia Foundation's Young Leaders' Conference, Moscow, Russia, September 21, 2003. As reported to the author by Nikolas K. Gvosdev. See Nikolas K. Gvosdev, "The Future Orientation of Russia: Let the Bids Begin," *Perihelion* (October 2003). Available online at: http://www.erpic.org/.

67. Aleksandr Platkovskii, "Vsya Rossiya Stanet Shen' Chzhenem," *Izvestiya* (June 28, 1997), 3. Cited in Lukin, *The Bear Watches the Dragon,* 211.

68. Alexei Mitrofanov, *Russia's New Geopolitics* (Harvard University, John F. Kennedy School of Government, Strengthening Democratic Institutions Project, July 1998), 8. Cited in Lukin, *The Bear Watches the Dragon,* 210.

69. Lukin, *The Bear Watches the Dragon,* 202-210.

70. Oleg Rakhmanin, "Vy o Nem Eshche Uslyshite," *Sovetskaya Rossiya* (February 25, 1997), 3. Cited in Lukin, *The Bear Watches the Dragon,* 207.

71. Remarks made at the Open Russia Foundation's Young Leaders' Conference.

72. Remarks made at the Open Russia Foundation's Young Leaders' Conference.

73. Lukin, *The Bear Watches the Dragon,* 202.

74. G. A. Stepanova, *Sistema Mnogopartiinogo Sotrudnichestva v Kitaiskoi Narodnoi Respublike* (Moscow: Institut Dal'nego Vostoka, RAN, 1999); *Kitaiskie Reformy i Rossiya.* 2 volumes (Moscow: Institut Dal'nego Vostoka, RAN, 2000); *Ekonomicheskie Reformy v Rossii i Kitae Glazami Rossiiskikh i Kitaiskikh Ekonomistov*; and *Ekonomicheskie Chudesa: Uroki dlya Rossii* (Moscow: OLMA-PRESS, 1994).

75. Lukin, *The Bear Watches the Dragon,* 203.

76. Author's observation, fourteenth annual conference *Kitai, Kitaiskaya Tsivilizatsiya, i Mir: Istoriya, Sovremennost', Perspektivy,* Institute of the Far East, Russian Academy of Sciences, Moscow, September 23, 2003.

77. Lin Yifu, Cai Fang, Li Zhou, *Kitaiskoe Chudo: Strategiya Razvitiya i Ekonomicheskaya Reforma* (Moscow: Institut Dal'nego Vostoka, 2001), translation of Justin Yifu Lin, Fang Cai, and Zhou Li, *The China Miracle: Development Strategy and Economic Reform* (Hong Kong: Chinese University Press, 1996).

78. Mikhail Titarenko, *Kitaiskie Reformy: Primer, Vyzov, ili Ugroza Rossii?* (Moscow: IDV RAN, April 1997), Unpublished manuscript, 2. As cited in Lukin, *The Bear Watches the Dragon,* 203.

79. Titarenko, *Kitaiskie Reformy,* 3-4.

80. Igor Baliuk, "K Voprosu o Vozmozhnosti Ispol'zovaniya Kitaiskogo Opyta Ekonomicheskikh Preobrazovanii v Usloviyakh Rossii," in *Kitai, Kitaiskaya Tsivilizatsiya, i Mir: Istoriya, Sovremennost', Perspektivy,* proceedings of the Fifth annual conference (Moscow: IDV RAN, 1994), 91. As cited in Lukin, *The Bear Watches the Dragon,* 206.

81. Andrei Ostrovskii, *Formirovanie Rynka Rabochei Sily v KNR* (Moscow: Institut Dal'nego Vostoka, Rossiiskaya Akademiya Nauk, 2003), 8.

82. See Andrei Ostrovskii, "Ekonomicheskie Reformy v KNR: Uroki dlya Rossii," *Teoriya i Praktika Ekonomicheskikh Reform v KNR* (Moscow: Institut Dal'nego Vostoka, Rossiiskaya Akademiya Nauk, 2000), 4-26.

83. Ostrovskii, "Ekonomicheskie Reformy v KNR," 5-6.

84. Ostrovskii, "Ekonomicheskie Reformy v KNR," 6.

85. Ostrovskii, "Ekonomicheskie Reformy v KNR," 4.

86. Ostrovskii, "Ekonomicheskie Reformy v KNR," 5.

87. Ostrovskii, "Ekonomicheskie Reformy v KNR," 6.

88. Boris Kulik, "Kliuchi k Uspekhu Reform: Oprobovano v Kitae," *Obozrevatel'* 12 (1994), 88. As cited in Lukin, *The Bear Watches the Dragon,* 206.

89. Ostrovskii, "Ekonomicheskie Reformy v KNR," 9-10.

90. Ostrovskii, "Ekonomicheskie Reformy v KNR," 25.

91. Anatolii Butenko, "Chetyrie Uroka: Sotsializm s Kitaiskoi Spetsifikoi," *Pravda,* August 30, 1995, 6.

92. Ibid.

93. See Mikhail Alexeev, "Economic Valuations and Interethnic Fears: Perceptions of Chinese Migration in the Russian Far East," *Journal of Peace Research* 40, no. 1 (January 2003): 89-106; Mikhail Alexeev, "Desecuritizing Sovereignty: Economic Interest and Responses to Political Challenges of Chinese Migration in the Russian Far East," in John D. Montgomery and Nathan Glazer, eds., *Sovereignty under Challenge: How Governments Respond* (New Brunswick, NJ: Transaction Publishers, 2002), 261-289; and Mikhail Alexeev, "Socioeconomic and Security Implications of Chinese Migration in the Russian Far East," *Post-Soviet Geography and Economics* 42, no. 2 (2001): 95-114.

94. Igor Malevich, *Vnimanie, Kitai* (Minsk: Kharvest, 2000).

95. See especially 79-81.

96. Andrei Devyatov, *Krasnyi Drakon: Kitai i Rossiya v Dvadtsat' Pervom veke* (Moscow: Algoritm, 2002).

97. Devyatov, *Krasnyi Drakon,* 185.

98. Quoted in B. Batjargal, *New Entrepreneurs in Post-Soviet Russia,* D. Phil. thesis, Oxford University, 1998, 302-303. As cited in Lukin, *The Bear Watches the Dragon,* 212.

99. "Russians' View of China is Positive," *Interfax,* November 28, 2002.

100. Andrei Ostrovskii, remarks at the roundtable "Novaya Strategiya dlya Rossii i Opyt Stran c Perekhodnoi Ekonomikoi," in *"Otechestvo" Otechestvu: Programma Preobrazovanii* (Moscow: Obscherossiiskaya Politicheskaya Obschectvennaya Organizatsiya "Otechestvo," 2001), 77-81.

101. Lukin, *The Bear Watches the Dragon.* 343, fn. 214.

102. Speech delivered at the Institute of the Far East, Russian Academy of Sciences, Moscow.

103. Interview with various scholars in Russia, July-September, 2003. Names and locations withheld to protect the identities of interviewees.

104. According to organizers of conferences and seminars on China in Russia, the media are regularly invited to such events, but they are told that the administrators of the various media do not want such things covered.

Chapter 7

Transition, Lesson-Drawing, and Culture

Those who cannot remember the past are condemned to repeat it.
–George Santayana[1]

Human beings, who are almost unique in having the ability to learn from the experience of others, are also remarkable for their apparent disinclination to do so.
–Douglas Adams[2]

I've just returned from a new Russia, now a country reaching toward democracy and our partner in the war against terror. Even in China, leaders are discovering that economic freedom is the only lasting source of national wealth. In time, they will find that social and political freedom is the only true source of national greatness.
–George W. Bush[3]

THE developmental paths Russia and China are following today head in seemingly opposite directions. In Russia, democracy is in retreat and the country seems to be backsliding once more into authoritarianism. Putin is not only bringing an end to the popular election of the country's 89 regional executives, he is also eliminating the single-mandate seats in the Duma and curbing smaller parties from the electoral process. Collectively, these measures strike a major blow to the development of grassroots democracy in Russia, however troubled its evolution has been thus far. As Cameron Ross recently suggested, Russia's qualified democracy is now being replaced by qualified authoritarianism, and where we previously described Russia as a "delegative" or "managed" democracy, we should now begin to refer to it as "electoral authoritarianism" or even "elective dictatorship."[4] While the country's economic product is growing at last, seemingly moving into a recovery stage, it is difficult for anyone who is familiar with Russia's economic situation to conclude that its economy is in overall good health. The economic recovery, in fact, seems to be

159

"floating on oil," insofar as most of the economic growth is attributable to the rising price of crude oil on the world market.[5]

Despite its setbacks, Russia still remains more democratic than China in almost every way. Nevertheless, China's path at least seems to be heading in the right direction, however slowly and cautiously. Even if the goal of democracy is still a long way off, liberalization is continuing unabated and grassroots democracy is slowly "trickling up" through the system. From the vibrancy of village elections to the transition to the fourth generation of leadership, there is room for optimism that the fifth modernization may not be a long way off. The most impressive accomplishments, of course, are in the economic sector, where the Middle Kingdom continues to register annual growth rates in excess of 10 percent, allowing China to displace Japan in 2004 as the third largest trading nation, just behind the U.S. and Germany.

FIGURE 7.1.
Political Rights and Civil Liberties in Russia and China, 1985-2004.

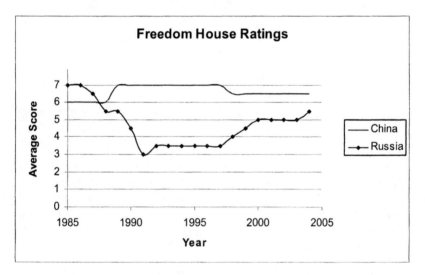

Source: *Freedom in the World* (Washington, DC: Freedom House, various years).

Note: Scores used for Russia for the years 1985 to 1990 are those for the Soviet Union, since a separate score for Russia was not calculated until 1991.

The unparalleled nature of the reform process in Russia and China can be seen more vividly by comparing the Freedom House ratings on political freedom and civil liberties for both countries for the period 1985-2004.[6] While China was considered more free than the Soviet Union in 1985, the two quickly crisscrossed each other's paths, and by 1987, as perestroika was launched in the Soviet Union and China began facing student unrest, the two switched positions. As a result of the clampdown at Tiananmen, by 1989 China had slid to the bottom of the scale, while the Soviet Union continued its steady liberalization until 1991. After an initial correction, due partly to the fact that the data used prior 1991 are for the Soviet Union, the ranking for both countries stayed stable until the late 1990s. Beginning in 1997, however, a new trend emerged, with China's rating improving slightly while Russia's began a somewhat steady depreciation. Today, as Russia continues to backslide into authoritarianism and China continues to slowly liberalize, their two paths may cross yet again—only this time with China outdistancing Russia.

Despite beginning its political and economic reforms earlier and pursuing them more ambitiously, the reform path chosen by Soviet and Russian leaders has not proven to be superior to that of the Chinese. In fact, many scholars would argue that the reverse is true. While in the areas of political reform and civil liberties Russia initially surpassed China, as the above analysis shows, the process is still far from complete. With Putin strengthening the Russian state and curbing freedoms while China's fourth generation continues with political reforms, it is possible that Russia may be surpassed in this area, too, in the years to come.

The Interdependence of Transition

From political leaders all the way down to ordinary citizens, transition societies have been aware of and influenced by events and processes unfolding throughout the Communist and post-Communist world. This degree of interaction means that events in one country reverberate across the planet, eliciting all types of responses. These facts make the transition from Communism one global, interdependent process. The tight intermingling of events and actors between 1989 and 1991 is perhaps still the best example of this, as the wave of transitions was in large measure impacted by interaction effects and lesson-drawing. Knowledge of events across the Communist world weighed in the thinking of reformers in all countries, and among publics as well. The impact of interaction effects and lesson-drawing are more expansive, therefore, than scholars such as De Nevers and Halperin have argued, as they reached all the way across the Communist world, not only segments of it.[7] Moreover, insofar as the Soviet Union attempted to emulate a Western-type model, one could actually say that this process reaches across the whole system, much like Waltz's idea of system socialization and the emulation of successful practices.[8]

If this is true, then the processes in most transition societies were contingent upon events in others, that is, the outcome of any particular transition was not the product of a solely domestic equation, but was also significantly influenced by forces external to the state. By logical extension, the absence of a particular example or event in another part of the Communist world would have fundamentally altered the way events played out. This leads us to question the methodology of comparative politics that is typically used to study democratic transitions. We must not be blind to the interaction that occurs between states, since all states and actors exist within a single international system. The condition of interdependence, therefore, must be taken into account, even if the focus of one's research is on domestic affairs.

This condition of interdependence allowed lessons to be drawn from both sides, only they most often were *negative* lessons, i.e., lessons about what undesirable outcomes may result as a consequence of following a certain course of reform. Gorbachev, for example, considered China's reforms too slow and narrow, and was convinced that the reform path chosen by the CCP, i.e., economic reform without political liberalization, would result in failure. It did quickly result in a crisis, but by resorting to the use of force, stability was regained and the country is proving itself able to pursue political evolution as opposed to succumbing to revolution. Gorbachev's lesson was not very helpful for himself, moreover, since the Soviet empire just as quickly collapsed under his leadership. The simultaneous extension of economic and political freedoms did not lead to support for his reform agenda, but to calls for more radical measures, ultimately resulting in the collapse of the system itself. Since that time Russia has had to travel down the hard road of post-Communist development, and has failed to take advantage of the successful experience of their eastern neighbor's economic policies, consistently rejecting China's experience as applicable to their society.

In the case of China, the interdependence of transition allowed the country's leaders to learn from the mistakes of the Soviet reform model and encouraged them to embark upon a different path than that of the Communist giant at their back door. China's reform strategy, therefore, has been largely shaped by the lessons members of the CCP leadership have drawn from the Soviet experience based upon their own perceptions of what led to the USSR's downfall and their own fears of what threats to CCP control loom on the horizon. This vicarious experience may prove to have been critical, since it led them to pursue reform much more cautiously than their old tutor. Whether or not China can continue to carry through reforms slowly, without reaching a breaking point at which revolutionary change becomes unstoppable without sever repression, is an issue we can only speculate about at this point. Even if China were to undergo a transition today, however, as opposed to in 1989, its long-term prospects are in fact much better. More capital is in private hands, a private economic sector is thriving, hundreds of thousands of citizens have had some experience with democracy through village and provincial elections, and the country has a national identity that is no longer hinged to the Marxist struggle against capitalism. These conditions would undoubtedly make a transition from CCP rule today easier than two decades ago.

While the interdependent nature of the transition process provided the opportunity for lesson-drawing, only China successfully drew lessons from their comrade's experience. Russia failed to do so, repeatedly rebuffing suggestions that China's experience was applicable. What then explains the predilection of the Chinese to draw upon Russia's experience and the failure of the Russians to do so? Having based their system on that of the Soviet Union, it was certainly natural for China to look to the USSR and later Russia as a source of ideas for policy innovation and as a bellwether of events to come. Indeed, China has a history of learning from the Soviet Union dating back to the example set by the success of the Bolshevik Revolution itself. Beginning as early as Mao's policy of "walking on two legs," however, China also proved itself quite willing to chart its own course, although still watching their Communist big brother closely.[9]

For their part, the Russians had always been the innovators when it came to Communism, having put Communist theory into practice for the first time successfully and supporting the emergence of other Communist states across the globe (although it must be added that Stalin was for a time even more supportive of the Guomindang, pragmatically calculating that their chances of success were greater than that of their Communist comrades). Since it was their system that they were exporting around the globe, it could be argued that it made little sense for Russian leaders to consider the experience of those who had emulated their system as applicable or even relevant to them. As discussed in the preceding chapter, however, many Russians, from ordinary citizens to policy advisors and even some politicians, did consider the Chinese experience relevant. The simple fact that China had emulated the Soviet system and not vice versa is therefore not a sufficient explanation for China's propensity for lesson-drawing and Russia's disinclination toward it.

Another explanation may be the magnitude of the events themselves. In the case of China, the most informative event for them was the collapse of the Soviet Union, an event of global proportions. There are no comparable lessons that China has to offer Russia, for learning from the success of economic reform is an issue of much less significance and importance than that of learning from a system collapse. There is also the issue of the disparity in levels of political and economic development, with Russia's leaders concluding that they have nothing to learn from a Third World country like China.

While these points at least partly explain the reasons why Soviet leaders dismissed Chinese-style reforms and why Russian leaders continue to ignore the lessons of China's remarkable economic success, we are still left to wonder whether or not lesson-drawing is a one-way process and under what circumstances it tends to take place. The truth is that Russia did draw lessons, however, only that they did not draw upon China's experience. In abandoning the Communist system, Gorbachev, Yeltsin, and many of their supporters were attempting to emulate a Western-style system, looking not to China for a model, but to the United States and Europe. In terms of their parliamentary system, religion law of 1991, federal design, etc., Russia was attempting to learn from Germany, France, and the United States. Unfortunately, such a model seems to be proving untenable for Russia, as it requires a liberal consciousness that is at this point beyond the grasp of the majority Russian culture, however much members of the country's alternative democratic culture may dream of such a society.

Perhaps just as clear as the Chinese leadership's attempt to learn from the mistakes of the USSR and the problems of post-Communist development in Russia has been their rejection of just such a Western-style system. While a Japanese model might have been appealing to some, the leaders in Beijing have been more affectionately predisposed toward a Singaporean model, which couples economic growth with political stability, albeit on the backs of political repression. This propensity was exemplified most clearly in the Chinese government's jumping on the Asian values bandwagon in the 1990s.[10] The example of South Korea and Taiwan, however, may be the model that reformers in Beijing are looking toward today, and this is a model that differs from that of Singapore in that genuine evolutionary changes are allowed to take place in the political sphere, with democracy only deferred but not declined.

Culture and Transition

While the above analysis provides a satisfactory explanation for the behavior observed in the preceding chapters, an important piece of the puzzle might still be missing. In fact, the explanation for such different reform agendas and their outcomes may rest outside of the policy realm altogether. If one is looking for an explanation as to why a certain society behaves one way while another behaves in a different manner, a factor that needs to be considered is culture. Recent scholarship is providing evidence that culture can impact how institutions function within a given society,[11] and it very well may be that culture may also help explain other aspects of political life, from the actual selection of institutions to the persistence of regime types.

In this sense, culture may help explain why Communism never really took hold in the Soviet Union and was eventually rejected there, and why it has been more adaptable in China. As Brzezinski said in the early days of reform, Communism in China faced the prospect of "organic absorption by the country's enduring traditions and values," while in Russia and Eastern Europe it faced "organic rejection."[12] In regards to Russia, Petro reached a similar conclusion when he explained that, "despite decades of trying, the Soviet regime ultimately failed in its effort to legitimize the rule of the Communist Party," as its ideology was not compatible with Russian culture at a fundamental level.[13]

In what specific ways was Communism incongruent with Russian culture? One area in particular that was a very tough sell for the Communists was atheism. In a country like Russia, with a thousand-year long tradition of Christianity, not to mention a system with a long history of a fusion of religion and politics, gaining legitimacy for an atheist state would be a tremendous challenge. Indeed, the poor record of Marxism and Western materialist-rationalist thought in Russia in the eighteenth century attested to that from the start.[14] Much like the church itself, which accommodated itself to the Communists in 1927 by swearing allegiance and support for a regime which had its own destruction as one of its primary goals, many Russians went along with atheism simply as a means to bide time. The revival of religion in Russia today also illustrates the degree to which Communist atheism left a spiritual vacuum among Russians, a void many Russians are today attempting to fill with a range of religious traditions.

If religion had been an integral part of Russian culture and presented the regime with a major obstacle, the atheistic policies of the Chinese Communists faced much less resistance among a culture that is almost unique among those of the world for not having been very closely identified with a particular religious tradition (that is, if one employs the more strict definition here and leaves out philosophical traditions such as Confucianism). Of course, the Chinese Communists did seek to promote atheism, but in comparison with the Soviets they had a much smaller scale problem to deal with and went about it with much less zeal, except perhaps during the turbulent days of the Cultural Revolution.

Another area in which Communism was more congruent with Chinese culture than Russian was the relative status of different social classes. In Russia, the Bolsheviks moved peasants and industrial workers up the social ladder and placed them above merchants and craftsmen, groups which had a rich tradition in Russia and were known for their contributions to trade and commerce. In contrast, the peasants had always been seen as attached to the land, as in fact they were for most of their history as serfs, and were seen as lazy and uncultured (*muzhiki*). Such a forced switch in social class prestige was to prove a difficult task. In China, by contrast, it was the merchants who had been lower than the peasants. In this rice culture civilization, tilling the land and producing food held some prestige, while craftsmen and traders were looked down upon, almost as parasites living off of society. In such a culture, maxims such as "profit is theft" resonated well, as did the glorification of the working class, which incidentally in Chinese unambiguously included the peasantry, since in Chinese there was no word for proletarian, and the more inclusive word "worker" was used (*gongren*) instead.

Finally, the Leninist rejection of Western imperialism was a tough sell in a multi-national empire like Russia that had played its part in European power politics for centuries, and which took great pride in its role as a great power (*derzhava*). Indeed, it did not take long at all for this tenet of Marxism to be twisted on its head in order to justify Soviet expansion into Eastern Europe on the pretext of "liberating" the workers of the region, thus fulfilling the dream of many a Russian tsar. Again by contrast, China's "empire" was largely the result of territorial acquisitions made by powers that had actually conquered the Chinese themselves, primarily the Mongols and Manchus, who then left the Middle Kingdom with an empire by default. Most significantly, however, was the anti-imperialist message that resonated well with a country in the midst of what would come to be called the "100 years of humiliation," under which China was carved up like a melon by the Western powers. The significance of the timing of the formation of the Chinese Communist Party should not be lost, moreover, a scant two years after the signing of the Treaty of Versailles which relinquished Shandong from Germany only to award it to the Japanese.

The degree of cultural congruence between Marxism-Leninism and the indigenous cultures of Russia and China no doubt explains part of the puzzle of why and how reform of these Communist systems was sought. In the case of Russia, it would make sense for a new generation of leadership to abandon an ideology that ran counter to its traditional culture. Likewise, in China it made perfect sense for the post-Mao generation to abandon the excesses of the system they had adopted from the Soviet Union while not abandoning Marxism altogether.

Beyond this, however, can culture explain the predilection for lesson-drawing? In fact, China's history is not one of learning from its neighbors, with the reverse more often the case. There remains a constant strand of learning from abroad, however, among a minority though significant Chinese social current. The example that held the greatest promise was that of the Guangxu Emperor and his famous "hundred days reforms," which potentially could have modernized China, had the emperor's aunt not removed him from the throne and continued to allow China to remain idle. The greatest example is perhaps Buddhism, a religion originally introduced from India with later pilgrims and monks making the voyage back to bring back new ideas and texts. Buddhism attests to China's ability to absorb foreign ideas and make them its own, a phenomenon which is perhaps occurring with Marxism today.

The irony of the situation is that Russia's record of learning from abroad is actually much longer than that of China. Peter the Great, the tsar who Westernized Russia and even gave it a capital that looked out onto Europe, is the earliest clear example, but Western currents from Peter on made their way into Russia, from Catherine the Great, who corresponded with the *philosophes*, to the Bolsheviks who gave a European idea a Russian home. As these examples make clear, Russia's propensity for learning is real, but it is one of learning from Europe more than elsewhere. This is precisely the point made by many Chinese scholars in the literature reviewed in chapter 5, who argued that the transition from Communism in the Soviet Union was one of attempting to adopt wholesale a Western system.

The implications of the significance of culture for political and economic transitions probably does not end with the transition itself, but almost certainly carries over into later stages of development. In this regard, it is no surprise that many are now turning to traditional Chinese culture as an explanation for the country's remarkable economic success. From the great respect attached to education to the high regard for hard work, the success of China's economic transition is certainly attributable as much to the cultural context in which it is occurring as the policies that shape it. Unfortunately, the same seems to be true for Russia. U.S. Federal Reserve Chairman Alan Greenspan—who also happens to hold a Ph.D. in economics—is reported to have said that he had always considered capitalism a part of human nature, but in the wake of the collapse of the Russian economy he came to realize that "it was not human nature at all, but culture."[15] Whether or not Russia can find a cultural basis for capitalism remains to be seen, although it appears that, although Orthodoxy might not be a hindrance to capitalism, it also does not appear to provide the fuel for rapid growth, either.[16]

The Future of Post-Communism

The labeling of historical epochs is always a somewhat messy process, but one must begin to wonder at what point we should stop referring to Russia as post-Communist. Given the strength of its legacy, however, and the perseverance of a sizable segment of the electorate that still favors parties that identify in some form with the country's Communist past, the labeling is still in many ways appropriate. In Russia today, there are still many who glorify the past and favor the retention of some form of a Communist identity. Contrary to Marxist tenets, the contemporary neo-Marxist groups in Russia are mixing nationalism with traditional culture, with extremist Marxist elements eliminated or marginalized. Parties and movements such as the CPRF, *Blok za Stalina*, the Soviet Communist Party and others all focus their messages on a loosely-combined mixture of Soviet glory, Russian nationalism, Communism (meaning the system of rule under the CPSU, *not* the Marxist ideal), anti-Semitism, xenophobia, egalitarianism, and even Orthodoxy. The marriage of the first two concepts is quite interesting, as it has resulted in the popularity of the idea of a Soviet motherland (*rodina*), thus combining the ideas of the cradle of Russian civilization and an ideological mantle which it wore for much of the twentieth century.

When one occasions unto an assembly of such groups, one is confronted with a daunting array of slogans and proclamations, such as the rich are thieves, property and natural resources should be renationalized, the country is being sold off, etc. There is even a healthy dose of anti-Americanism, with one particularly explicit display labeling George Bush as the master (*khozyain*) to Putin's servant (*slug*), while another labels America "terrorist #1" and Putin as Cain.[17] The messages of such groups are inconsistent from one to the next, and they have great difficulty identifying a common set of values and positions.[18] While this is true even of the most well-organized of them, i.e., the Communist Party,[19] the situation is even worse among the others. Coupled with the fact that such groups are content with demonstrating on occasion and have rejected violence as a means of achieving their ambitions, it is probably only a matter of time before they, too, become a thing of the past. But one must wonder: if things had been done differently, how large might this segment have been? What would have been the result of an accommodation of such people with other more progressive elements? These are questions, of course, Chinese leaders take very seriously.

The popularity of centrism in Russia today and the existence of the neo-Communist movement seem to suggest that in fact Russia might have responded favorably to a Chinese model of transition from Communism. Certainly a large segment of the population would have clung onto a changed Communist message and identity. Witness the popularity of *siloviki*-politicians, political figures who have moved into politics from the military or security services, including Putin himself.[20] While the number of neo-Communists is shrinking with every election, this is only because they are giving way to the centrist movement, whose message combines pride for the country's past with great power ambitions for the future.

The window of opportunity for such a path is closed, however, and indeed it is no longer needed. Russia is on a new path, and such voices will remain just that—voices, as such groups are politically moderate in their means of action. They vote in large numbers, they demonstrate quite frequently, and they publish a range of newspapers, books, and pamphlets. But, their appeal remains limited and they remain marginalized. Whatever representation they do achieve in government, moreover, quickly becomes moderated by the realities of parliamentary politics, such as the need to work with others, to get reelected, committee assignments, etc. There is no turning back the clock, however, and their historical time has lapsed.

The real question is whether or not time is running out for China's Communists, or whether their success with implementing reform over the past two decades has given them a new lease on life. While it is tempting to conclude that China has passed over its regime crisis and now enjoys relative stability, it is still premature to draw any final conclusion. We must bear in mind that before the late 1980s no one was predicting the collapse of Communism in the Soviet Union and Eastern Europe either. While many of the key factors that played a role in the collapse of the Soviet Union are absent or impotent in China today, in the final analysis an eventual collapse still cannot be ruled out.

A collapse, for example, might eventually be sparked not by a leader who comes to power and, like Gorbachev, attempts to implement radical changes overnight, but rather by a leader who fails to keep the speed of reform on pace with the expectations of an increasingly efficacious citizenry. While slow and controlled reforms such as those carried out in China over the past quarter century may, therefore, seem superior to one centered on rapid change, they are more likely to be seen as unsatisfying by those who wish revolutionary change. No matter how controlled the process, the business of Communist reform is still very tricky and fraught with difficulties. Liberalization is a double-edged sword, since it gives people some of the freedoms they desire, but this freedom can be used to protest the very regime that just gave them this freedom. The process of liberalization is thus a dangerous one, as it tests a regime's commitment to reform and the people's commitment to the regime.

If China does eventually collapse, however, it will not be the "inevitable collapse" that so many have talked about. The country faced a crisis moment between 1989-1991, and successfully survived it. While the country may find itself in a crisis moment again in the future, the Communist regime may survive that one as well. If it does not, however, the collapse will be attributable to a set of circumstances unique to that particular moment in the history of the regime, and indeed of the world. Communist systems can reform and liberalize, and evolve into a more democratic system with a less severe rupture and transition to democracy than the model witnessed in Eastern Europe and the Soviet Union between 1989-1991. Interestingly, evidence in support of this position may be gleaned from the recent Orange revolution in Ukraine. While the democratic revolution that swept through Ukraine in the fall of 1991 ushered in a fledgling democracy that slowly evolved into authoritarianism yet again, the true democratic transition ended up being one that was conducted within the very institutions that had up to that point been home to the authoritarian leadership. In this sense, China may be able to make an eventual transition to democracy by way of an Orange revolution, not a Soviet-style collapse. And the dynamic of such a transition would hopefully be distinct from that of the Soviet Union as well, with its attendant disintegration and ethnic conflict.

Much of this book has been devoted to tracing the evolutionary paths of these two countries, and highlighting the numerous differences in the reform processes pursued over the past quarter of a century. In terms of substance, speed, and sequencing, the reform paths chosen in Moscow and Beijing were very distinct. As we look forward to the future of Russia and China and the ultimate outcome of the monumental transformations attempted, we are still left with uncertainty, although hopefully we are able to see things more clearly. When it comes to the issue of whether or not these unparalleled reforms will remain unparalleled in their outcomes, however, all we can conclude at this point is, in the words of Zhou Enlai in reference to the French Revolution, "it is still too soon to tell."

Notes

1. George Santayana, *Life of Reason, Reason in Common Sense* (New York: Scribner's, 1905), 284.

2. Douglas Adams and Mark Carwardine, *Last Chance to See* (New York: Ballantine, 1990).

3. Commencement Speech, United States Military Academy, West Point, June 1, 2002.

4. Cameron Ross, "Federalism and Electoral Authoritarianism under Putin," *Demokratizatsiya* 13, no. 3 (Summer 2005), forthcoming.

5. Goldman, "Anders in Wonderland."

6. To generate an overall picture, I average together the two scores for political freedom and civil liberties.

7. De Nevers, *Comrades no More*, and Halperin, "Learning from Abroad."

8. Kenneth Waltz, *Theory of International Politics* (New York: McGraw-Hill, 1979), 74-77, and 127-128.

9. Rozman, *The Chinese Debate about Soviet Socialism*, and "China's Soviet Watchers in the 1980s."

10. Kishore Mahbubani, "The Pacific Way," *Foreign Affairs* 74, no. 1 (January/February 1995): 100-111; For more on this topic, including the fiction of "Asian"

values and the distortion of Confucianism which serves as its basis, see Amartya Sen, "Human Rights and Asian Values," *The New Republic*, July 14, 33-40; and Wm. Theodore de Bary, *Asian Values and Human Rights: A Confucian Communitarian Perspective* (Cambridge, MA: Harvard University Press, 1998).

11. Robert Putnam, *Making Democracy Work: Civic Traditions in Modern Italy* (Princeton: Princeton University Press, 1993); Lawrence Harrison and Samuel Huntington, eds., *Culture Matters: How Values Shape Human Progress* (New York: Harper Collins, 2001).

12. Brzezinski, *The Grand Failure*, 147.

13. Petro, *The Rebirth of Russian Democracy*, 59.

14. William B. Husband, *"Godless Communists": Atheism and Society in Soviet Russia, 1917-1932* (De Kalb, IL: Northern Illinois University Press, 2000).

15. Quoted in Lawrence Harrison, "Culture Matters," *The National Interest* (Summer 2000): 56.

16. Such was the conclusion reached by myself and Peter Berger following a conference we held on the topic of "The Spirit of Orthodoxy and the Ethic of Capitalism," Institute for Human Sciences, Vienna, Austria, March 7-9, 2005. See also Christopher Marsh and Nicolai Petro, "Orthodoxy, Civil Society, and Russia's Dual Transition," paper presented at the Annual Convention of the AAASS, Boston, December, 4-7, 2004.

17. Author's observation during demonstration outside Lenin Museum, Moscow, July 6, 2003.

18. Interviews by the author with political activists, Moscow, July 2-18, 2003.

19. Luke March, *The Communist Party in Post-Soviet Russia* (Manchester, UK: University of Manchester Press, 2002).

20. Marsh, *Russia at the Polls*, 126-128, particularly the box on "A Commanding Presence in Russia's Regions."

Bibliography

Adams, Douglas, and Mark Carwardine. *Last Chance to See*. New York: Ballantine, 1990.

Akimov, V.I. and S.S. Emel'yanova. "Dynamika razvitiya ekonomiki Kitaya." *Problemy Dal'nego Vostoka* 2 (1984): 43-52.

Alexeev, Mikhail. "Desecuritizing Sovereignty: Economic Interest and Responses to Political Challenges of Chinese Migration in the Russian Far East." In *Sovereignty under Challenge: How Governments Respond*, edited by John D. Montgomery and Nathan Glazer, 261-289. New Brunswick, NJ: Transaction Publishers, 2002.

———. "Economic Valuations and Interethnic Fears: Perceptions of Chinese Migration in the Russian Far East." *Journal of Peace Research* 40, no. 1 (2003): 89-106.

———. "Socioeconomic and Security Implications of Chinese Migration in the Russian Far East." *Post-Soviet Geography & Economics* 42, no. 2 (2001): 95-114.

Almond, Gabriel. *A Discipline Divided: Schools and Sects in Political Science*. Thousand Oaks, CA: Sage, 1990.

———. "National Politics and International Politics." In *The Search for World Order*, edited by Albert Lepawsky, Edward Buehrig, and Harold Lasswell. New York: Appleton-Century-Crofts, 1971.

Analiticheskii Tsentr Gossoveta KNR o Vnutripoliticheskoi Situatsii v Rossii. Moscow: Institut Dal'nego Vostoka, Rossiiskaya Akademiya Nauk, 2000.

Åslund, Anders. "Russia's Economic Transformation under Putin." *Eurasian Geography & Economics* 45, no. 6 (2004): 397-420.

Åslund, Anders. "Putin's Second Term is Likely to Differ from His First: A Rebuttal." *Eurasian Geography & Economics* 45, no. 6 (2004): 435-438.

Aukutsionek, Sergei, Igor Filatochev, Rostislav Kapelyushnikov, and Vladimir Zhukov. "Dominant Shareholders, Restructuring and Performance of Privatized Companies in Russia: An Analysis and Some Policy Implications." *Communist Economies & Economic Transformation* 10, no. 4 (1998): 495-518.

Bao Xifen. "Sravnenie Reform v Kitae i Rossii." In *Kitaiskie Politologi o Kharaktere i Rezul'tatakh Perestroiki v Rossii v "Epokhu El'tsina."* Moscow: Institut Dal'nego Vostoka, Rossiiskaya Akademiya Nauk, 2000.

Baum, Richard, ed. *Reform and Reaction in Post-Mao China: The Road to Tiananmen*. New York: Routledge, 1991.

———. "Epilogue: Communism, Convergence, and China's Political Convulsion." Pp. 183-200 in *Reform and Reaction in Post-Mao China: The Road to Tiananmen*, edited by Richard Baum. New York: Routledge, 1991.

Berman, Harold. "Freedom of Religion in Russia: An Amicus Brief for the Defendant."
    Pp. 275-76 in *Proselytism and Orthodoxy in Russia: The New War for Souls*, edited
    by John Witte and Michael Bourdeaux. Maryknoll, NY: Orbis Books, 1999.
Billington, James. "Orthodox Christianity and the Russian Transformation." Pp. 51-65 in
    Proselytism and Orthodoxy in Russia: The New War for Souls, edited by John Witte
    and Michael Bourdeaux. Maryknoll, NY: Orbis Books, 1999.
Blasi, Joseph, Maya Kroumova, and Douglas Kruse. *Kremlin Capitalism: Privatizing the
    Russian Economy.* Ithaca, NY: Cornell University Press, 1997.
Borevskaya, N.E. "Model' lichnosti po-maoistski." *Problemy Dal'nego Vostoka* 2
    (1982): 151-158.
Bova, Russell. "Political Dynamics of the Post-Communist Transition: A Comparative
    Perspective." *World Politics* 44, no. 1 (October 1991): 113-138.
Bovt, Georgy. "The Russian Press and Civil Society: Freedom of Speech vs. Freedom of
    Market." Pp. 91-104 in *Civil Society and the Search for Justice in Russia*, edited by
    Christopher Marsh and Nikolas Gvosdev. Lanham, MD: Lexington Books, 2002.
Bransten, Jeremy. "The East: Ten Years After 1989 – The Revolutions That Brought
    Down Communism." *Radio Free Europe/Radio Liberty* (October 8, 1999).
Brook, Timothy, and B. Michael Frolic. *Civil Society in China.* Armonk, NY: M.E.
    Sharpe, 1997.
Brubaker, Rogers. "Nationhood and the National Question in the Soviet Union and Post-
    Soviet Eurasia: An Institutionalist Account." *Theory and Society* 23, no. 1 (February
    1994): 47-78.
Brzezinski, Zbigniew. *The Grand Failure: The Birth and Death of Communism in the
    Twentieth Century.* New York: Charles Scribners, 1989.
Buckley, Mary. *Redefining Russian Society and Polity.* Boulder, CO: Westview Press,
    1993.
Bunce, Valerie. "Should Transitologists be Grounded?" *Slavic Review* 54, no. 1 (Spring
    1995): 111-127.
Bush, George, and Brent Scowcroft. *A World Transformed.* New York: Alfred A. Knopf,
    1998.
Bunce, Valerie. "Comparing East and South." *Journal of Democracy* 6, no. 3 (Fall 1994).
Carothers, Thomas. "The End of the Transition Paradigm." *Journal of Democracy* 13, no.
    1 (Spring 2002): 5-21.
Casanova, Jose. "Church, State, Nation and Civil Society in Spain and Poland." Pp. 101-
    153 in *The Political Dimensions of Religion,* edited by Said Arjomand. Albany, NY:
    SUNY Press, 1993.
Chang, Gordon. *The Coming Collapse of China.* New York: Random House, 2001.
Chang, Sasha. *China Country Briefing.* Beijing: Bank One, NA, 2001.
Chen Xinming. *Sulian yanbian yu shehuizhuyi gaige.* Beijing: Zhonggong zhongyang
    dangxiao chubanshe, 2002.
Cheng, Jie, and Yang Zhong. "Defining the Political System of Post-Deng China: Emerg-
    ing Support for a Democratic Political System." *Problems of Post-Communism* 45,
    no. 2 (January-February 1998): 30-42.
Clemens, Walter. *Baltic Independence and Russian Empire.* New York: St. Martin's
    Press, 1990.
Collier, David, and Richard Messick. "Prerequisites versus Diffusion: Testing Alternative
    Explanations for Social Security Adoption." *American Political Science Review* 69,
    no. 4 (Winter 1975): 1299-1315.
Colton, Timothy. *Transitional Citizens: Voters and What Influences them in the New
    Russia.* Cambridge, MA: Harvard University Press, 2000.

————. *The Dilemma of Reform in the Soviet Union.* New York: Council on Foreign Relations, 1986.

Coye, Molly Joel, and Jon Livingston, eds. *China Yesterday and Today.* Second edition. New York: Bantam Books, 1979.

Davis, Nathaniel. *A Long Walk to Church: A Contemporary History of Russian Orthodoxy.* Second Edition. Boulder, CO: Westview Press, 2003.

D' Encausse, Helene Carrere. *The End of the Soviet Empire: The Triumph of the Nations.* New York: Harper Collins, 1993.

Deng Maomao. *Deng Xiaoping, My Father.* New York: Basic Books, 1995.

De Nevers, Renée. *Comrades no More: The Seeds of Change in Eastern Europe.* Cambridge, MA: MIT University Press, 2003.

Devyatov, Andrei. *Krasnyi Drakon: Kitai i Rossiya v Dvadtsat' Pervom veke.* Moscow: Algoritm, 2002.

Dickson, Bruce. "Unsettled Succession: China's Critical Moment." *National Interest* (Fall 1997): 64-72.

Ding, X. L. "Who Gets What, How? When Chinese State-Owned Enterprises Become Shareholding Companies." *Problems of Communism* 46, no. 3 (1999): 32-33.

Dittmer, Lowell. *China Under Reform.* Boulder, CO: Westview, 1994.

————. *Sino-Soviet Normalization and its International Implications, 1945- 1990.* Seattle: University of Washington Press, 1992.

Dogan, Mattei and Dominique Pelassy. *How to Compare Nations: Strategies in Comparative Politics.* Chatham, NJ: Chatham House, 1990.

Dolmatov, V.A. "Maoizm – ideinii i politicheskii protivnik mirovogo revoliutsionnogo dvizhenya." *Problemy Dal'nego Vostoka* 3 (1980): 196-199.

Dowdle, Michael William. "Constructing Citizenship: The NPC as Catalyst for Political Participation." Pp. 330-52 in *Changing Meanings of Citizenship in Modern China*, Merle Goldman and Elizabeth Perry. Cambridge, MA: Harvard University Press, 2002.

Dragadze, Tamara. "Azerbaijan and the Azerbaijanis." Pp. 269-90 in *The Nationalities Question in the Post-Soviet States*, edited by Graham Smith. New York: Longman, 1996.

Dreyer, June Teufel. "Encroaching on the Middle Kingdom? China's View of its Place in the World." Pp. 85-103 in *US-China Relations in the Twentieth-Century: Policies, Prospects, and Possibilities*, edited by Christopher Marsh and June Teufel Dreyer. Lanham, MD: Lexington Books, 2003.

Ekonomicheskie Chudesa: Uroki dlya Rossii. Moscow: OLMA-PRESS, 1994.

Ekonomicheskie Reformy v Rossii i Kitae Glazami Rossiiskikh i Kitaiskikh Ekonomistov: Sbornik Statei. St. Petersburg: Sankt-Peterburgskii Gosudarstvennii Universitet, 2000.

Ekonomicheskie Reformy v Rossii i Vengrii: Opyt Sravnitel'nogo Issledovaniya. Novosibirsk: IEiOPP SO RAN, 1996.

Ernst & Young International, Ltd. *Doing Business in the Russian Federation.* Moscow: Ernst and Young, 2002.

Evans, Carolyn. "Chinese Law and the International Protection of Religious Freedom." *Journal of Church and State* 44 (Autumn 2002): 749-774.

Eyestone, Robert. "Confusion, Diffusion, and Innovation." *American Political Science Review* 71, no. 2 (June 1977): 441-447.

Fewsmith, Joseph. *China Since Tiananmen: The Politics of Transition.* Cambridge, UK: Cambridge University Press, 2001.

Fish, M. Stephen. *Democracy From Scratch: Opposition and Regime in the New Russian Revolution.* Princeton, NJ: Princeton University Press, 1995.

Friedgut, Theodore. *Political Participation in the USSR.* Princeton, NJ: Princeton University Press, 1979.

Froese, Paul. "Forced Secularization in Soviet Russia: Why an Atheistic Monopoly Failed." *Journal for the Scientific Study of Religion* 43, no. 1 (2004): 35-50.

Gans-Morse, Jordan. "Searching for Transitologists: Contemporary Theories of Post-Communist Transitions and the Myth of a Dominant Paradigm." *Post-Soviet Affairs* 20, no. 4 (2004): 320-349.

Gao Fang. *Sulian dongou jubian yuanyin yanjiu.* Beijing: Zhongguo renmin daxue chubanshe, 1992.

Gibson, James. "Social Networks, Civil Society, and the Prospects for Consolidating Russia's Democratic Transition." *American Journal of Political Science* 45, no. 1 (2001): 51-69.

Gilboy, George, and Eric Heginbotham. "China's Coming Transformation." *Foreign Affairs* 80, no. 4 (July-August 2001): 26-39.

Gilley, Bruce. *Tiger on the Brink: Jiang Zemin and China's New Elite.* Berkeley: University of California Press, 1998.

Gleason, Gregory. "National Self-Determination and Soviet Denouement." *Nationalities Papers* 20, no. 2 (March 1992): 1-8.

Goldman, Marshall. "Anders in Wonderland: Comments on Russia's Economic Transformation Under Putin," *Eurasian Geography & Economics* 45, no. 6 (2004): 429-434.

———. "China Rethinks the Soviet Model." *International Security* 5, no. 2 (Fall 1980): 49-65.

Goldman, Merle. "The Reassertion of Political Citizenship in the Post-Mao Era: The Democracy Wall Movement." Pp. 159-86 in *Changing Meanings of Citizenship in Modern China,* edited by Merle Goldman and Elizabeth Perry. Cambridge, MA: Harvard University Press, 2002.

Gong Dafei, Xu Kui, and Yang Zheng, eds. *Sulian jubian xin tan.* Beijing: Shijie zhishi chubanshe, 1998.

Gorbachev, Mikhail. *Gorbachev: On My Country and the World.* New York: Columbia University Press, 2000.

———. *Zhizn' i Reform,* Vol. 1. Moscow: Novosti, 1995.

Gorbachev, Mikhail and Zdenek Mlynar. *Conversations with Gorbachev: On Perestroika, the Prague Spring, and the Crossroads of Socialism.* New York: Columbia University Press, 2002.

Gourevitch, Peter. *Politics in Hard Times: Comparative Responses to International Economic Crises.* Ithaca, NY: Cornell University Press, 1986.

Gray, Virginia. "Innovation in the States: A Diffusion Study." *American Political Science Review* 67, no. 4 (December 1973): 1174-1185.

Greeley, Andrew. "Coleman Revisited: Religious Structures as a Source of Social Capital." *American Behavioral Scientist* 40, no. 4 (1997): 587-594.

Gudoshnikov, L.M. "Samorazoblachenie maoizma." *Problemy Dal'nego Vostoka* 1 (1981): 201-205.

Gunther, Richard, P. Nikiforos Diamandouros, and Hans-Jurgen Puhle. "O'Donnell's 'Illusions': A Rejoinder." *Journal of Democracy* 7, no. 3 (October 1996): 151-59.

Guo, Gang. "Party Recruitment of College Students in China." *Journal of Contemporary China* 14, no. 43 (May 2005): 371-393.

Gurtov, Mel, ed. *The Transformation of Socialism: Perestroika and Reform in the Soviet Union and China.* Boulder, CO: Westview, 1990.

Gvosdev, Nikolas K. *Emperors and Elections: Reconciling the Orthodox Tradition with Modern Politics.* Huntington, NY: Troitsa Books, 2000.

Hague, Rod, Martin Harrop, and Shaun Breslin. *Political Science: A Comparative Introduction.* New York: Worth, 1998.

Halperin, Nina. "Learning From Abroad: Chinese Views of the East European Economic Experience, January 1977-June 1981." *Modern China* 11, no. 1 (1985): 77-109.

Hanson, Philip. "Putin and Russia's Economic Transformation." *Eurasian Geography & Economics* 45, no. 6 (2004): 421-428.

Harrison, Lawrence and Samuel Huntington, eds. *Culture Matters: How Values Shape Human Progress.* New York: Harper Collins, 2001.

Higley, John, Judith Kullberg, and Jan Pakulski. "The Persistence of Postcommunist Elites." *Journal of Democracy* 7, no. 2 (1996): 133-147.

Homer, Lauren B. and Lawrence A. Uzzell. "Federal and Provincial Religious Freedom Laws in Russia: A Struggle for and against Federalism and the Rule of Law." Pp. 284-320 in *Proselytism and Orthodoxy in Russia: The New War for Souls*, edited by John Witte and Michael Bourdeaux. Maryknoll, NY: Orbis Books, 1999.

Hough, Jerry. *Democratization and Revolution in the USSR, 1985-1991.* Washington, DC: Brookings Institution Press, 1997.

Hu Jian. "Eluosi jingji zhuangui moshi de sikao – jianlun zhonge jingji zhaungui de bijiao." *Dongou Zhongya Yanjiu* 2 (2001): 79-84.

Huang Weiting. *Sugong wangdang shinian ji.* Jiangxi: Jiangxi Gaoxiao Chubanshe, 2002.

Huang Yunshan. "Eluosi zhengzhi shenghuo fazhan wu nian." *Jingri Dongou Zhongya* 1 (1997).

Hudson, George. "Civil Society in Russia: Models and Prospects for Development." *Russian Review* 62, no. 2(2003): 212-222.

Huntington, Samuel. *The Third Wave: Democratization in the Late Twentieth Century.* Norman, OK: University of Oklahoma Press, 1991.

Husband, William B. *"Godless Communists": Atheism and Society in Soviet Russia, 1917-1932.* De Kalb, IL: Northern Illinois University Press, 2000.

International Monetary Fund, The World Bank, Organization for Economic Co-operation and Development, and European Bank for Reconstruction and Development. *A Study of the Soviet Economy*, Vol. 1. Paris: OECD, 1991.

Kaple, Deborah A. *Dream of a Red Factory.* Oxford: Oxford University Press, 1994.

Kapralov, P.B., A.M. Krygalov, and A.V. Ostrovskii. "Nekotorye tendentsii v sotsial'no-ekonomicheskoi politike kitaiskogo rukavodstva." *Problemy Dal'nego Vostoka* 4 (1980): 105-116.

Kitaiskie Politologi o Kharaktere i Rezul'tatakh Perestroiki v Rossii v "Epokhy El'tsina." Moscow: Institut Dal'nego Vostoka, Rossiiskaya Akademiya Nauk, 2000.

Kitaiskie Reformy i Rossiya. 2 volumes. Moscow: Institut Dal'nego Vostoka, RAN, 2000.

Kornai, János. *The Socialist System: The Political Economy of Communism.* Princeton, NJ: Princeton University Press, 1992.

Kovács, János Mátyás. "Rival Temptations and Passive Resistance: Cultural Globalization in Hungary." Pp. 146-182 in *Many Globalizations: Cultural Diversity in the Contemporary World*, edited by Peter Berger and Samuel Huntington. Oxford: Oxford University Press, 2002).

Lambert, Tony. "The Present Religious Policy of the Chinese Communist Party." *Religion, State & Society* 29, no. 2 (June 2001): 121-129.

Landman, Todd. *Issues and Methods in Comparative Politics: An Introduction.* London: Routledge, 2000.

Lane, Ruth. *The Art of Comparative Politics.* Needham Heights, MA: Allyn and Bacon, 1997.

Lawrance, Alan. *China Under Communism.* London: Routledge, 1998.

Li, He. "The Role of Think Tanks in Chinese Foreign Policy." *Problems of Post-Communism* 49, no. 2 (March-April 2002): 33-43.

Li, Lianjiang, and Kevin O'Brien. "The Struggle over Village Elections." Pp. 129-44 in *The Paradox of China's Post-Mao Reforms,* edited by Merle Goldman and Roderick MacFarquhar. Cambridge, MA: Harvard University Press, 1999.

Lin, Yifu, Fang Cai, Zhou Li. *Kitaiskoe Chudo: Strategiya Razvitiya i Ekonomicheskaya Reforma.* Moscow: Institut Dal'nego Vostoka, 2001.

Lin, Justin Yifu, Fang Cai, and Zhou Li. *The China Miracle: Development Strategy and Economic Reform.* Hong Kong: Chinese University Press, 1996.

Liu Guoguang, Wang Luolin, Li Jingwen, Liu Shucheng, and Wang Tongsan, eds. *Economics Blue Book of the People's Republic of China, 1999: Analysis and Forecast.* Armonk, NY: M. E. Sharpe, 1999.

Liu Zuxi, ed. *Dongou jubian de genyuan yu jiaoxun.* Beijing: Dongfang chubanshe, 1995.

Lou Fang. "Eluosi: cong jihua dao shichang de jiannan guodu — toushi 21 shiji jingji gaige mubiao." *Dongou Zhongya Yanjiu* 6 (2001): 32-36.

Lu Nanquan. "Sulian jubian de genben yuanin." *Shijie jingji* 9 (1996).

————, and Jiang Changbing, eds. *Sulian jubian shencengci yuanyin yanjiu.* Beijing: Zhongguo shehui kexue chubanshe, 1999.

————, Jiang Changbing, Xu Kui, and Li Jingjie. *Sulian xingwangshi lun.* Beijing: Renmin chubanshe, 2001.

Lukin, Alexander. *The Bear Watches the Dragon: Russia's Perception of China and the Evolution of Russian-Chinese Relations Since the Eighteenth Century.* Armonk, NY: M.E. Sharpe, 2003.

————. "The Initial Soviet Reaction to the Events in China in 1989 and the Prospects for Sino-Soviet Relations." *The China Quarterly* 125 (March 1991): 119-136.

Lutz, James M. "Emulation and Policy Adoptions in the Canadian Provinces." *Canadian Journal of Political Science* 22, no. 1 (July 1989): 147-154.

Ma, Hgok, Ka-ho Mok, and Anthony B. L. Cheung. "Advance and Retreat: The New Two-Pronged Strategy of Enterprise Reform in China." *Problems of Post-Communism* 48, no. 5 (2001): 52-61.

Mackerras, Colin, Pradeep Taneja, and Graham Young. *China Since 1978: Reform, Modernisation and "Socialism with Chinese Characteristics."* New York: St. Martin's Press, 1994.

Mahbubani, Kishore. "The Pacific Way." *Foreign Affairs* 74, no. 1 (January/February 1995): 100-111.

Malia, Martin. *The Soviet Tragedy: A History of Socialism in Russia, 1917-1991.* New York: Free Press, 1994.

Malevich, Igor. *Vnimanie, Kitai.* Minsk: Kharvest, 2000.

March, Luke. *The Communist Party in Post-Soviet Russia.* Manchester, UK: University of Manchester Press, 2002.

Marsh, Christopher. "The Challenge of Civil Society." Pp. 141-58 in *Russia's Policy Challenges: Security, Stability, and Development,* edited by Stephen Wegren. Armonk, NY: M. E. Sharpe, 2003.

————. *Russia at the Polls: Voters, Elections, and Democratization.* Washington, DC: CQ Press, 2002.

————. "Power Capabilities, External Recognition, and Sovereignty: The Case of Lithuanian Independence." *East European Quarterly* 35, no. 1 (2001): 75-92.

————, Helen Albert, and James W. Warhola. "The Political Geography of Russia's 2004 Presidential Election." *Eurasian Geography & Economics* 45, no. 4 (July 2004): 188-205.

————, and Paul Froese. "The State of Freedom in Russia: A Regional Analysis of Freedom of Religion, Media and Markets." *Religion, State & Society* 32, no. 2 (2004): 137-149.

————, and Mark Heppner. "When Weak Nations Use Strong States: The Unintended Consequences of Intervention in Kosovo." *Nationalities Papers* 31, no. 3 (September 2003): 281-293.

McCormick, Barrett, and Jonathan Unger, eds. *China After Socialism: In the Footsteps of Eastern Europe or East Asia?* Armonk, NY: M.E. Sharpe, 1996.

Misra, Kalpana. *From Post-Maoism to Post-Marxism.* New York: Routledge, 1998.

Muromtseva, Z.A. "Modernizatsiya sel'skogo khozyaistva KNR: Voprosy kapital'nikh vlozhenii." *Problemy Dal'nego Vostoka* 1 (1985): 96-106.

Naimark, Norman. "Ich will hier raus?: Emigration and the Collapse of the German Democratic Republic." Pp. 72-95 in *Eastern Europe in Revolution,* edited by Ivo Banac. Ithaca, NY: Cornell University Press, 1992.

Naletova, Inna. "Orthodox *Yarmarki* as a Form of Civic Engagement." Pp. 85-90 in *Burden or Blessing? Russian Orthodoxy and the Construction of Civil Society and Democracy,* edited by Christopher Marsh. Boston: Institute on Culture, Religion and World Affairs, Boston University, 2004.

Nathan, Andrew. "Authoritarian Resilience: China's Changing of the Guard." *Journal of Democracy* 14, no.1 (2003): 6-17.

Nathan, Andrew and Perry Link, eds. Compiled by Zhang Liang. *The Tiananmen Papers: The Chinese Leadership's Decision to Use Force Against Their Own People – In Their Own Words.* New York: Public Affairs, 2001.

Nolan, Peter. *China's Rise, Russia's Fall: Politics, Economics and Planning in the Transition from Stalinism.* New York: St. Martin's Press, 1995.

Novaya Rossiya: Desyat' Let Reform Glazami Rossiyan. Moscow: Institut Kompleksnykh Sotsial'nykh Issledovanii, Rossiiskaya Akademiya Nauk, October 2001.

O'Brien, Kevin J. *Reform Without Liberalization: China's National People's Congresses and the Politics of Institutional Change.* New York: Cambridge University Press, 1990.

————. "Villagers, Elections, and Citizenship." In *Changing Meanings of Citizenship in Modern China,* edited by Merle Goldman and Elizabeth Perry, 212-231. Cambridge, MA: Harvard University Press, 2002.

O'Donnell, Guillermo. "Illusions About Consolidation," *Journal of Democracy* 7, no. 1 (April 1996): 34-51.

O'Donnell, Guillermo, Philippe C. Schmitter, and Laurence Whitehead, eds. *Transitions from Authoritarian Rule: Prospects for Democracy.* Baltimore: Johns Hopkins University Press, 1986.

Oi, Jean C. "The Fate of the Collective after the Commune." Pp. 15-36 in *Chinese Society on the Eve of Tiananmen: The Impact of Reform,* edited by Debora Davis and Ezra Vogel. Cambridge, MA: Council on East Asian Studies, Harvard University, 1990.

————. *Rural China Takes Off: Institutional Foundations of Economic Reform.* Los Angeles and Berkeley, CA: University of California Press, 1999.

Olson, William J. "A New World, a New Challenge." Pp. 3-12 in *Managing Contemporary Conflict: Pillars of Success*, edited by Max Manwaring and William J. Olson. Boulder, CO: Westview, 1996.

Organization for Economic Cooperation and Development. *Investment Guide for the Russian Federation*. Paris: Organization for Economic Cooperation and Development, 1996.

Otsenki Kitaiskimi Politologami Vnutrennei Situatsii v Rossii v Kanun Parlamentskikh i Prezidentskikh Vyborov. Moscow: Institut Dal'nego Vostoka, Rossiiskaya Akademiya Nauk, 1999.

Ostrovskii, Andrei. "Ekonomicheskie Reformy v KNR: Uroki dlya Rossii." In *Teoriya i Praktika Ekonomicheskikh Reform v KNR*. Moscow: Institut Dal'nego Vostoka, Rossiiskaya Akademiya Nauk, 2000.

———. *Formirovanie Rynka Rabochei Sily v KNR*. Moscow: Institut Dal'nego Vostoka, Rossiiskaya Akademiya Nauk, 2003.

———. "Novaya Strategiya dlya Rossii i Opyt Stran c Perekhodnoi Ekonomikoi." Pp. 77-81 in *"Otechestvo" Otechestvu: Programma Preobrazovanii*. Moscow: Obscherossiiskaya Politicheskaya Obschectvennaya Organizatsiya "Otechestvo," 2001.

Owens, Brad. "The Independent Press in Russia: Integrity and the Economics of Survival." Pp. 105-24 in *Civil Society and the Search for Justice in Russia,* edited by Christopher Marsh and Nikolas Gvosdev. Lanham, MD: Lexington Books, 2002.

Pan Deli. "Lun sulian jubian de sixiang zhengzhi genyuan." *Dongou Zhongya Yanjiu* 5 (2001): 2-7.

———. "Sugong xianjingxing de sangshi yu sulian jubian – xuexi 'sangedaibiao' sixiang, dui sulian jubian yuanyin zai renshi." *Dongou Zhongya Yanjiu* 6 (2001): 1-8

Pan Guang. "Zhizhengdang de zhidao sixiang guanxi dao guojia de xingwang – cong sulian jieti kan 'sangedaibiao' sixiang de zhongyao yiyi." *Dongou Zhongya Yanjiu* 6 (2001): 9-14.

Pei, Minxin. *From Reform to Revolution: The Demise of Communism in China and the Soviet Union*. Cambridge, MA: Harvard University Press, 1994.

———. "Domestic Changes in China and Implications for American Policy." Pp. 43-62 in *U.S.-China Relations in the Twenty-first Century : Policies, Prospects and Possibilities*, edited by Christopher Marsh and June Tuefel Dreyer. Lanham, MD: Lexington Books, 2003.

Pei Yuanying. "A Multi-Dimensional View of Russian Diplomatic Strategy." *Foreign Affairs Journal* (Beijing) 65 (September 2002): 55-59.

Perry, Elizabeth. "China in 1992: An Experiment in Neo-Authoritarianism." *Asian Survey* (January 1993): p. 12-21.

Petro, Nicolai. *The Rebirth of Russian Democracy: An Interpretation of Political Culture*. Cambridge, MA: Harvard University Press, 1995.

———. "Perestroika from Below: Voluntary Socio-Political Associations in the RSFSR." Pp. 102-35 in *Perestroika at the Crossroads*, edited by Alfred Rieber and Alvin Rubinstein. Armonk, NY: M. E. Sharpe, 1991.

Politologi KNR o Sovremennoi Politicheskoi Zhizni Rossii. Moscow: Institut Dal'nego Vostoka, Rossiiskaya Akademiya Nauk, 1998.

Portyakov, V.Y., and S.V. Stepanov. "Spetsial'nie ekonomicheskie zony kitaya." *Problemy Dal'nego Vostoka* 1 (1986): 37-46.

Pu Guoliang. "Lun suweiai tizhi de lishi diwei jiqi shijian jiaoxun." *Dongou Zhongya Yanjiu* 1 (2001): 70-75.

Putnam, Robert D. *Making Democracy Work: Civic Traditions in Modern Italy.* Princeton, NJ: Princeton University Press, 1993.
———. "Diplomacy and Domestic Politics: The Logic of Two-Level Games." *International Organization* 42, no. 3 (Summer 1988): 427-460.
Raffe, David, and Russell Rumberger. "Education and Training for 16-18 Year Olds in the UK and USA." *Oxford Studies in Comparative Education* 2, no.2 (1992): 135-157.
Ragin, Charles. *The Comparative Method: Moving Beyond Qualitative and Quantitative Strategies.* Berkeley: University of California Press, 1987.
Ramet, Sabrina. *Nihil Obstat: Religion, Politics, and Social Change in East-Central Europe and Russia.* Durham, NC: Duke University Press, 1998.
Ratnikov, S.R., and D.A. Radikovskii. "Diskussiya v KNR o puti razvitiya strany." *Problemy Dal'nego Vostoka* 4 (1984): 115-127.
Rose, Richard. "Comparing Forms of Comparative Analysis." *Political Studies* 39, no. 3 (1991): 446-462.
———. *Lesson-drawing in Public Policy: A Guide to Learning across Time and Space.* Chatham, NJ: Chatham House, 1993.
Rossiya: Ot "Epokhi El'tsina" k "Epokhe Putina." Moscow: Institut Dal'nego Vostoka, Rossiiskaya Akademiya Nauk, 2000.
Ross, Cameron. "Federalism and Electoral Authoritarianism under Putin." *Demokratizatsiya* 13, no. 3 (Summer 2005), forthcoming.
Rozman, Gilbert. *The Chinese Debate about Soviet Socialism, 1978-1985.* Princeton, NJ: Princeton University Press, 1987.
———. "China's Soviet Watchers in the 1980s: A New Era in Scholarship." *World Politics* 37, no. 4 (July 1985): 435-74.
———. "Chinese Studies in Russia and their Impact, 1985-1992." *Asian Research Trends* 5 (1994): 143-160.
———. "Moscow's China Watchers in the Post-Mao Era: The Response to a Changing China." *China Quarterly* 94 (June 1983): 215-42.
———. *A Mirror for Socialism: Soviet Criticisms of China.* Princeton, NJ: Princeton University Press, 1985.
———. "Sino-Russian Relations in the 1990s: A Balance Sheet." *Post-Soviet Affairs* 14, no. 2 (1998): 93-113.
———. "Sino-Russian Relations: Mutual Assessments and Predictions." In *Rapprochement or Rivalry: Russia-China Relations in a Changing World,* edited by Sherman Garnett, 147-176. Washington, DC: Carnegie Endowment for International Peace, 2000.
———, ed. *Dismantling Communism: Common Causes and Regional Variations.* Washington, DC and Baltimore: Woodrow Wilson Center Press and Johns Hopkins University Press, 1992.
Rustow, Dankwart. "Transitions to Democracy: Toward a Dynamic Model." *Comparative Politics* 2, no. 3 (April 1970): 337-363.
Sakwa, Richard. *Gorbachev and His Reforms, 1985-1990.* Englewood Cliffs, NJ: Prentice Hall, 1990.
Santayana, George. *Life of Reason, Reason in Common Sense.* New York: Scribner's, 1905.
Sartori, Giovanni. "Concept Misformation in Comparative Politics." *American Political Science Review* 64, no. 4 (December 1970): 1040-1041.
Savage, Robert. "Diffusion Research Traditions and the Spread of Policy Innovation in a Federal System." *Publius: The Journal of Federalism* 15, no. 4 (Fall 1985): 1-27.

Scalapino, Robert. "The People's Republic of China at Fifty." *NBR Analysis* (National Bureau of Asian Research) 10, no. 4 (1999): 11-15.

Schmitter, Philippe C. with Terry Lynn Karl. "The Conceptual Travels of Transitologists and Consolidologists: How Far to the East Should they Attempt to Go?" *Slavic Review* 53, no. 1 (Spring 1994): 173-185.

Seeley, John Robert. *An Introduction to Political Science.* London: Macmillan, 1886.

Service, Robert. *A History of Twentieth-Century Russia.* Cambridge, MA: Harvard University Press, 1997.

Shambaugh, David, ed. *Is China Unstable? Assessing the Factors.* Armonk, NY: M. E. Sharpe, 2000.

Shi, Tianjian. "Mass Political Behavior in Beijing." In *The Paradox of China's Post-Mao Reforms,* edited by Merle Goldman and Roderick MacFarquhar. Cambridge, MA: Harvard University Press, 1999.

———. *Political Participation in Beijing.* Cambridge, MA: Harvard University Press, 1997.

Skocpol, Theda. *States and Social Revolutions.* Cambridge, MA: Harvard University Press, 1979.

Slider, Darrell. "Privatization in Russia's Regions." *Post-Soviet Affairs* 10 (1994): 367-396.

Smidt, Corwin, ed. *Religion as Social Capital: Producing the Common Good.* Waco, TX: Baylor University Press, 2003.

Smirnov, D. A. "Maoistskaya kontseptsiya 'novoi demokratii' – pravorevizionistskaya versiya 'natsional'nogo' sotsializma." *Problemy Dal'nego Vostoka* 4 (1979): 92-105.

Snyder, Jack. *From Voting to Violence: Democratization and Nationalist Conflict.* New York: W. W. Norton, 2000.

Soled, Debra, ed. *China: A Nation in Transition.* Washington, DC: CQ Press, 1995.

Statistical Yearbook of China, 2000. Beijing, 2001.

Stepanova, G. A. *Sistema Mnogopartiinogo Sotrudnichestva v Kitaiskoi Narodnoi Respublike.* Moscow: Institut Dal'nego Vostoka, Rossiiskaya Akademiya Nauk, 1999.

Supyan, Victor. "Privatization in Russia: Some Preliminary Results and Socioeconomic Implications." *Demokratizatsiya* 9, no. 1 (2001): 137-154.

Sun, Yan. *The Chinese Reassessment of Socialism, 1976-1992.* Princeton, NJ: Princeton University Press, 1995.

Su, Chi. "Soviet China-Watchers' Influence on Soviet China Policy." *Journal of Northeast Asian Studies* 2 (December 1983): 25-49.

Tan Zhoujian. "Itogi El'tsinskoi Epokhi i Perspektiby Ekonomicheskogo Ravitiya Rossii." In *Kitaiskie Politologi o Kharaktere i Rezul'tatakh Perestroiki v Rossii v "Epokhy El'tsina".* Moscow: Institut Dal'nego Vostoka, Rossiiskaya Akademiya Nauk, 2000.

Tanner, Murray Scot. "The National People's Congress." In *The Paradox of China's Post-Mao Reforms,* edited by Merle Goldman and Roderick MacFarquhar, 100-128. Cambridge, MA: Harvard University Press, 1999.

———. *The Politics of Lawmaking in Post-Mao China: Institutions, Processes, and Democratic Prospects.* New York: Oxford University Press, 1998.

Tanner, Murray Scot and Chen Ke. "Breaking the Vicious Cycles: The Emergence of China's National People's Congress." *Problems of Post-Communism* 45, no. 3 (1998): 29-47.

Thakur, Ramesh, and Carlyle A. Thayer, eds. *The Soviet Union as an Asian Pacific Power: Implications of Gorbachev's 1986 Vladivostok Initiative.* Boulder, CO: Westview, 1987.

Tian Juanbao. "Jiekesiluofake." *Jingri Sulian Dongou* 3 (1990): 17-21.

Tilly, Charles, ed. *Formation of National States in Western Europe.* Princeton, NJ: Princeton University Press, 1975.

Tishkov, Valery. *Ethnicity, Nationalism, and Conflict in and after the Soviet Union: The Mind Aflame.* Thousand Oaks, CA: Sage, 1997.

Tökés, Rudolf. *Hungary's Negotiated Revolution: Economic Reform, Social Change and Political Succession.* Cambridge, UK: Cambridge University Press, 1996.

Tubilewicz, Czeslaw. "Chinese Press Coverage of Political and Economic Restructuring of East Central Europe." *Asian Survey* 37, no. 10 (1997): 927-943.

Tucker, Nancy Bernkopf. "China as a Factor in the Collapse of the Soviet Union." *Political Science Quarterly* 110, no. 4 (Winter 1995-96): 501-518.

Vanhanen, Tatu. *Prospects of Democracy: A Study of 172 Countries.* London: Routledge, 1997.

Vardys, V. Stanley, and Judith Sedaitis. *Lithuania: The Rebel Nation.* Boulder, CO: Westview Press, 1997.

Walker, Jack. "The Diffusion of Innovations Among the American States." *American Political Science Review* 63, no. 3 (1969): 880-899.

Waltman, Jerold. *Copying Other Nations' Policies: Two American Case Studies.* Cambridge, MA: Schenkman, 1980.

Waltz, Kenneth. *Theory of International Politics.* New York: McGraw-Hill, 1979.

Wang Jincun. "Osobennosti Rossiiskoi modeli perestroiki ekonomiki i prichiny ee porazheniya." Pp. 19-28 in *Analiticheskii Tsentr Gossoveta KNR o Vnutripoliticheskoi Situatsii v Rossii.*

Wang Shouze. "Guanyu egong de chengsheng he yeliqin de xuanju." *Jingri Dongou Zhongya* 5 (1996): 7-11.

Wang Zhengquan. "Sulian kuatai de genben yuanyin." *Eluosi Yanjiu* 4 (December 2001): 9-12.

White, Douglas R., Andrey Korotayev, and Daria Khaltourina. *Using SPSS: Analysis and Comparison in the Social Sciences.* Unpublished manuscript, 2004.

White, Stephen. *Gorbachev and After.* Cambridge, UK: Cambridge University Press, 1993.

———. *Russia Goes Dry: Alcohol, State and Society.* Cambridge, UK: Cambridge University Press, 1996.

———, and Ian McAllister. "Orthodoxy and Political Behavior in Postcommunist Russia." *Review of Religious Research* 41, no. 3 (2000): 359-372.

White, Tyrene. "Political Reform and Rural Government." Pp. 37-60 in *Chinese Society on the Eve of Tiananmen: The Impact of Reform,* edited by Debora Davis and Ezra Vogel. Cambridge, MA: Council on East Asian Studies, Harvard University, 1990.

Wilson, Jeanne. "'The Polish Lesson': China and Poland 1980-1990." *Studies in Comparative Communism* 23, nos. 3-4 (Autumn/Winter 1990): 259-268.

Witte, John, and Michael Bourdeaux, eds. *Proselytism and Orthodoxy in Russia: The New War for Souls.* Maryknoll, NY: Orbis Books, 1999.

Woo, Wing Thye. "The Art of Reforming Centrally Planned Economies: Comparing China, Poland, and Russia." *Journal of Comparative Economics* 18 (1994): 276-308.

Wuthnow, Robert. "Mobilizing Civic Engagement: The Changing Impact of Religious Involvement." Pp. 331-63 in *Civic Engagement and American Democracy,* edited by Theda Skocpol and Morris Fiorina. Washington, DC: Brookings Institution, 1999.

Xu Poling. "Zhongdongou yu eluosi jingji zhuanxing shinian: duibi yu jiejian." *Dongou Zhongya Yanjiu* 1 (2001): 22-29.

Xu Zhixin. "Eluosi duiwai zhengce de jiaoxun." *Dongou Zhongya Yanjiu* 2 (2002): 54-58.

———. "Lun sulian shibai de jingji genyuan." *Dongou Zhongya Yanjiu* 3 (2001): 1-10.

Yali Peng. "Democracy and Chinese Political Discourses." *Modern China* 24, no. 4 (Oct. 1998): 408-444.

Yang, Benjamin. *Deng: A Political Biography*. Armonk, NY: M. E. Sharpe, 1998.

Zahariadis, Nikoloas. *Theory, Case, and Method in Comparative Politics*. Ft. Worth: Harcourt Brace, 1997.

Zhang Shengfa. "Sulian jieti yuanyin zai tan." *Eluosi Yanjiu* 4 (December 2001): 16-27.

Zhang Shuhua. "Minzhu de jianxin yu shenhua de pomie – dui eluosi shinian zhengzhi zhuangui de fenxi yu fansi." *Dongou Zhongya Yanjiu* 4 (2001): 12-19.

Zhao, Suisheng, ed. *China and Democracy: Reconsidering the Prospects for a Democratic China*. London: Routledge, 2000.

———. "Chinese Nationalism and Authoritarianism in the 1990s." In *China and Democracy: Reconsidering the Prospects for a Democratic China*, edited by Suisheng Zhao, 253-270. London: Routledge, 2000.

Zhou Shangwen. "Sugong changqi buneng zuodao sangedaibiao yingchu de jiaoxun." *Eluosi Yanjiu* 4 (December 2001):10-13.

———. "Zhong'e jingjin zhuangui chushi tiaojian de bijiao." *Elousi Yanjiu* 2 (2003): 39-42.

Zuo Fengrong. "Daozhi sugong baiwang de ji ge guanjianxing yinsu." *Eluosi Yanjiu* 4 (December 2001): 28-34.

———. *Zhiming de cuowu – sulian duiwai zhanlue de yanbian yu yingxiang*. Beijing: Shijie zhishi chubanshe, 2001.

Zweig, David. *Democratic Values, Political Structures, and Alternative Politics in Greater China*. Peaceworks no. 44. Washington, DC: United States Institute of Peace, 2002.

Periodicals Consulted

Banyue Tan
Beijing Review
Hongqi
Izvestiya
Los Angeles Times
Moscow Times
Moskovskie Novosti
Nanfang Zhoumo
New York Times
Nezavisimaya Gazeta
Pravda
Renmin Ribao
Rossiskaya Gazeta
The Guardian
The Independent
The International Herald Tribune

Index

About the Author

Christopher Marsh is Associate Professor of Political Science and Church-State Studies and Director of Asian Studies at Baylor University. Dr. Marsh completed his undergraduate and master's degrees at Central Connecticut State University, and his Ph.D. in Political Science at the University of Connecticut. He has also held research appointments at Tsinghua University in Beijing and the Institute of the Far East of the Russian Academy of Sciences in Moscow. Dr. Marsh maintains close research ties with the Institute on Culture, Religion, and World Affairs at Boston University and the Institute for Multidisciplinary Social Research of the Russian Academy of Sciences.

Dr. Marsh's research interests center on Communist studies and transition politics, with a focus on Russia and China. His previous books include *Russia at the Polls: Voters, Elections, and Democratization* and *Making Russian Democracy Work: Social Capital, Economic Development, and Democratization*. Dr. Marsh is also the author of numerous journal articles published in such places as *The National Interest, Demokratizatsiya, Nationalism and Ethnic Politics, Journal of Baltic Studies, American Journal of Chinese Studies*, and *Communist and Post-Communist Studies*. Dr. Marsh is currently at work on his next book project, an investigation into the role played by religion and ethnic identity in post-Communist separatist movements.